The Organization of the Future

DRUCKER FOUNDATION
FUTURE SERIES

ABOUT THE DRUCKER FOUNDATION

The Peter F. Drucker Foundation for Nonprofit Management, founded in 1990, takes its name and inspiration from the acknowledged father of modern management. By providing educational opportunities and resources, the foundation furthers its mission "to lead social sector organizations toward excellence in performance." It pursues this mission through the presentation of conferences, video teleconferences, the annual Peter F. Drucker Award for Nonprofit Innovation, and the annual Frances Hesselbein Community Innovation Fellows Program, as well as through the development of management resources, partnerships, and publications.

Since its founding, the Drucker Foundation's special role has been to serve as a broker of intellectual capital, bringing together the finest leaders, consultants, authors, and social philosophers in the world with the leaders of social sector voluntary organizations.

The Drucker Foundation believes that a healthy society requires three vital sectors: a public sector of effective governments, a private sector of effective businesses, and a social sector of effective community organizations. The mission of the social sector and its organizations is to change lives. It accomplishes this mission by addressing the needs of the spirit, mind, and body of individuals, the community, and society. This sector and its organizations also create a meaningful sphere of effective and responsible citizenship.

The Drucker Foundation aims to make its contribution to the health of society by strengthening the social sector through the provision of intellectual resources to leaders in business, government, and the social sector. In the first nine years after its inception, the Drucker Foundation, among other things:

- Presented the Drucker Innovation Award, which each year generates several hundred applications from local community enterprises; many applicants work in fields where results are difficult to achieve.

- Worked with social sector leaders through the Frances Hesselbein Community Innovation Fellows program.

- Held twenty conferences in the United States and in countries across the world.

- Developed six books: a *Self-Assessment Tool* (revised 1998) for nonprofit organizations; three books in the Drucker Foundation Future Series, *The Leader of the Future* (1996), *The Organization of the Future* (1997), and *The Community of the Future* (1998); *Leader to Leader* (1999); and *Leading Beyond the Walls* (1999).

- Developed *Leader to Leader,* a quarterly journal for leaders from all three sectors.

For more information on the Drucker Foundation, contact:

The Peter F. Drucker Foundation for Nonprofit Management
320 Park Avenue, Third Floor
New York, NY 10022-6839 U.S.A.
Telephone: (212) 224-1174
Fax: (212) 224-2508
E-mail: info@pfdf.org
Web address: www.pfdf.org

The Organization of the Future

FRANCES HESSELBEIN
MARSHALL GOLDSMITH
RICHARD BECKHARD
EDITORS

 Jossey-Bass Publishers • San Francisco

Jossey-Bass books and products are available through most bookstores. To contact
Jossey-Bass directly, call (888) 378-2537, fax to (800) 605-2665, or visit our website at
www.josseybass.com.

Substantial discounts on bulk quantities of Jossey-Bass books are available to corporations, professional associations, and other organizations. For details and discount information, contact the special sales department at Jossey-Bass.

 Manufactured in the United States of America on Lyons Falls Turin Book. This
paper is acid-free and 100 percent totally chlorine-free.

The poetry from T. S. Eliot in Chapter Seven is an excerpt from "Little Gidding" in *Four
Quartets*, copyright 1943 by T. S. Eliot and renewed 1971 by Esme Valerie Eliot, reprinted
by permission of Harcourt Brace & Company. English language rights throughout the world
excluding U.S.A. granted by Faber and Faber Limited.

Library of Congress Cataloging-in-Publication Data

The organization of the future / Frances Hesselbein, Marshall
  Goldsmith, Richard Beckhard, editors. — 1st ed.
    p.   cm. — (Drucker Foundation future series)
  Includes index.
  ISBN 0-7879-0303-5 (hardback)
  ISBN 0-7879-5203-6 (paperback)
  1. Organizational change.   I. Hesselbein, Frances.
II. Goldsmith, Marshall.   III. Beckhard, Richard, date.
IV. Series.
HD58.8.07284 1997
658.4'06 — dc21   96–45826

| *HB Printing* | 10 9 8 7 6 5 4 3 | FIRST EDITION |
| *PB Printing* | 10 9 8 7 6 5 4 3 2 1 | |

Contents

Preface

Peter F. Drucker once considered writing a book called *The Future That Has Already Happened*. In it he would explain how we can find meaning in the events happening outside our windows, events that are visible but not yet seen. In *The Organization of the Future*, we have gathered forty-six of the most talented writers, observers, and practitioners to share their perspectives on what is happening outside the window and how it will make a difference tomorrow.

Like *The Leader of the Future*, the first book in the Drucker Foundation Future Series, *The Organization of the Future* rides in on a wave of massive, accelerating change. Giants Peter Drucker and Charles Handy open and close the book. In between, some of the world's great intellects look at the way organizations do the key work of the society in all three sectors, they examine the ways in which the work of the organization will change, and with urgency, they underscore the essential role of the organization—public, private, and social.

This book is for leaders, those who now lead organizations and those who will in the future. It is for members, workers, supporters, customers, and stakeholders everywhere. Organizations are a human enterprise and, as Peter Drucker says in his introduction, their highest purpose is "to make the strengths of people effective and their weaknesses irrelevant." Throughout the chapters in this book, the need for organizations is unquestioned. The authors provide a variety of forms and operating plans for organizations today and tomorrow; at the same time, each recognizes the indispensable role of organizations to human accomplishment and achievement.

It is our hope that as you begin to read *The Organization of the Future*, you will find in its remarkable diversity a few applicable messages that can help to move your organization into an uncertain, yet exuberant, future.

Guideposts

This book is designed to be perused—read not in one sitting, but a chapter or two at a time, to be thought about, deliberated, held in our leadership book bag as a companion on the journey to the future. The structure of the book gives guidance to the reader, providing guideposts on the road.

If the urgency of the moment, for you, is shaping the future of your organization, Part One brings "Shaping Tomorrow's Organizations," with chapters that examine preparation, generational shifts, the soul and size, design and competencies, for a new world of organizations. If "New Models for Working and Organizing" are your special need, Part Two ranges from concept to architecture, from mission to shape.

Part Three, "Organizing for Strategic Advantage," is about strategy and the strategic context. Here we see people as the heart of the organization, the civic character—learning, winning, and organizing around capabilities. Communication, technology, knowledge, and information converge in Part Four, "Working and Organizing in a Wired World." Here, the chapters offer unique perspectives into our increasingly interconnected, wired world.

All the shaping, organizing, working, and winning will have little effect if new concepts of leading and managing people are missing. In Part Five, "Leading People in the Organization of the Future," our authors explore new ways of thinking about the skills, emotions, cultures, competencies, and capabilities that are essential to leading people into the future. Part Six, "New Definitions of Organizational Health," includes work-life balance and the health, diversity, and social results needed for the next challenge.

The Only Gift

All of the book's distinguished thinkers, authors, and leaders gave their time and thinking as a personal contribution to the future and to the work of the Drucker Foundation. Their contributions provide insight, wisdom, and experience to leaders of all organizations across the globe. Through these contributions, the forty-six authors confirmed Ralph Waldo Emerson's observation: "The only gift is a portion of thyself." We are deeply grateful that we can share their gifts with you.

The Drucker Foundation Future Series

Starting with the first book, *The Leader of the Future*, and continuing with this one, the Drucker Foundation Future Series seeks to provide the latest and most innovative thinking on the future of leadership, organization, community, and change. Each volume examines a different facet of the jewel of organizational life, but all focus on the critical function of organizations that was so precisely defined by Peter Drucker in *Managing in a Time of Great Change*, "to put knowledge to work—on tools, products, and processes; on the design of work; on knowledge itself." We wish you continued success in making strengths effective and weaknesses irrelevant. We strive to do the same in this and upcoming volumes in the Drucker Foundation Future Series.

October 1996   Frances Hesselbein
                                                 Easton, Pennsylvania

                                                 Marshall Goldsmith
                                                 Rancho Santa Fe, California

                                                 Richard Beckhard
                                                 New York, New York

SPECIAL THANKS TO THE PUBLICATION TEAM

The Organization of the Future is the result of the efforts of scores of people who coordinated their efforts toward a common goal. We are honored to work with these friends and colleagues who further our mission.

First, our heartfelt thanks go to the forty-six authors whose work makes up this book. We are deeply grateful for their gifts. Their intellectual contributions provide extraordinary energy to the Drucker Foundation as it pursues its mission: "to lead social sector organizations toward excellence in performance."

Attracting and involving the authors and making their works into a book required the contributions of the following extraordinary people:

Marshall Goldsmith, whose bright idea it was to recruit our friends to write articles on leadership and the future as a contribution to the work of the Drucker Foundation and to publish them in a book, *The Leader of the Future*. He continues as an editor and a recruiter of friends and articles for the books that have become the Future Series, and as an energized and energizing member of the Foundation's Board of Governors.

Richard Beckhard, distinguished author, editor, organization development consultant, and retired professor of the Sloan School of Management at the Massachusetts Institute of Technology, who recruits his friends to write, edits the Future Series, and is a member of the Foundation's Board of Advisors.

Alan Shrader, our editor at Jossey-Bass, who shepherded the flock of Drucker Foundation publications and worked as our partner in developing new publications for leaders in all sectors.

Rob Johnston, vice president of the Drucker Foundation, who serves as managing editor of the Future Series, coordinating the efforts of three editors and scores of authors.

Pat Rose of Keilty, Goldsmith & Company in California and *Asa Danes*, *Debra Lewis*, and *Amy Sazama* of the Drucker Foundation in New York, who coordinate the collection of biographies, letters of agreement, and manuscripts from all our author contributors.

Each member of the publication team played a unique and indispensable role. We are deeply grateful.

October 1996

Frances Hesselbein
President and Chief Executive Officer
The Drucker Foundation

PETER F. DRUCKER

Introduction

Toward the New Organization

For over a century, starting in the 1860s, the trend worldwide was toward an employee society of big organizations. This trend seemed inexorable and irreversible. The world best-seller in 1965 was a book by a French politician and journalist, Jean-Jacques Servan-Schreiber, titled *Le Défi américain* (The American Challenge). Servan-Schreiber predicted that, by 1990 or so, four-fifths of the world's manufacturing would be in the hands of, at most, fifteen American multinational companies, each employing hundreds of thousands of people worldwide. But just when this book had sold millions of copies, the tide turned. Production and sales in the world economy have more than tripled in these thirty years, but since the mid-sixties, most of the then-existing big businesses—American, British, German, French, Swiss, and even Japanese—have lost market share worldwide. Adjusted for inflation, few have grown at all, except by merger or acquisition. One example: in the last ten years, since the mid-eighties, U.S. exports of manufactured goods have almost doubled. About 80 to 90 percent of that growth has come from small or medium-sized companies. In fact, where we used to speak of economies of scale, we now increasingly speak of *diseconomies* of scale.

The trend toward an employee society of big organizations gathered rapid momentum after World War I and, especially, after World War II. In 1914, before the outbreak of World War I, the great majority of people in the workforce in every developed country were not independent or self-employed. They were employees—as the great majority of workers have been since prehistoric times. But they did not work for an organization. They worked for a master or a mistress as hired hands and sharecroppers, as domestic servants, as salespeople in small stores, or as apprentices and journeymen in crafters' shops. Only blue-collar workers in manufacturing plants worked for an organization, and they were still a small minority—no more than a tenth of the workforce, even in highly industrialized countries.

By 1965, at least four-fifths of the workforce in the developed world—the United States, Germany, the United Kingdom, and Japan—had become employees of organizations. In fact, President Lyndon Johnson's Great Society programs, such as Medicare, *assumed* that by 1990 or 1995 practically everyone in the U.S. workforce would have become an employee in a big organization (and thus have both employer-paid health insurance and an employer-paid pension). But just as everyone had accepted this forecast, the tide turned. The great majority of today's workforces in highly developed countries do indeed work for—or at least with—an organization. But increasingly, they work not as employees of an organization but as temporaries, for an "outsourcing" contractor, as specialists providing expert services, and so on. We are moving toward a network society rather than an employee society.

For over a century, from their beginnings in the 1860s and 1870s, organizations were based on ownership. The typical company owned, or at least controlled, whatever it considered its business. Independent suppliers and distributors existed, but they were "outside." The company itself was based on command and control, anchored in ownership. That is still the structure of traditional businesses, but increasingly, command and control is being replaced by or intermixed with all kinds of relationships: alliances, joint ventures, minority participations, partnerships, know-how, and marketing agreements—all relationships in which no one controls and no one commands. These relationships have to be based on a common understanding of objectives, policies, and strategies; on teamwork; and on persuasion—or they do no work at all. And where the old command-and-control organization based on ownership was meant to be permanent, many of the new relationships are temporary and ad hoc.

The multinational business is not, as most people assume, an invention of the post–World War II period. It goes back to the fifteenth century, to the world's first financial "superpower," the Florence-based Medici bank. It was the world's first true multinational, with sixteen or eighteen branches covering all of Europe. In both manufacturing and finance and even in retailing, multinationals held a substantially larger share of the world's business in the decades before the First World War than they do even today. But *multinational* meant then, as it did for the Medici, having separate businesses in separate countries under common ownership. The Swiss subsidiary of the U.S.-based National Cash Register Company made and sold the same U.S.-designed products as every other National Cash Register subsidiary, but it was run as a Swiss company, was staffed by Swiss nationals (except maybe for an American comptroller), made all its products in Switzerland, and sold them exclusively in Switzerland. To this day, most British "know" that the Ford Motor Company and the Woolworth Corporation are "true-blue" English companies and that Ivory soap is made by an English company. But Ford and Woolworth are, of course, wholly owned subsidiaries of U.S. companies, and Ivory soap is made by the wholly owned subsidiary of America's Procter & Gamble. But until fairly recently, these subsidiaries were run as autonomous—or at least separate—English companies.

Increasingly, companies, even quite small ones, have to be run as "transnational" businesses. Their market may still be local or regional, but their competition is global. Their strategy also has to be global, in respect to technology and finance, products and markets, information and people. This is also true for organizations other than businesses. The small management school where I teach, for instance, has to base its curriculum on the assumption that it competes not only with management schools in Southern California and the United States but also—in fact, primarily—with management schools in half a dozen European countries and even with management schools in New Zealand. Increasingly our prosperity, indeed our survival, depends on enrollment from foreign countries, and especially from Asia and Europe, in our Executive Management Program. And management schools in Switzerland and France are rapidly becoming our most serious competitors in attracting students.

A good many writers, seeing all these changes and all this turmoil, are writing of "the end of organizations." That, however, is the one thing we can predict with certainty will not happen. To be sure, theoretically, anarchy—the absence of organization—is by far the most consistent and most persuasive theory. The only flaw is that it does not work. Organizations will be needed even more than before. Precisely because there will be so much ambiguity, so much flexibility, so many variations, far more clarity will be needed in respect to mission, values, and strategy; in balancing long-range and short-range goals; in defining results. Above all, absolute clarity will be needed as to who makes ultimate decisions and who is in command in a crisis.

What we mean by *organizations* is indeed changing. The first definition of an organization—it might be called the first theory of the organization—comes from the way the Prussian king Frederick the Great, in the mid-eighteenth century, defined his invention of the modern army. "An army," he said, "has three parts: infantry walks; cavalry rides; artillery is being pulled." An organization, in other words, is defined by how different work is being done. This basic concept underlay all military organizations through World War II. But it was also the concept that underlay the first attempt to define business organizations: the theory of the manufacturing business, which was developed around the time of World War I by a French executive, Henri Fayol, the head of what was then Europe's largest coal mining company. The purpose of the organization is to get the work done. This requires a structure that puts similar work, like engineering, manufacturing, and selling, into departments. After World War I and Alfred Sloan's reorganization of General Motors Corporation (and culminating in the 1950s with the decentralization of the American General Electric Company), we superimposed on Fayol's model a structure called the "business unit." It tries to balance the *internal* concern for getting the work done with the *external* concern of serving the market. It is still the most widely accepted approach and underlies all of the present discussion of balancing "core competencies" and "market focus" as well as the present concern with reengineering.

But now a totally different approach is emerging, not replacing the older approaches but being superimposed on them: it says that the purpose of organizations is to get results *outside*, that is, to achieve performance in the market. The organization is, however, more than a machine, as it is in Fayol's structure. It is more than economic, defined by results in the marketplace. The organization is, above all, *social.* It is people. Its purpose must therefore be to make the strengths of people effective and their weaknesses irrelevant. In fact, that is the one thing only the organization can do—the one reason why we have it and need to have it.

But as important as these shifts may be in the theory of the organization and the resulting shifts in its structure, even more important is the fact that we are rapidly moving away from the belief that there has to be one theory of the organization and one ideal structure, the belief that underlay Frederick the Great's definition of an army, Fayol's "typical manufacturing company," and the business units of Sloan's General Motors and Jack Welch's General Electric. A good many of the contributors to this volume still seem to believe that there is—or should be—one ideal organization. But the very diversity of their contributions makes it clear that organizations will increasingly be fashioned differently: for different purposes, different kinds of work, different people, and different cultures. The organization is not just a tool. It bespeaks values. It bespeaks the personality of a business, a nonprofit enterprise, a government agency. It is both defined by and defines a specific enterprise's results. The most novel fact, and this volume clearly expresses it, is that we are rapidly moving toward a plurality and a pluralism of organizations. We are rapidly moving toward *the new organizations*.

Part I

Shaping Tomorrow's Organizations

1
JAMES A. CHAMPY

Preparing for Organizational Change

James A. Champy, chairman of the Consulting Group, Perot
Systems Corporation, is the leading authority on the management
issues surrounding business reengineering, organizational change,
and corporate renewal. He is coauthor of Reengineering the
Corporation, *which has sold more than two million copies. His*
book Reengineering Management *was named by* Business
Week *as one of the best business books of 1995. His newest*
book, coedited with Nitin Nohria, was published in March 1996.
A compilation of Harvard Business Review *articles on change,*
it is titled Fast Forward.

I often describe organizational change today as a "journey." To many managers, it's a journey that never ends. Some tell me that the journey is leaving them breathless. My advice: learn to "breathe" differently and anticipate what you are likely to encounter. This chapter is about anticipation and preparation.

Any major change effort must begin by describing the journey's destination. It may be a dramatic improvement in operating performance, but not just financial performance. Focusing on cost reduction may lead only to downsizing, with no real improvement in the organization's effectiveness. Objectives might also include improvements in service, quality, growth, or return on investment. Sometimes the objective is expressed in terms of creating more shareholder value. The "destination" of a pharmaceutical company was a 50 percent reduction in its drug development and approval time, from eight to four years. A telecommunications company's objective was to install a new service in one day, rather than the thirty days it had previously taken. The goal of a major health care provider was to let customers see a physician at the time most convenient for them, not the clinic.

Such ambitious objectives are the hallmark of what has become known as reengineering. Besides ambition, reengineering is characterized by the recognition that the organization of work need not follow function, but rather should follow processes that cross functional lines, and by the frequent need to design the flow of work from scratch, starting over rather than just incrementally changing what exists today. Reengineering usually is a journey in uncharted waters.

But sometimes the journey's objective is even more ambitious than changing the work flow and operating performance of a company. Many companies find themselves in industries that are dramatically changing. The forces of change may be emerging technologies, such as the Internet, or conditions of deregulation, privatization, and open trade. Often, a combination of these factors causes fundamental industry restructuring. These changes raise profound questions of strategy. How does a newspaper publisher profit in the information age, when news is freely available in digital form and advertisers have multiple channels for broadcasting their messages? What does a retail bank do with its investment in the bricks and mortar of a branch network in the face of the onslaught of "virtual" banks and home banking? How does an electric utility learn to compete and grow in markets that are relatively flat? What is the "business" of a hospital in a health care industry whose future has yet to be clearly defined?

The answers to these questions will demand much more than the reengineering of a company's processes; it will require that the business itself be reinvented. The journey of business reinvention will take place in even more turbulent waters than the journey of reengineering. Reinvention is characterized by changes in many elements of the organization at once. Processes will be redesigned, new opportunities and strategies will emerge, organizational structures and relationships will shift both inside and outside the company, new information technology infrastructures will be required, the work of managers will change, and we will require new behaviors from our people. All this will add to a manager's breathlessness, as shareholders and customers demand that change happen quickly.

Faced with such dramatic and multifaceted change, managers must cast away the strategic planning approaches of the past. This is not a simple journey from A to B. It has too many unknowns, too many perceived barriers. Yet we must know the journey's business objectives in substantive terms, and we must anticipate the challenges and breakdowns along the way. Like reengineering, reinvention is a journey that requires an inclination to action, rather than an inclination to study; it is marked by breakdowns from which we must recover and move on. Here are some of the conditions and events to anticipate and prepare for, whether you are reengineering or reinventing the business.

Breakdown at the Top

Major change programs must be top-down and vision-driven, and they require broader participation in the design and implementation phases. However, no workforce that I know of has ever arrived at the office or plant on Monday morning and voted to transform the company. At least initially, major change programs must be actively led by senior management.

Senior management teams often appear to be in agreement about the need for and direction of change. It's easy to buy into broad strategy statements: "We want to be number one in customer service"; "Let's become the low-cost, high-quality provider"; "We must lead the market with innovation." But, usually within the first three months of a major change program, as members of the senior management team confront the real implications of change, their effort breaks down. Sometimes the breakdown is visible and results in confrontation. That's good. This provides an opportunity to debate the issues and concerns, get resolution, and move on. Sometimes, however, the breakdown is quiet. It goes underground. There is a hope that "this, too, shall pass." As one senior manager who was mobilizing a company for change told me, "People just stopped coming to my meetings." When this happens, the breakdown may take the form of a slowing down of change activities. Eventually, the change program dies.

Whatever the manifestation of the breakdown, the senior management team must restart the effort by getting agreement on at least three issues:

the business case for the change ("Why must we go through this?"), the scope and scale of the change ("What processes are we going to reengineer?" or "How much of the business must change?"), and the governance process for managing the change ("Who will be accountable for the design and for the results?"). It would, of course, be best to have determined this at the launch of the change program. However, managers are typically anxious to move on and, thus, wind up fooling themselves into believing that they have agreement. Or they may have agreement, but only about an abstract objective. Whatever the case, the quality of the debate on these three issues will tell you whether you're ready to start—or restart.

Changing Scope

I once had a very sophisticated manager ask me how he could tell whether he was in the right place with his change program. He said he was particularly concerned because the scope of the program kept changing. Was he out of control or was everything okay? My answer was, "It depends, of course, but you're probably okay." Changes in scope are common. As I suggested earlier, today's change programs are marked by ambition. Companies are looking for big results over a short period of time. But this ambition is often tempered with concerns about risk. How much can we change at once? Won't we be risking the business?

This leads to schizophrenic behavior. Usually, the initial scope is big; a few months into the effort, the scope is narrowed because of concerns about risk and manageability. As the program moves to implementation, the people running it discover that the narrower scope won't deliver the required business results, so they expand the effort.

This is a natural phenomenon. What's important is to keep checking to see if the scope of the change effort will produce the business results you require. Here's some added advice on managing risk: every large organizational change is risky, and breakdowns are inevitable. I have never experienced a control system that could prevent all of them. And when the breakdowns happen, it usually takes the superhuman efforts of a number of people to allow the company to recover, particularly without the breakdown becoming visible to customers. Business risk is minimized by having the kind of person on your team who will respond appropriately when breakdowns occur.

Scale

It may be counterintuitive, but I have now concluded that the larger the scale of a change program, the more likely it is to succeed. I must admit that this assertion is often challenged. The argument is that a large-scale program is "too much, too fast" for the human condition. I'm told that organizations and people cannot change that quickly. A more incremental, evolutionary approach is required, so the argument goes.

As you might expect, I disagree. A change program aimed at incremental improvements creates too many fronts on which to fight battles. Sometimes the battles are quiet. You don't even know that they are going on. And sometimes, in fact, nothing *is* going on! People are just involved in continuing discussions or study—no action is being taken. The organization's antibodies are quietly killing the change effort. If the change program is large, however, and it has senior management's commitment, the organization must confront all that is required to manage the change. No hiding, no return to the current state. The results—or lack of results—are also visible. But in the end, remember that the degree of industry change and management ambition will determine the scale of a company's business and organizational change. The change may make us breathless, but we may not have the option of slowing it down.

Everything Changes

Sometimes, a large change program can begin with a narrow focus: reengineering order fulfillment or customer service or new-product development. But be prepared for a lot more to change than a business process and don't expect to keep the change localized. When a business process changes, required skills and jobs change. A new organizational structure usually results. The old reward and recognition systems will no longer work. The work of managers changes as people become more self-managed. By anticipating these shifts, managers can accelerate the change process. Not all of the shifts will be initially visible, but for those that are, early attention can prevent your having to redo or restart a change program.

For example, thinking ahead about what resulting management or governance structures might look like can give you a lot of perspective on how to manage the change process itself. If structures or managers are likely to change, the management of the change process may have to occur outside of the company's normal governance process. Thinking ahead about structure and managers will also help you anticipate how to manage the transition from the old to the new way of operating. Will the designers of business and organizational changes be the implementors of the change? Will program sponsorship and leadership shift during the journey? Might you run two businesses for some period of time: one with the new operating model, one with the old? Or will you immediately make the transition from the old to the new way of operating? Anticipating how these shifts will occur can also be helpful in sorting through employee and staffing issues.

On the issue of keeping change localized, recognize that most major performance improvements come from changes that cut across organizational boundaries. Getting products to market more quickly does not just involve the research and development function. It will also involve manufacturing, marketing, sales, and distribution. Significantly improving customer service doesn't just mean answering the phone more quickly. It is likely to also include redesigning products so that defects show up less frequently and the service phone doesn't ring at all.

Many organizational changes today directly attack fragmentation. Companies are recognizing that the supremacy of departments and functions has led to bureaucracy and internally focused management. To significantly improve the business, organizational boundaries must become more porous. So whether you are attacking fragmentation directly or getting there through some process change objective, expect the change to go further than you may have originally planned.

Conversation Versus Communication

There is an endless stream of advice on the need for constant communication about any change program. But having observed many companies carefully execute communication programs, I am now convinced that broadcasting messages is not enough. What's required is conversation, not just communication. Listen for a moment to a manager who has made that discovery: "I regularly give the chairman's talk: why we need to change and where we are going. But I know that it's not enough. So we've produced videotapes that make the case, published newsletters, and used all types of media. But I know that's still not enough. What we need is for the person who runs the cafeteria to understand what we're up to well enough to communicate to everyone who works in that area why we are doing this, where we are going, and what it means for all of us."

You should anticipate two needs that people have during a major change program. The first is the need to believe that the company's management knows what it's doing, where its markets are going, and how it's going to accomplish change. The second is the need to understand what the change means to individuals in the organization. The challenge in responding to this second need is that, early in most organizational changes, no one may know what these changes will mean to the individual. Concerns cannot be met by one-way forms of communication. We must mobilize managers to have conversations with people across the organization about the drivers and implications of the change program. It's in the give and take of discussion that people will discover the truth about what's likely to happen.

Fear and Cynicism

Be prepared to encounter fear and cynicism. The fear comes from the real possibility of job loss or job change. Reengineering does not mean automatic downsizing, but many managers use these terms interchangeably. Often, the intention is, in fact, to downsize the organization. Cynicism can come from distrusting that managers will do what they say and suspecting that their jargon is disguising their real intent. Additionally, many organizations have had a succession of change programs that have produced few results.

Some of the fear and cynicism can be addressed in the conversations that you have with people; fear will not go away if it is legitimate, but much of the cynicism can be dispelled if managers act authentically on what they say.

Focusing on More Than Performance

Here's one last piece of advice. Most organizational changes today are made in the name of improved business performance. This should continue to be the objective. But while you are driving toward this result, also be thinking about creating a company that is agile, that can sustain multiple changes, and that is a good place in which to work. You don't want to put in place an organization that, five years from now, can't respond quickly to the next wave of industry change. Keep asking whether you are just replacing one form of organization with another that is equally rigid. Nimbleness and agility should be your principal design criteria.

2

JAY A. CONGER

How Generational Shifts Will Transform Organizational Life

Jay A. Conger is chairman and executive director of the Leadership Institute at the University of Southern California. He is one of the world's experts on leadership. Author of over sixty articles and four books, he researches executive leadership, the management of organizational change, and the training and development of leaders and managers. A recent book, Learning to Lead *(1992), is the culmination of a two-year research effort examining the field of leadership training. It was described by* Fortune *magazine as "the source" for understanding leadership training. His newest book,* Spirit at Work *(1994), explores the search for community and meaning in the workplace.*

Certain parts of the world have seasonal winds that affect the moods of local inhabitants when they appear. Though invisible, these winds bring temperature and barometric changes that produce tangible physiological effects. A parallel could be drawn with the different generations of humankind. Though composed of the same biological creatures, each generation has a distinct "wind" or character. As members of a generation pass through, they influence a society in ways that are different from those of their predecessors. From the perspective of organizational life today, these influences are particularly important. I say this because two significant transitions are occurring simultaneously: (1) a generation of Baby Boomers

17

is now of the age where they are entering the executive suite and (2) for the first time, the Baby Buster generation, or Generation X, is old enough to include front-line managers. These transitions will dramatically reshape expectations about what constitutes effective management in the organization of the future.

As one example of this, within the space of a single generation the word *boss* has completely changed its meaning. No longer a positive sign of accomplishment and authority, such a term now symbolizes distance from others, an unreasonable toughness, and other not-so-attractive connotations. Instead, among the Boomer and X generations, there is a desire to lead more as a symbolic peer. Recently, I had lunch with a Baby Boomer CEO. Afterward, he climbed into the front seat of his chauffeured company car so that he could be "up front" with a driver he knew. The very next week, I had lunch with the sixty-year-old president of a retailing company. This time, the executive slipped into the back seat of his chauffeured company car. Both knew their drivers well, and both had made important statements about their relationship vis-à-vis employees way down the line. Something remarkable has happened during the space of a single generation to cause this profound shift.

And if you think that Generation X is simply a copycat version of its older siblings, the Boomers, then take a look at the differences in the two groups' attitudes toward women bosses. According to an article by S. Mitchell in the February 1996 issue of *American Demographics*, 61 percent of the young women of Generation X say that they would prefer to work for a woman boss, as compared to 26 percent of women in the Boomer generation. Although only 22 percent of X'er men prefer a woman boss, some 52 percent say it doesn't matter which gender they report to. Something quite fundamental and important is occurring, not only within these two generations but also between them.

Today's Workplace Generations

Three generations are working in today's organizations. What makes each of them special is that they have experienced certain historical events unique to their specific generation. For example, most of the Silent Generation, born between 1925 and 1942, missed out on combat in World War II and instead were the children of war and of the Great Depression. They would not only become the youngest-marrying generation in the history of the United States, but also the generation that would experience the largest increase in divorce of any of today's age brackets.

Behind the Silent Generation comes the well-publicized Baby Boomer generation—a group born between 1943 and 1960. They started off their college years with sit-down protests in deans' offices and stereos blasting rock music. They were raised in an era of phenomenal national wealth, which would later translate into an indulged and somewhat narcissistic generation nicknamed the yuppies. Demographers of the Boomer generation summarize their character as largely individualistic.

The most recent generation, born between 1961 and 1981, is gradually filling in the wake of the Boomers. These young people are officially called the Baby Busters, because of the drop-off or "bust" in births following the Boomer generation. We know them more popularly as Generation X, after the title of a best-selling book about them. They are the children of dual-career couples and of parents whose marriages ended in record national divorce rates. In contrast to the Boomers, this is the group that chose majors in business and economics rather than in political science and psychology, as their parents' generation did. With this generation, the adolescent idealism so characteristic of the Boomers gave way to a more pragmatic and cynical realism.

From the vantage point of organizations, we are particularly interested in these fundamental differences between the generations because they tell us about expectations and motivations. For example, a direct link exists between attitudes toward formal authority and the way individuals prefer to be managed. Those with a strong respect for formal authority will accept, or at least tolerate, a more domineering, control-oriented boss. Those with an aversion toward formal authority will demonstrate little tolerance of domineering superiors and may even rebel against or depart from their authority. Motivation to perform under such circumstances is likely to tumble.

We normally associate variations in reactions to formal authority with a person's *stage* in the life cycle. In other words, we assume that adolescents are more likely to distrust and rebel against authority. After all, the teenage years are the time when individuals search for personal identity, and rebellion is an important part of that process. The critical question is whether this distrust of authority persists into midlife and beyond, becoming what we call a structural change between generations. In itself, this would be a remarkable historical event. What I am going to argue is that we are indeed experiencing this remarkable historical event—a major structural change between the generations in their willingness to respect formal authority. This fundamental shift began with the Baby Boomers and continues today with the Busters, setting these two generations distinctly apart from previous generations.

The Silent Generation was in essence the end of the line of "command" generations. After all, their parents were the last living generation in which a majority served in the military and had great respect for it. They are a generation whose lifetimes have seen strong and admired political and military leaders restore the well-being of the society and achieve victory in a world war. They are also the generation for whom the term "organization man" was coined because of the loyalty commanded by and given to the corporation. Coming out of these times, the Silent Generation retained high respect for formal authority and for the effectiveness of the command model. But all of that has changed with their children, the Baby Boomers.

The Baby Boomers

The Baby Boomers saw the vulnerability of authority. They witnessed a failed war in Vietnam, the assassination of two Kennedys and Martin Luther King Jr., the disgrace of a president after Watergate, the OPEC oil crisis, and environmental disasters like Three Mile Island. To this generation, authority looked unreliable and, often, just plain wrong. Unlike their parents, they thought it reasonable to challenge authority directly. Their college years were marked by scenes in which students took over college administration offices to protest what was seen as an unfair war in Vietnam—challenges to authority that were largely unimaginable to the Silent Generation.

This generation's reluctance to accept formal authority with ease is also tied to seeds of independence planted in their childhoods. For example, from public opinion surveys taken over an entire century in the United States, we can trace how independence has grown as a positive character trait for children. Surveys starting in 1890 found that only 16 percent of parents believed that independence was an important characteristic for their children. By the end of the 1970s, however, approximately 75 percent of all parents felt that independence was *the most important* character trait.

Although numerous forces lie behind the importance placed on independence, several have been particularly influential. One was a new mood of child rearing that appeared with the publication of the book *Dr. Spock's Baby and Child Care*, with its strong emphasis on teaching children to be independent. This book would become the bible of child rearing for the parents of the Baby Boomers. Then came the commercial introduction in the 1960s of the contraceptive pill, which gave women a greater sense of control. Combined with the successes of the women's movement, these two forces would ultimately create a new and dramatically heightened sense of autonomy for women. The migration of women into the labor force in massive numbers, jumping from 31.5 percent of the labor force in 1960 to almost 60 percent in 1992, would only further reinforce these feelings. Finally, education played a critical role in undermining traditional authority. The Baby Boomers were participants in the greatest and most dramatic wave of education in history. This trend has continued with Generation X. As greater numbers of students went on to college and graduate school, they found themselves in learning environments where they were encouraged and expected to criticize the books and ideas they were studying. They were actually graded on their ability to challenge one another's thinking and even the professor's thinking in classroom discussions.

All of these forces are creating a new generation of leaders who will shun the stereotypical commander's role. Instead, we will see a more informal, team-based leadership role emerge among them. They will share responsibility more easily, communicate more frequently, and challenge the hierarchies of their organization more comfortably.

Generation X

Like the Boomers, the Busters possess a strong sense of determination and willingness to work, but it is balanced by a desire to place boundaries on the infringement of work on their personal lives. The comments of a young banker are representative of what I have found:

I'm definitely willing to work long hours during the week. But I think there is a limit to it. I think you need some time for yourself, for your family, for recreation. I sense that there's more of a concern about quality-of-life issues. It's not really wanting the expensive vacation. It's just wanting to enjoy life. I don't think that just having things will satisfy us. It's related to the uncertainty of life. Life isn't the way it was in the fifties and sixties. There are so many nasty things that can happen along the way. There are diseases, there's crime—I mean, you're so bombarded constantly with all these negative aspects, so it makes you think you might as well enjoy some of life.

In general, several important historical forces are shaping Generation X to be less loyal to organizations and therefore to traditional authority than even the Boomers have been. Let's start with the notion of limits to work. Although this value may change as Generation X members move into midlife, where career demands soar, it appears for now to be a trademark of this generation. Interview after interview confirms a sense of being willing to work hard but not at the expense of one's personal life. This attitude has its roots both in the childhood homes of X'ers and in the organizations where their parents work.

First of all, this is the generation of dual-career couples. No generation in recent history has seen so many working couples. Remembering that X'ers are individuals who were born between 1961 and 1981, the statistics on women participating in the labor force who have children under the age of six jumped from 18.6 percent in 1960 to 59.9 percent in 1992. As a result, Generation X is the first generation to bear both the advantage of dual-family incomes and the downside of more absent parents. Simultaneously, as more mothers have entered the workforce, divorce rates have climbed at the steepest rate in history. At today's current rates, approximately half of all marriages in the United States will end in divorce. A heightened divorce rate and dual careers actually go hand in hand as women with incomes worry less about the poverty that can come with divorce.

What we may witness with members of Generation X is a wish not to replicate their own childhood experiences, with parents who were less available. Instead, there appears to be a growing desire to build more traditional family lives. As a twenty-five-year-old male manager explained to me, "You really need to be careful not to give 100 percent of yourself to the job, because there will be nothing left over for your partner when you get home at the end of the day." Having time at home with the family is a priority they felt their parents only partially pursued. In interviews, I have consistently heard the comment, "We are not living to work but working to live, choosing a life that we want to have as opposed to just bringing home a paycheck." This attitude makes the members of Generation X far less willing to see their identity as tightly linked to any organization. They prefer to see themselves as an independent lot who can move if they don't like where they are.

The second set of forces undermining Generation X's respect for formal authority comes from organizations themselves. Witnessing waves of corporate downsizing just as they were graduating from college, young people quickly and rightly sensed that company loyalty was a thing of the past. The once-secure workplace havens of AT&T and IBM have dismissed tens of thousands of employees. The contract of lifetime loyalty, which began to slide with the Boomer generation, is practically nonexistent for younger generations. Nowhere is the evidence of this more apparent than in X'ers' expectations about their careers. When asked how many employers they expect to have over the course of their careers, Generation X'ers will typically state, "Three to five." When they are asked why, they will say that members of their generation expect to lose their jobs at some point. Just as important, they have the sense that better opportunities, better salaries, better challenges, better locations always lie in the next move to another organization, not in waiting patiently to move up the hierarchy. As with the generation before them, they believe that loyalty rests with yourself and your teammates, not with your corporation.

As with the Baby Boomers, managing this generation as their "boss" will only backfire. Instead, they will be seeking superiors who are mentors and coaches, who lead more by effective persuasion than by command. Given the relative absence of community in their childhood lives, X'ers will be drawn toward managers and organizations that create a genuine sense of community. As managers themselves, members of Generation X will strive to do the same for their subordinates or, as they will call them, their teammates.

Conclusion

The generational shifts just described will play a powerful role in shaping how employees of the organization of the future will prefer to be managed and led. Clearly, more informal, team- and persuasion-based approaches will succeed with the Boomers and Generation X. The dilemma that we face as managers, however, is that these generational transitions are like a riptide; their force is not completely visible on the surface. Instead, we experience their pull in the individual incidents of a day that leave us wondering why forty-year-old Mark would rather accept a team decision than make his own. Or why twenty-nine-year-old Ashley left our firm after two fast-track promotions to start her own business. If, as managers of the organization of the future, we do not understand these dynamic forces, we are likely to be tumbled in their surf.

3   MICHAEL HAMMER

The Soul of the New Organization

Michael Hammer, one of the world's foremost business thinkers, is the originator of both reengineering and process centering, ideas that have transformed the modern business world. Formerly a professor of computer science at the Massachusetts Institute of Technology, he is founder and director of several high-technology firms and the author of the international best-sellers Reengineering the Corporation: A Manifesto for Business Revolution *(1993),* The Reengineering Revolution: A Handbook *(1995), and* Beyond Reengineering: How the Process-Centered Organization Is Changing Our Work and Our Lives *(1996). In 1996 he was named by* Time *magazine as one of America's twenty-five most influential individuals.*

An organization is more than a set of products and services. It is also a human society, and like all societies, it nourishes particular forms of culture, "company cultures." Every company has its own language, its own version of its history (its myths), and its own heroes and villains (its legends), both historical and contemporary. The whole flourishing tangle serves to confirm old-timers, and to induct newcomers, in the corporation's

Note: This chapter is adapted and edited from *Beyond Reengineering: How the Process-Centered Organization Is Changing Our Work and Our Lives,* by Michael Hammer (New York: Harper-Business, 1996). Copyright © 1996 by Michael Hammer. Reprinted by permission of Harper-Collins Publishers, Inc.

distinctive identity and its particular norms of behavior. In myriad ways, formal and informal, it tells them what is okay and what is not.

Despite their many differences, great similarities exist across most contemporary organizational cultures. Certain themes resonate almost everywhere: avoiding blame and responsibility, treating coworkers as competitors, feeling entitled, and not feeling intense and committed. This commonality is hardly surprising. After all, most of today's corporations were born and raised in the same business environment, subject to the same pressures and issues. And because nurture definitely dominates nature in the business world, most companies, facing a common context, developed a common culture.

The key feature of the environment in which most contemporary organizations came of age is that by and large, for the last two hundred years, demand exceeded supply. It would be an exaggeration to say that corporate growth in this era was purely demographic—a simple matter of the growing numbers and purchasing power of consumers—but it wouldn't be much of one. On the whole, from the last quarter of the eighteenth century to this, the last quarter of the twentieth century, producers have consistently had the upper hand over consumers. Except during downturns in the business cycle, there were always more people—or companies—who wanted to buy than there were goods or services to satisfy them. Whether it was automobiles, telephone service, or soft drinks, the dominant concern for the modern corporation was to keep up with an apparently insatiable demand. The primary goal was to not make mistakes. With a market waiting to be taken, brilliance and innovation were unnecessary; caution and plodding could be counted on to carry the day. So why take risks? The highest values—planning, control, and discipline—were those needed to capitalize on a ready market.

This business context fostered company cultures that were strangely at odds with America's independent and democratic spirit. You might suppose that nothing could go more against the American grain than having to make a career, or at least a living, in an organization that was at once paternalistic, controlling, and bureaucratic. Here was a hat trick, if there ever was one, against personal freedom! Yet, in fact, so it was for everyone except those lucky few who scrambled their way through bureaucratic warrens and up the hierarchical pole. Almost everyone else, workers and managers alike, found life in the industrial-era corporation stifling and disheartening. Inventiveness was frustrated by protocol and work rules. Ambition expressed itself more in politics than in productivity. Craftsmanship was a thing of the past and creativity a thing of the future, reserved for after hours.

Why did people put up with this for so many years? The answer is obvious: security. Even Americans were never so in love with freedom, independence, and risk—were never, in a word, so *entrepreneurial*—that they would blithely brush aside the value of employment security. To oversimplify (but again, not by much), at the heart of the old company culture was a deal: obedience and diligence in exchange for security, security for obedience and diligence. The deal was not always simply struck. Many workers had to unionize and strike to get real security, not to mention higher pay; management had to supervise and bureaucratize to get the other side of the bargain. But the deal was there, and it held for the better part of the modern era.

No longer. A historic chain reaction is under way—enormous changes in the business environment forcing deep changes in company cultures—and the cumulative effect is a deal breaker. The rise of the demanding customer is the crucial precipitating factor in the chain reaction that is doing in the security-for-obedience-and-diligence deal. When the customer comes first in the environment, something has to adjust in the company culture. Customers care nothing for our management structure, our strategic plan, or our financial structure. They are interested in only one thing: results, the value we deliver. A customer focus forces an emphasis on results and on fashioning a culture that supports their delivery.

The effect of the modern customer on the security-for-obedience-and-diligence deal can be felt already. When a customer calls the tune, everyone in a company must dance. But this means letting go of commands; no system that depends on segregating wisdom and decision making into a managerial class can possibly offer the speed and agility customers demand. It also means letting go of metaphors like "hands." Customers require whole human beings possessed of hands, heads, and hearts to serve them.

In the new regime, managers are not the deciders of the fate of employees; customers are. The company does not close plants or lay off workers; customers do, by their actions or inactions. Samuel Gompers might plausibly throw his slogan of "More!" in the face of a monopolist or oligopolist. His antagonists controlled their markets and their customers; if they wished, they could give employees a bigger cut of their pie. Now, it verges on the comic to read screeds against "giant and powerful multinational corporations." The corporations I know are closer to pitiful, helpless giants, all running scared of their customers. When the customer comes first, the company and its employees must perforce come second. Our needs must be subordinated to those of the people for whom we are creating value.

Like it or not, security, stability, and continuity are out, because there simply isn't anyone on the scene who can provide them. The company can't because the customer won't. Companies are not cold or cruel or heartless. They are merely running as fast as they can to keep up with demanding and unforgiving customers. The people who work in them will have to do the same. A sign should now hang in every factory, office, and work site: "You're on your own." It's not that no one cares about you; it's just that no one can do anything about it.

But the new regime also offers compensation to managers for withdrawing the power of command and to employees for withdrawing its protection from customers and the market. It offers freedom and personal growth. The essence of the new deal in the modern organization is an exchange: initiative for opportunity. The company offers its employees the opportunity, and often the educational means, to achieve personal success; in return, the employees promise the company to exercise initiative in creating value for customers and thereby profits for the company.

Obedience and diligence are now irrelevant. Following orders is no guarantee of success. Working hard at the wrong thing is no virtue. When customers are kings, mere hard work, without understanding, flexibility, and enthusiasm, leads nowhere. Work must be smart, appropriately targeted, and adapted to the particular circumstances of the process and the customer. Imagination, flexibility, and commitment to results are needed. If the results aren't achieved, you can no longer claim, "But I did what I was told and I worked very hard." It doesn't matter. You are accountable for results, not for effort.

Without protection, there is no reason to obey, and with obedience goes its cousin, loyalty. Loyalty to the company as a cultural artifact is

replaced by commitment to business succes
of the organization man—that putting th
was dispensation from further responsib
cess—is now ridiculous. Without resul
is an empty gesture. If it no longer gu
it can no longer guarantee success ro
work are by themselves quaint relics, about as
business success as the ability to make a perfect dry m
nizations must now urge employees to put loyalty to the custom
alty to the company, because that is the only way the company will tr

No longer is the company the "head," the employee the "hand." The employee is now assumed to be a mature, capable, self-reliant adult. The company does not promise to take care of the employee, which is just as well, because such a promise would be a false and empty one. "Taking care of your employees" implies a degree of control over your environment in which you can really intercede with the forces around you to shelter people from the impact of these forces. This promise may have been realistic once but is laughable now. Instead of protection, the company owes its people opportunity: the chance to do well, to succeed, to grow in their careers. Instead of "training and retraining," a model in which the employee is the object of external forces, the new deal is "the offer of training." An employee who leaves the company should be able to do so as a more capable and knowledgeable individual than he or she was on arrival. But there's a proviso to this: *provided* the employee takes advantage of the opportunity. Gone is the notion that somehow the company has the obligation to develop you.

Whether these changes are good or bad is a value judgment that must be made by every individual. Some will consider the new regime to be liberating and empowering; they will see it as conveying dignity and autonomy to every employee, by eliminating the controlling and confusing network of rules that has confined most people in their work lives. Others will see it as a harsh and cruel new world, a Darwinian jungle where only the fittest survive—and that only temporarily.

I prefer to simply call it realistic. For too long the large organization has provided a fantasy environment in which people could pretend that there was such a thing as security. By working hard and following the rules,

tainties of the outside world could be kept at bay. The organiza-
vided a buffer against reality, a comfortable zone of predictability
tability. So long as demand exceeded supply and customers were
ile and subservient, the fantasy could continue. But no longer. Corpo-
ations do not dominate their landscapes, controlling their customers and
securely deciding their own futures, any more than start-ups do. The large
company and its employees must get used to the environment and lifestyle
to which their entrepreneurial cousins adapted long ago—an environment
of uncertainty and anxiety, but also of exhilarating freedom. It may not be
to everyone's liking, but there is no going back.

In effect, the qualitative difference between large companies and small
ones, between young companies and established ones, between those who
create markets and those who control them, is gone. It has been replaced
by a mere quantitative difference. Large businesses are no longer very different from small ones; to paraphrase Ernest Hemingway's comment, they
simply have more people. And if a large corporation is, in effect, becoming more like a small company, then everyone who works in it must start
acting and thinking like an owner of a small company. Our new role model
is no longer the corporate manager but the entrepreneur. No one needs to
tell the owner of a small company about the need to stay close to the customer, to remain flexible, to reduce nonvalue-adding overhead, to respond
quickly to new situations. The owner sees with absolute clarity the connection between the way the business performs and the owner's own personal success and future prospects. The small businessperson will do
whatever it takes to succeed, knowing that the past is no indicator of the
future, the luxury of coasting is gone, there is no guarantee of future
employment, and success at one thing means nothing without success at
everything else.

How do all these new cultural elements look when they're brought
together? For that, let's look at GPU Generation Corporation, a medium-
sized electric power producer that operates plants in New Jersey and Pennsylvania. Their previously regulated and monopolistic industry is now in
the throes of deregulation, and a cross-section of people from across the
company have worked together to articulate the kinds of attitudes and
philosophies that everyone will need to share if the company is to make
it. The following are some excerpts from their work:

"In the GPU Generation Corporation, our only measure of success is to find out who our primary, paying customers are (or will be), find out what they want, and give it to them at a better overall value than anyone else."

"Nothing we do is more important than creating the best value for our customers. No other work matters at all."

"Serving and creating value for the customer means that each member of the firm must be treated as a professional who, whenever possible, is in charge of the whole job, not just pieces of it. Stop checking with the boss. You know what's best and you have an obligation to serve your customer and not keep asking for permission. If you need assistance, ask for it."

"To be effective, you must have both freedom and autonomy while at the same time acting professionally."

"If we are successful at becoming truly focused on creating value for our customers, we shouldn't need bosses in the traditional sense at all. We will already know what to do. We will need only to be kept informed and coached so we can be even more effective at what we do."

"Nobody hands us anything. We work for what we have, every day. We can't stand for anyone who does not want to contribute to our team."

This is not theory; this is reality. The twenty-first-century organization is characterized by responsibility, autonomy, risk, and uncertainty. It may not be a gentle environment, but it is a very human one. Gone are the artificial rigidities and disciplines of the conventional corporation. In their place is a world full of the messiness, challenges, and disappointments that characterize the world of real human beings.

4

RIC DUQUES
PAUL GASKE

The "Big" Organization of the Future

Ric Duques is chairman and chief executive officer of First Data Corporation (FDC). In 1989, when American Express Information Services Corporation (ISC) was formed from the Data Based Services Group, he became ISC's first president. In 1992, ISC was renamed First Data Corporation and its initial public offering was completed. Paul Gaske is the managing director of Keilty, Goldsmith & Company, where his clients include American Express, Cablevision Systems, Champion International Corporation, FDC, Nortel, and Pfizer. Before joining the firm, Gaske was a professor at San Diego State University, the University of Oregon, and the University of Southern California.

With the recently completed merger with First Financial Management Corporation, First Data Corporation (FDC) is now the seventy-fourth largest company in the United States in market capitalization, with a workforce of over thirty-six thousand employees. It is the market leader or a strong number two in a full range of transaction-, payment-, and information-processing services. FDC has consistently grown at an annual rate of 20 percent or more in both revenue and profitability since its formation in 1989 by American Express as Information Services Corporation. Since its initial public offering in April 1992 at twenty-two dollars per share, FDC's stock price has increased nearly 350 percent, recently selling at seventy-five dollars per share. By virtually any standard, FDC, to this point, must be considered successful. And yet, when we look at the FDC organization of the future, the operative word is *change*. The challenges of rapid growth and a dynamic industry require a thorough reexamination of organizational structure, corporate responsibility, and company culture. It is particularly sobering, as Gary Hamel noted at the FDC 1996 Senior Management Conference, to observe that big, market-dominant companies rarely sustain market leadership over time and rarely create or develop innovative or breakthrough products or services once they've reached the top. As much as we would like to take a deep breath, relax, and enjoy arriving at our destination, it is quite clear that the journey toward becoming a great, big company has just begun. The path toward greatness requires a combination of past practices and new activities.

In this chapter, we will try to describe some elements of the FDC organization of the future. Clearly, the challenges we face are shared by other fast-growing, entrepreneurial companies who aspire to achieve or retain positions of market leadership. We are at the transitional point of an unparalleled opportunity in our company's development, one that could position us extraordinarily well for the future or lead us down the path to mediocrity (or worse). The accelerated rate of change in our industry will create rewards for the swift and severe punishment for those who don't change quickly.

The foundation of our business is, and must remain, building and sustaining client loyalty and retention. We have set a standard beyond "satisfaction" in the FDC vision statement: "Every client *recommends* FDC." To shape our focus on client recommendation, we have embraced the Service-Profit Chain as a framework for communicating business strategy, guiding managerial decision making, and affirming FDC values. Developed by a group of Harvard professors and external consultants, the Service-Profit Chain documents the economic impact of client retention on profitability and growth through the "Lifetime Value of Customers" concept. Service quality and value underpin client retention. High employee satisfaction and loyalty promote high-quality service. We believe that for clients to recommend FDC in a sustainable way, FDC employees must also be able to recommend FDC as a place to work. Figure 4.1 illustrates the interrelationships between the components of the Service-Profit Chain.

Figure 4.1. The Service-Profit Chain.

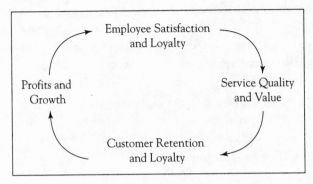

Profits and Growth → Employee Satisfaction and Loyalty → Service Quality and Value → Customer Retention and Loyalty → Profits and Growth

The Service-Profit Chain has been especially valuable in drawing attention to four critical factors necessary to sustain the revenue growth, profitability, and market leadership associated with great companies.

Factor 1: Act like a Small Company

Arrogance often comes with increased size. Whether it is the product of latent "bullying" tendencies or the ability to exert substantial influence through sheer mass, growth often causes resentment toward the market leader from its customer base. This may happen because the market leader becomes increasingly inflexible or unresponsive to client requests or needs. The market leader may require the client to be more adaptable to fit the leader's needs rather than the leader adapting to the client's needs. The personal attention offered when the company was smaller or the client was new may have faded. Customization or new features may take longer because of an increased backlog or heightened pressure to standardize processes in the name of efficiency. For example, the huge changes in market leadership in the personal computer industry during recent years are direct consequences of the companies' ability or inability to listen to customers and to quickly and effectively introduce new products and services to satisfy changing customer needs.

Through our vision, "Every client *recommends* FDC," we recognize that the loyalty and retention of current clients are the cornerstones of our continued viability as a market leader. None of the characteristics of "big-ness" described above would lead to client recommendation. In the future, if not today, organizational flexibility will beat organizational muscle. Yet a flexible big company is currently an oxymoron in many quarters, likened to the challenge of turning a battleship around in a bathtub.

"Acting small" means behaving like a small company that needs to sat-isfy its clients and retain them in order to survive. In the language of the Service-Profit Chain, it means managing the business for zero defections. So, how does a market-leading big company act like a small company in the future? Here are some thoughts:

1. *Organize by product or service, not size.* If anything, a consequence of bigness is an inability to deal with customers individually. Large orga-nizations often organize the client service function by client size (volume of business done with the company) more than by the client's products and services (and how the company can add value to the client's business). Big organizations often lump revenues and expenses in larger buckets, thus making it next to impossible to determine the profitability of individual accounts and blurring the company's ability to make prudent investment decisions on new products or services. We need to focus as obsessively on why clients defect as on attracting new clients. You know your organiza-tion is too large if losing a client doesn't bother you (or worse, if you don't know you've lost a client).

2. *Develop a deep and trusting relationship with the current client base.* The ability to add ongoing value to current clients is critical for their long-term satisfaction, retention, and recommendation. Listening to current clients represents perhaps the best source for developing and testing new prod-ucts and services. Dedicating resources to individual clients or client fam-ilies (rather than following the current trend toward centralizing client services and depersonalizing client contact) represents a tremendous opportunity to "act small" in a high-payoff way. Clients buy more, and more quickly, from suppliers who know them well and whom they trust. A "high-tech, high-touch" perspective with current clients not only should benefit the clients, but should produce more highly satisfied internal employees who truly find rewards in the ability to add value to individual clients and to develop meaningful relationships with them.

3. *Get back in the mindset and habit of making things yourself.* Small entrepreneurial companies typically are highly dependent on individual creativity and internal development of ideas. This stems in part from their desire for a competitive advantage and in part from the reality of scarce resources. Big companies often buy what they don't have through acquisition, licensing, or other strategies. Unfortunately, this can become the norm for development, and it often results in clumsy attempts to make acquired products "fit" client needs. Thus, the big company quickly gets out of practice in making client-based changes occur and is viewed as slow or unresponsive.

Although these attributes may help FDC and other companies "act small," we and other big companies are considering some specific changes to ensure a smaller mindset:

1. *Put a governor on the size of individual businesses and split them out as separate P & L's as they grow.* We have noted the success of big "small" companies, like Asea Brown Boveri, Corning, and 3M, who insist on using small operating units. An additional benefit of this policy is the required development of a broader cadre of management talent, because the number of managers with direct P & L responsibility increases substantially.

2. *Place revenue goals on the development of new products or services.* For example, 3M requires that 25 percent of total revenue be generated from products developed within the past five years. 3M can do this because of its institutional mandate to "think small" with respect to clients, organizational structure, and product development. More big companies, including FDC, need to stretch themselves in generating new revenue streams. The safest way to do so is to listen closely to current clients and bring an increased focus on helping them succeed in their markets.

3. *Develop metrics around agility and responsiveness, as judged by your clients.* We need to zero in on what the key measures of "acting small" are and drive ourselves to achieve them with our client base. Major weapons used by smaller or "boutique" competitors are agility, flexibility, responsiveness, and attention, some of the benefits of being small. The big company that can compete on these terms is far better positioned for sustainable growth than one that cannot.

Factor 2: Create the Urgency for Innovation

One of the frightening historical realities of big, market-dominant companies is their poor record of developing breakthrough products and services once they have achieved that market dominance. Obviously, this failing plays a major role in their fall from grace.

A number of actions can be taken to stimulate innovation in big, market-dominant companies. Perhaps the most important is to instill the 3M "make a little, sell a little" philosophy in the various company businesses. At FDC, for example, historically, we have been much more likely to go out and buy new products through acquisition of small companies, often at inflated prices. In some cases, we have even acquired capabilities from outside the company that already existed in other parts of the company or were nearly fully developed. Our track record on these investments has been spotty at best, owing to both the speculative nature of such acquisitions and our lack of systematic attention to internally generated innovation. The writeoffs we have taken over the years would have made a tremendous research pool for internal research and development efforts.

One key to "make a little, sell a little" work is having a current-client focus. Our current clients are both the source of innovative ideas and the laboratories for testing them in a collaborative manner. Also key is knowing when to discard ideas as unworkable. We have to look at innovation much as a farmer thins a crop to increase the yield: many more projects will always be under way than will ever see the marketplace, but we should purposefully stop some efforts in order to have the resources for others to flourish.

Dedicated resources for innovative projects must also be assured. For example, at FDC we are contemplating the establishment of a substantial corporate strategic investment fund to underwrite internal projects without adversely affecting the business's P & L. We are also hoping that such a fund would encourage the sort of cross-business initiatives that are increasingly warranted by client needs. Accompanying the fund will be a rigorous and quick business case evaluation process and an agreed-upon timetable for continuing or discontinuing initially funded projects.

Ultimately, our goal is to revitalize the entrepreneurial spirit that marks a small, nimble company. The change for FDC is to balance making deals to acquire innovative products with making innovative products. For both the company and its employees, pride of ownership comes from creative opportunities for developing products or enhanced value-added services. We are also aware that today's talented employees who are unable to make a difference and innovate become tomorrow's founders of start-up companies, future competitors, or—ironically—future acquisition targets.

Factor 3: Create a Lean, Value-Added Corporate Function

For the big, market-dominant company, a large centralized staff is like Hamburger Helper—adding bulk but no content. This does not minimize the value-added role that the corporate function can and must play, but it does illustrate that neither size nor centralization of authority are predictors of sustained high company performance.

The corporate role in the future must center on striking a number of delicate balances. For example, corporate leadership must work to unencumber the businesses without being reckless. Ideally, the corporate function should be viewed as an enabler rather than an obstructionist while setting the parameters in which the field can operate freely. To do so requires a shift from "How can we control individual businesses, then help them grow?" to "How can we help to grow the individual businesses, within appropriate parameters?"

Corporate leadership should also be the catalyst for leveraging organizational capability—sharing, information dissemination, and the like. Whether through developing internal communication networks for sharing best practices, developing a system for identifying companywide candidates for key organizational positions, or scheduling and coordinating technology conferences, the corporate function should add value by leveraging organizational talent across the company. In addition, it should be an organizationwide vehicle for communicating success stories and recognizing outstanding achievement. It also needs to sponsor and cultivate the development of leaders in the present and for the future, ensuring the quality and depth of leadership required to sustain growth and maintain market dominance.

Perhaps the most direct way to change the perceived role of management is to redefine key positions and responsibilities. In FDC's largest division, for example, a senior corporate officer in an "administrative" role has become the designated troubleshooter and field resource on issues related to employee satisfaction. Her charter is to work for one to three months in selected areas that require improved responsiveness and that could benefit dramatically from implementing strong employee-satisfaction practices. This includes acting as a coach to local general management and supervisory levels, developing teams to implement process improvement initiatives, and establishing measurements and metrics for each assignment with continuous monitoring of results. Not only is this an appropriate companion to integrating the Service-Profit Chain into the fabric of FDC culture, but it is a demonstration of commitment to "walking the talk" on employee and client satisfaction. Perhaps most important, this effort is also intended to dramatically redefine the value and relevance of staff support roles.

The success of such an effort requires access into selected areas to be unencumbered by political or turf barriers. It also requires the executive's focus for the period assigned to be absolute: arbitrarily moving an individual to another assignment or "crisis du jour" would unequivocally signal a lack of commitment to employees. And it requires absolute right of access and full support from all executive leaders, because the time and effort to fight for these things is nonexistent.

These tasks comprise the corporate jobs of the future, whether at the headquarters or field level. Ideally, many of the responsibilities routinely delegated to outside consultants will be performed by dedicated internal resources. When an organization gets so large that managers can't make decisions without outside consulting help, it's time to simplify the organization. We believe that the corporate responsibility is to facilitate such simplification. By doing so, the agility and flexibility required to sustain market leadership and growth can be enhanced.

Factor 4: Create an Energizing Culture

Enemies of sustained market leadership include complacency and arrogance. But they can also include unrelenting pressure to perform, high stress levels, and ongoing concerns around job security. Employee burnout is as much a threat to the organization of the future as complacency, especially given downsizing trends and the relentless drive to improve efficiency by doing more with less.

Just as the big company must act small to stay competitive, it should feel small to the individual employee. To do so, the following elements should become part of the culture:

1. *Maintain clear articulation of and strong adherence to organizational values.* This should be a constant across the business; it promotes the ability to personalize the values in day-to-day decision making.

2. *Remain accountable for employee and client satisfaction at the local level.* For example, while FDC corporate function is interested in how satisfied FDC employees are as a group, measured by the annual employee survey, it is far more concerned about individual units and businesses and how it can support efforts to improve satisfaction at the local level. Although some broad corporationwide initiatives may be relevant, the bulk of the real impact is exerted at the local level.

3. *Associate low levels of fear with innovation.* The worst message to send regarding new ideas is that you encourage their development, then punish their developer if the ideas prove unsuccessful. After all, the "thinning" process is essential for innovative growth; knowing when to stop doing something is more important and difficult than knowing when to start something. What we must communicate is that discontinuing an idea, or "failing," is an opportunity to do something else and a learning experience. We learn more from our failures than from our successes. If anything, the advancer of an innovation should ultimately be the most frequent recommender of a decision to kill a project.

4. *Associate security with earning, rather than having it be an entitlement.* Management must send the clear and unequivocal message that job security is directly linked to contributions to company growth and profitability and must support it by a reward-and-recognition system that is consistent with a meritocracy. As Judith Bardwick has observed in *Danger in the Comfort Zone*, such a shift to a performance-based culture invokes fear in individuals who are accustomed to being rewarded for length of service or for being an "average" performer. The death of the "job for life" mindset may

seem contrary to a focus on employee satisfaction and loyalty. However, employees of the big company of the future will remain committed to the company if:

- The company continues to invest in their development
- The company recognizes contributions in a fair and equitable way
- The company ensures that high performers are provided with security (high performers don't get laid off when layoffs occur)
- Work remains challenging and fun and workers understand how their role makes a difference

The ongoing success of companies like 3M, ServiceMaster, and Southwest Airlines is due in no small measure to their company cultures. Culture is a critical factor in the decision to affiliate with a company. It affects an individual's performance as an employee and influences decisions to stay or leave. To sustain market leadership, organizational culture must be aligned with and supportive of business objectives. FDC's embracing of the Service-Profit Chain as a framework for realizing its vision, "Every client *recommends* FDC," is a de facto recognition of the importance of culture in a competitive enterprise.

The challenges of achieving substantial growth and market leadership are difficult. But perhaps the greater challenge is staying on top once you've gotten there. In the future, it will be even more difficult to stay on top, and a sure prescription for failure is standing still. By thinking and acting like a small company, pursuing internal innovation vigorously, redefining corporate responsibility, and aligning company culture, the FDC of the future (and the big organization of the future) should have a greater opportunity to become a long-term success rather than an also-ran.

5

JEFFREY PFEFFER

Will the Organization of the Future Make the Mistakes of the Past?

Jeffrey Pfeffer is Thomas D. Dee Professor of Organizational Behavior in the Graduate School of Business at Stanford University. He is the author of Organizations and Organization Theory, Power in Organizations, Organizational Design, Managing with Power: Politics and Influence in Organizations, *and* Competitive Advantage Through People: Unleashing the Power of the Work Force *and is coauthor of* The External Control of Organizations: A Resource Dependence Perspective, *in addition to more than ninety articles and book chapters.*

Americans often don't know or pay much attention to history. American business writers seem to know even less. Today we are bombarded with breathless descriptions of the virtual organization, the networked organization, and the boundaryless organization. We are told about the "new employment contract," a nice way of saying that long-term careers in a single organization are a thing of the past and that we are all contingent workers now. Each of these presumed innovations is hailed as some new way of organizing that will solve all (or at least most) of the problems of competitiveness and change that bedevil contemporary organizations.

A big problem exists with all of this—namely, that the "new" organizational forms aren't new at all. In fact, this was how enterprise was organized more than one hundred years ago. The same holds true for the "new" employment arrangements. Long before internal labor markets and career hierarchies, long before long-term attachments between employees and employers, work was organized on a spot market basis, albeit without the help of Manpower and the other temporary help services and outside contractors we have today. Furthermore, believe it or not, there is evidence that the competitive environment and the march of technology were even more dynamic and stressful in past periods of our economic history than they are today.

Our ignorance of the past has a very real cost, the substantial likelihood that without understanding the evolution of organizations and the employment relation up to this point, we will be prone to remake old mistakes. In a continuing search for what is new and trendy, we may fail to appreciate the strengths as well as the weaknesses of some recent organizational arrangements. Leaders can gain three benefits from a deeper understanding of history: first, a fresh perspective from seeing that what looks new is really old; second, a fuller appreciation of the hidden costs of these "new" arrangements (and note that by the time we learn, we may ourselves be case studies in history); and third, an understanding of the appropriate steps needed to sustain a competitive advantage and avoid being swept up in fads and fashion.

A Brief History of the Economy

Before there were organizations, there were markets. In an economy in which more than 90 percent of us work for others, the idea of being an employee is unexceptional. "We forget the time when complete dependence on wages had for centuries been rejected by all who regarded themselves as free men," writes labor historian Christopher Hill in an article in the journal *Past and Present*. By the late 1700s, a system called "putting out" had emerged in textile manufacture and subsequently spread to other enterprises as well. Under this system, workers owned their own equipment and set their own hours. However, the merchant entrepreneur owned the raw materials and sold the finished product in the market. This person was essentially a trader, standing between the various producers of subassemblies, the final product, and the market.

This system was ultimately replaced by the practice of inside contracting, in which centralized work factories were established. Those who worked in the factories, however, were still independent of the factory owners. "The inside contractors made an agreement . . . to make a part of their product and receive a certain price for each completed unit," notes economist Dan Clawson in his book *Bureaucracy and the Labor Process*. "Inside contractors had complete charge of production in their area, hiring their own employees and supervising the work process." Inside contracting was used by such well-known manufacturers as Singer Sewing Machine, Pratt & Whitney, Reed & Barton Silversmiths, and Baldwin Locomotive.

Even when these early organizations began to hire their own employees, the organizations were frequently quite small, and the employment relation had little continuity, resembling more a spot labor market than anything else. For example, Robert Lacey's history of the Ford Motor Company, *Ford: The Men and the Machine*, reported that by 1913, turnover had reached nearly 400 percent at the Highland Park, Michigan, plant. When the directors decided to issue a Christmas bonus to workers who had been with the company for at least three years, only 640 qualified out of some 15,000 employees. Thus, the hallmarks of the new organization—an absence of vertical integration of production and the use of contract and temporary help—were the dominant mode of organizing work more than one hundred years ago.

Nor is competitive challenge a new phenomenon. A study by Larry Griffin, Michael Wallace, and Beth Rubin published in the *American Sociological Review* noted that from 1890 to 1928, close to 600,000 enterprises failed. The failure rate during this period was more than twice the post–World War II average. The turn of the century also witnessed one of the most vigorous waves of mergers in history. The absolute number of mergers in 1899 and 1929 was not topped again until 1967, and the merger rate was much higher than it was in 1967 because, of course, many more enterprises existed by then. This turbulent economic landscape resulted in a concern with costs and productivity reminiscent of today's. A superintendent of the Mesabi iron mine, responding to the question of what he wanted to do more than anything else, said, "Cut a dollar a ton off the cost of ore."

Finally, in an era in which much is made about rapid technological change, consider the fact that one hundred years ago we witnessed the development of electric power, the telephone, and the telegraph; the invention of the gasoline engine; and the building of a national railway network, as well as other industrial inventions of similar economic magnitude. Suddenly, national markets and rapid communication extended across vast distances. In fact, data show that the number of patents issued in the United States per million inhabitants was higher in the early 1900s than it was in the 1970s and 1980s, say Robert Eccles and Nitin Nohria in *Beyond the Hype,* and absolutely no evidence exists of an upward trend in technological change, at least as measured by patent data. Indeed, Eccles and Nohria have argued that little is new under the management sun. Much of the overheated rhetoric used to characterize present-day trends is good for mobilizing action and possibly for selling consulting services or books and articles, but it is not very useful for understanding how today's world differs from that of the past.

Lessons from History

Vertical integration and organizational expansion occurred for the same reason that the employment relationship evolved: firms wanted to achieve more control over critical uncertainties that were crucial to their success. With respect to the workforce, it was difficult to achieve a competitive advantage through people, or even to run an organization, with extremely high levels of turnover and limited attachment of employees to their employers. With the introduction of the assembly line, interdependence was increased; the line cannot operate unless every position is staffed. With the increased investment in capital equipment, downtime was an increasingly significant expense.

Henry Ford's decision to offer a substantially higher wage, five dollars a day (roundly criticized, by the way, by the *Wall Street Journal* at that time, further evidence that little has really changed), was not done just to have more people who could afford to buy his cars or because he was a nice fellow. With demand for Fords outstripping the company's ability to make them, Ford wanted a reliable, dedicated workforce who would show up for work so production could be assured. "Henry Ford always liked to present the Five Dollar Day as a hardheaded matter of 'efficiency engineering' with 'no charity in any way involved,' and he took pleasure in subsequently reporting it to be 'one of the finest cost-cutting moves we ever made,'" writes Lacey.

Similarly, contracting for parts or subassemblies or services inevitably places a firm at the mercy of those providing the service. The consumer electronics industry offers a nice case study of this process. First, U.S. manufacturers of televisions, radios, and similar appliances believed they could contract out manufacturing. But because manufacturing and product design are closely interrelated, soon these firms were also contracting out important parts of the design process, retaining a marketing and distribution function. This process creates competitors, and the Japanese and Korean firms that did first the manufacturing and then the product development soon decided to move into marketing and distribution and thereby take over the entire market. A similar process occurred with automobiles where, once again, firms that were initially contract manufacturers soon came to be full-blown competitors—for example, Mitsubishi in the case of Chrysler.

The counterargument to all of this is that times have changed, that developments in information technology permit coordination across a distributed supply chain even if the elements of that chain are outside the organization's boundaries, and that corporations have learned to work with suppliers in a model that is often ascribed to the Japanese: building a network of interrelated organizations that share detailed cost and technology knowledge and act effectively as a single unit. Similarly, the labor market has changed, and one can now easily acquire contract labor or temporary help—after all, Manpower is the largest private sector employer in the United States—and not be burdened with either the fixed costs of permanent employment or the difficulties of administering personnel.

This additional capacity to contract and manage across boundaries is undoubtedly real, and certainly the degree of integration that could be observed at Ford's River Rouge plant, where not only cars but the steel, glass, and many other materials and parts that went into them were manufactured, is neither necessary nor economically efficient. But it is also the case that one cannot achieve competitive advantage—the ability to earn above-normal economic returns over a sustained period of time—simply through acquiring resources on the market. Anyone can hire personnel from temporary help agencies and any firm can contract with the numerous manufacturers that have grown up to provide manufacturing in the electronics industry. It is customarily the case that things that can be bought have little enduring value as a basis of competitive success, simply because one's competitors can readily buy them also.

The evidence suggests that it is much more difficult to duplicate an organization's culture and way of operating than its technology, its strategy, or even its products or services. That is why culture and organizational capability are increasingly important sources of organizational success. But if this is true, then it must follow that firms need to implement high-performance or high-commitment work practices and build relationships with both customers (because customer acquisition is typically more costly and more difficult than customer retention) and employees. How can one succeed on the basis of culture and organizational capability in a virtual organization, which must surely also have a virtual culture? Organizations with a strong culture avoid turnover and don't run their employment relationship like a spot market. Retaining and building capability requires keeping those in whom the tacit knowledge resides, as many organizations have discovered to their chagrin after they have lost employees and the associated wisdom they represented.

The problem with many of the "new" organizational and employment arrangements is that the apparent cost savings, which are often actually illusory, appear real and immediate and the long-term detrimental competitive consequences are in the future, uncertain, and, in any event, difficult to unambiguously trace to bad decisions. It is little wonder that the lessons of history are so poorly learned. For instance, many retailers employ mostly part-time help, use as few of them as possible, pay them little, and thereby seek to minimize their labor costs. One department store chain that was notable for these practices was the Emporium Capwell Company, now defunct. That organization perfected what I call the "neutron bomb" theory of retailing (the neutron bomb destroys people but not things); it had plenty of nice merchandise but no one to sell it. Of course, minimizing labor costs is not the goal of retailers. If it were, they could simply close down, at which point their labor costs would be zero. Nordstrom is successful, although its retail clerks typically make twice the industry average. New United Motors Manufacturing pays the highest wage in the automobile industry. But with a production system that provides more than 50 percent higher productivity than the plant it replaced and with quality levels among the highest in the industry, the organization still comes out way ahead.

An employee, even if she or he is very poorly paid and therefore seemingly cheap, is still much too expensive if the person does not have the knowledge, experience, or commitment to do what is required to make the business profitable. By contrast, well-paid employees may be very cost-effective. A study of oil refineries uncovered one that paid its crew some 35 percent more than other refineries in the same region. But because the refinery hired better-qualified workers, trained them in multiple skills, and paid a wage sufficient to retain this skilled labor force, its total maintenance outlay was some 25 percent *less* than the next best refinery, according to an article by Richard Ricketts in the *Oil and Gas Journal*.

With the exception of Norwest Bank and a handful of others, banks in the United States have followed retailers in their labor market policies and competitive strategy. Pursuing a strategy of short-term cost reductions, banks have employed part-time help who were trained only in the skills required to do their jobs; the organizations have deemphasized career development and promotion. This has resulted in employee turnover rates that are much higher in banks in the United States than those in most countries of the industrialized world. With a turnover rate, for instance, for commercial loan officers of some 33 percent, "relationship" banking becomes a one-night stand. The loss of U.S. banks' market share in demand deposits (mutual funds today control more financial assets), loans, and credit cards (two of the three largest issuers of credit cards in the United States today are not banks) to their competition contrasts with the experience in other countries such as Germany, where banks have pursued a market strategy that is not based just on customer acquisition (how many solicitations from banks did you receive last week?) but also on customer retention and selling a range of services to the existing customer base.

The Courage to Be Different

The temptation to follow trends and fashion is often overpowering. In our search for the new we sometimes reinvent the old. Levi Strauss and Company's innovative gainsharing programs for manufacturing employees, introduced in the United States in the late 1980s, were based on the Scanlon Plan of the 1930s and were acknowledged as such. Interest in employee share ownership has come in waves, writes Eric Abrahamson in the *Academy of Management Review*, with the biggest wave cresting in the late 1920s. Steve Barley and Gideon Kunda have shown, in an article for the *Administrative Management Quarterly*, that management interest in using normative or cultural bases of motivation on the one hand, or external measures and financial incentives on the other, has waxed and waned over time.

What is important is to recognize that following the crowd will probably not permit an organization to outperform the crowd. If a given firm does what its competitors do, how much better can its performance be? That is why the exceptional performers, like Southwest Airlines, Norwest, and Wal-Mart Stores, have always been willing to avoid following conventional wisdom and to do things differently. Southwest eschewed a hub-and-spoke system, once described as a way of bringing the maximum number of unhappy people together at the same place at the same time, and instead offered point-to-point service. Wal-Mart operated its own trucking and distribution system even as Kmart and other competitors were contracting out this seemingly peripheral function. In hindsight, it is easy to see how distribution has played such a crucial role in this chain's success and how useful controlling its own trucking fleet has been, but hindsight is always like that.

There are several enduring truths about organizations and management. One is the norm of reciprocity, which exists in all nationalities and cultures. We cannot expect dedication and loyalty from employees unless we are willing to make some reciprocal commitment to them. Another truth is the idea of core competence or capability. Contracting out core tasks has often been a recipe for disaster, in the 1890s as well as the 1990s. This is because contracting out leaves the foundation of competitive success in the open market. A third truth is that to succeed you must understand the basic forces and ideas that shape modern economic life, reject trends if they don't make sense, and never substitute rhetoric for judgment.

Implications for Leaders

To avoid getting caught in the dilemma of not changing when change is required or of blindly following fads, it is useful to ask yourself a few simple questions and keep the answers firmly in mind.

1. *What is the key to our competitive success?* One of the things that distinguishes Southwest, Nordstrom, and, for that matter, Whole Foods Market, the rapidly growing natural foods grocery store chain, is that these firms are clear about what they are in business to do: to sell merchandise, to fly planes on time with high levels of customer satisfaction, and to distribute wholesome and healthy foods and educate consumers in the process. Systems, procedures, policies, strategies, and all the other accoutrements are means to those ends, not ends in themselves.

2. *What are the core capabilities or competencies required in the firm's competitive marketplace, and what can we do to maintain an advantage in these core skills?* Investments in building core capabilities are not expenses; they are what will be required to secure advantage over time. It is trite to note that we are all in a service business today; even products are sold on the basis of the services they provide and the services provided by the manufacturer. Yet many companies fail to build and maintain their service capability, which requires them to invest in people. Do an experiment. Call Charles Schwab, Fidelity Investments, and Wells Fargo Bank and see how long it takes to get through and the skill with which your questions are answered. Then forecast who will succeed in the financial services marketplace. Not surprisingly, what you will experience on the phone reflects the policies and strategies for developing and retaining people (or not doing those things) that constitute the firms' employment relations strategy.

3. *Are the organization's policies for recruiting, selecting, paying, training and developing, and organizing its workforce consistent with the core capabilities it needs to succeed in its marketplace?* In many organizations I have seen, the answer is no. Policies have built up like deposits in caves, and the alignment with what the organization needs to do is poor.

4. *What really distinguishes our organization from those with which it competes?* If the answer is the culture, the people, and the skills and capability they represent, then be sure to evaluate planned policies and decisions in terms of whether they will build or destroy those assets. It is common for firms to understand the concept of brand equity—that advertising and product quality build a brand image that is worth money in the bank. It is less common, but no less important, for firms to recognize the "equity" that resides in their workforce and to make decisions accordingly.

6

ORIT GADIESH
SCOTT OLIVET

Designing for Implementability

*Orit Gadiesh is chairman of the board of Bain & Company, an
international strategy consulting firm. She has worked extensively
in corporate portfolio restructuring, global strategy development,
and change implementation. She sits on many boards, including
the Publications Review Board of Harvard Business School Press
and the board of directors of the SEI Center for Advanced Studies
in Management at the Wharton School. Scott Olivet is a vice
president of Bain & Company. He has done extensive work on
strategy and operational issues in telecommunications, consumer
products, transportation, and financial services. He is leader of
Bain's practice in organizational effectiveness and change strategies.*

The challenges facing businesses today are documented everywhere—
movable business boundaries, booming global markets, explosive competition, shifting demographics, and a steadily increasing pace of change.
Companies strive to adapt, building the organizations of tomorrow with
new strategies, novel operating techniques, and fresh ways of thinking
about what they do. In recent years, we have seen a growing reliance on
another adaptive lever as well: structural redesign. A company organized
by function reconfigures on the basis of customer segments, or it moves to
reduce decision time by eliminating organizational layers.

But redesign has a poor track record. Many of the companies that
restructure will restructure again a few years later. Some of these repeated

redesigns are the result of external change; the first restructuring loses its relevance and power. More often than not, however, the company is simply disappointed with the results of the first redesign and so undertakes a second. This disappointment has less to do with the specific structures chosen than with the way those structures are designed and put into place. In company after company, we find that the objectives of the redesign are unclear, the redesign ignores critical parts of the organization, or the redesign is only partially executed. No matter what the organizations of the future are to look like, partial execution of a partial design, measured against unspecified objectives, is no recipe for success.

In all organizational redesigns, the ultimate aim is the same, to increase the company's ability to implement its strategies and decisions. We call this goal *implementability* because we see it as roughly analogous to the goal of designing products for manufacturability. Products that are *not* designed for manufacturability may look great on paper, but they often suffer from two serious faults. They can't be made at the required cost, and they can't be made without trade-offs that reduce overall performance, which means that they fail to meet expectations. The same weaknesses plague organizations that are not specifically designed for implementability, and they will plague even well-designed organizations if their designs are inadequately executed. Moreover, when the results of redesign are disappointing, company leadership is too quick to start over with another new design. Some companies repeat the cycle endlessly.

Redesigning a company has three formidable requirements:

1. Company leaders must generate a good answer to the question, "Granted that we need to change, why do we need a new structure?"

2. Company leaders must design for implementability. The new structure's first priority must be to facilitate the day-to-day implementation of company decisions and processes.

3. In executing the new structure, company leaders must be thorough, rigorous, and counterintuitively patient.

Asking Why

The most common objectives of a new structure are to respond to changing business boundaries or customer buying patterns, to reduce costs, to reset priorities, to shift personnel and align capabilities, or to shake things up. Changing the organizational structure can help you to achieve any of these objectives, but it is not necessarily the best method or the best place to start. Structure is likely to be only one piece of the total solution.

The first thing you have to do is question whether a structural change is appropriate at all. Be honest: What are the real root causes of your slow growth and inability to change? How will your customers know if the redesign has been successful? On Monday morning, what do you want to do differently? Perhaps what drives the struggle between manufacturing and sales over new-product development is not company structure but a lack of clear goals and strategies or a compensation system that rewards parochial behavior. Is structure really the best lever for removing the true inhibitors? Analyze your alternatives the same way you would if you were making an operational improvement.

Understanding your objectives will help you to analyze the trade-offs you'll have to make in the design process, in the design itself, in the process of putting the new design in place, and in monitoring results. A highly participatory, very public design process may be appropriate in responding to customer demands for a single point of contact but less appropriate when the imminent issue is the sale of a business unit. When you are choosing your structure, every option will have pluses and minuses. You may be trading cost for flexibility or speed for consistency. You will make trade-offs in the rollout as well. For example, the way you announce the change will affect employee reactions. If your goal is to shake things up, you may want to make a sudden announcement and include major personnel shifts. When the change is massive and requires careful management, a gentler announcement and slower rollout may be more appropriate. Because structural redesigns always have a cost, including disruption to customers and employees, lost productivity, and direct cash outlays, they should not be undertaken lightly. Restructure only if you have to and if you're certain the investment is worth making. But remember, you cannot make informed trade-offs if your objectives are not clear.

Designing for Implementability

Once you know exactly what you want to achieve with a new organizational design, it is time to work on the blueprints. We'd love to be able to describe a design machine that always churns out the right answer, or to tell you that certain designs are perfectly suited to certain competitive situations or to certain stages in a company's life cycle. But magic formulas do not exist. We find no correlation at all between particular structures and satisfied or dissatisfied general managers. What drives dissatisfaction is the mismatch between the expectations for a new design and the improvements it actually generates. And what causes this mismatch is not the structure per se but the failure to design it thoroughly and then to execute it thoroughly. Organizational restructurings fail to have their intended effect because companies make the mistake of designing:

- *The top but not the bottom.* They designate the primary structure—market-based rather than geographic, for example—but they do not explicitly design the rest of the vertical structure.

- *The vertical but not the horizontal.* They map out the vertical hierarchy—which functions will be grouped under which market segments—but they give no attention to the coordinating mechanisms that cut across organizational units.

- *The relationships but not the decisions or processes.* They focus on who reports to whom and whether they are connected by dotted or solid lines, but they fail to plan how individuals and groups will make decisions or deliver products and services to customers.

- *The jobs but not the teams.* They write individual job descriptions to clarify each new position, but they ignore the accountabilities of groups, from departments to coordinating teams.

- *The structure but not the supports.* They focus entirely on structure and fail to design new processes, skill-building requirements, performance management systems, rewards, and information systems.

By designing only part of the organization, they neglect to consider how the organization will actually function. These overlooked elements have always mattered, but developments like the increasing complexity of global organizations and the increasing need for speed in all company processes make them even more important. The fact is that companies must be tremendously quick on their feet even as the growing complexity of their internal relationships tends to slow them down. To overcome these conflicting forces, companies need to pay close attention to every aspect of designing for implementability.

Designing the Entire Vertical Hierarchy

Choosing your basic method of organizing work—product, function, geography, customer or market, process, or some hybrid—is an important decision. Any structure you choose will have some advantages and disadvantages. For example, functional structures build strong functional expertise, but they often produce long product development cycles. Designing the entire vertical hierarchy in detail can shine a light on these trade-offs and help you to figure out how to manage them or how to use other design elements to mitigate them. In fact, designing tiers two, three, and four of the organization can often be as important as designing tier one. What matters most to individuals and teams is the person to whom they report and to whom they owe loyalty, so the design of lower tiers has a greater impact on their behavior, decision making, and work flow. Input from managers on their own piece of the structure is critical, but top leaders still need to oversee the trade-offs and make sure that all the various pieces are properly integrated.

In a recent restructuring of a global consumer products company, we debated the benefits of a regional versus a product structure and decided on the former. We then found ourselves in an even tougher debate over whether to base the second-tier, regional structure on function, customer, or country. Among other things, we grappled with the question of where to manage manufacturing: although organizing by country would make the company more responsive to customer needs, individual country markets were too small to realize important economies of scale. Closer examination of this trade-off made it clear that for maximum economic efficiency, some manufacturing decisions should be made at a global level. Designing the entire vertical structure helped us to identify inherent tensions in our first proposal, showed us that we needed a global manufacturing chief to make cross-regional decisions, and raised questions about our earlier choice of an exclusively regional structure. We then reconsidered every function and process and, as a result, developed a regional-functional hybrid as the basic structure.

Designing the Coordinating Mechanisms

One common restructuring mistake is to redesign only what appears on paper. But what's on paper is usually the vertical structure alone, which is only a small part of the real organization. Moreover, the company has changed and evolved since that structure was adopted. When you are analyzing what isn't working in today's company, you need to compare your ideal with how the company actually functions, not with someone's long-forgotten notion of how it *ought* to function.

Focusing on how the organization actually works means giving lots of attention to the cross-organizational coordination and decision making that are called horizontal processes or coordinating mechanisms. Coordinating mechanisms vary widely in form and function, from permanent teams for cross-functional tasks to coordinating groups for process management to special-project task forces to ad hoc experience-sharing conferences. Regardless of the form they take, no company of any size can achieve implementability without them. They cushion trade-offs, speed and simplify decision making, facilitate the development of core capabilities, send signals as influential as any that come from the vertical structure, and promote a culture of unity and common purpose.

But to do all these things effectively, horizontal processes must be explicitly designed. All too often, senior leaders provide some general direction about the type of coordination they desire, then leave it to others to design the actual mechanisms. For various reasons, this rarely works. One difficulty is conflicting interests. People asked to design and manage coordinating mechanisms are not likely to do their best to create processes powerful enough to override the wishes of their own departments. Yet one of the purposes of a good horizontal process is to counteract precisely this kind of vertical overcontrol.

Even coordinating mechanisms that are meant to be informal or voluntary will work best if they are deliberately integrated with each element of the organizational system. Coordinating mechanisms are like all other aspects of structure. For the greatest impact, they must be explicitly designed.

Designing the Decision-Making Process

We have interviewed hundreds of senior managers about the ways an organization's structure can inhibit growth. One common response has to do with the design of business processes, a subject that has been treated extensively in several recent books and articles. However, the most common response has to do with decision making. Managers complain that they lack the decision-making power to do their jobs and that top leadership is unable to make decisions quickly. Ineffective decision making has many causes, from the complexity of the business environment to conflicting management styles and philosophies. But one of the most frequent causes is the company's failure to design the decision process—to identify key decisions, specify how they're to be made, and see to it that the process does not clash with the organizational structure or supporting mechanisms.

It's hard to find an organization where no decision crosses an organizational boundary, where decision making never involves groups with different objectives, where the responsibilities of teams and individuals, staff and line, never conflict. These are the points of intersection where gridlock tends to occur. The organization stops dead in its tracks, not on the substance of an issue but on how a decision will be made. If it's implementability you're after, you must be as clear about decision making as you are about product and service delivery. You must:

- Designate the key decisions needed to execute a strategy
- Identify the critical issues, data, and analyses required
- Enumerate the roles and accountabilities of each individual and group involved
- Describe the process and timing by which the necessary people and information will all come together

Our experience tells us that it is often best to start with a diagnosis of how decisions are made today. Two tools can help you do this. The first, called decision mapping, is a form of process mapping for key decisions. It produces a visual, chronological record of all the players who touch the decision and of the often convoluted path that decisions follow through your organization. Mapping real past decisions is a great help in uncovering rework inefficiencies and in evaluating the effectiveness of your company's current decision-making process. It also gives executives a factual base they can use to correct their perceptions of how things work. The second tool is a matrix that can help you design your new decision-making process. This matrix identifies key company decisions along one axis and the major players for each decision along the other, then delineates the role—recommend, agree, input, or decide (RAID)—that each individual or group will play in each decision. If you ask managers from different parts of the company to create one RAID matrix for how things work today and a second one for how things ought to work, you will be amazed at the extent of their disagreement about current practices and even about who is involved. Obviously, the differences on the second RAID matrix—the proposed new process—will be even greater. But a grasp of all these different views is exactly what you are after. They are a major cause of decision gridlock.

Whether decision design precedes or accompanies other aspects of structural design, it will make the work easier. If you *begin* with decision analysis, you will quickly discover which dimension of the primary structure—geography, product, function, or customer—is the most logical driver of key decisions. If you do decision analysis *after* proposing a primary structure, it will highlight all the points of conflict where your proposed structure might hinder decisions. Either way, decision design will help you to define the decision-making process, identify the skills you'll need at the table, and make sure those skills are present.

Designing Team Charters and Accountabilities

A typical large company contains any number of teams that deal with matters like procurement and product development, and an increasing variety of such groups and teams have responsibilities that cross geographic or other boundaries. As a result, it is no longer enough to write job descriptions for individuals. You must also design team charters and accountabilities to give these groups direction, clarify objectives, establish goals and measures, set limits, and help their managers make trade-offs.

A clear charter can also head off the tendency of groups and teams to feel that they have to solve all of a company's problems before they can address their own. The members of a group supposedly chartered to look at tactical sales force effectiveness spent almost a year examining questions beyond their scope—which customer segments the company should serve, who the sales force should report to, how funding for new products should be decided—instead of focusing on the particular improvements they had been asked to clarify. Company leaders can eliminate this type of "scope creep" and wasted time by writing a description of every group's objectives, powers, responsibilities, and decision-making roles. If more and more of the work in your company is being done by teams, then you must start giving them the same direction and guidance you have traditionally given to individuals.

Designing the Alignment

"Structure should follow strategy" is an adage you've heard again and again. In fact, it's an adage you are now honoring by redesigning your structure to fit your company's latest strategic innovations. You will probably find, however, that no matter how clear the strategy is to the chief executive, your design team will soon be begging for detailed clarifications. You'll find it a useful and time-saving exercise to begin the design process by articulating the strategy in detail, then translating the details into a set of design principles. It is essential that everyone embark on the task of organizational design with the same set of assumptions. However, given the growing amount of work done across national and cultural boundaries by self-managed teams, a clear strategy by itself is no longer an adequate guide for structural design. We would revise the adage to read, "Structure should follow organizational ideology and strategy," because, increasingly, what keeps organizations in alignment is a shared understanding of the company's purpose and core values. Moreover, unlike strategy and tactics, ideology is by definition constant and therefore a better anchor for design consistency.

Yet even strategy and ideology are not enough. You must also see to it that all the elements of company ideology, strategy, structure, process, rewards, and people are in alignment. If you don't make this happen—and it won't happen naturally or easily—you'll wind up with mixed signals. Let's say that you've instructed sales to sell only the most profitable business. To align interests and rewards, you must now invest in systems that will give your salespeople data on product profitability, and you must stop rewarding them solely on the basis of total revenue. Every piece of the puzzle must promote organizational goals and not stand in their way.

You won't necessarily put everything in place at once, but it is important to have a clear picture of how it all fits together. One good way to do this is to draw three columns on a piece of paper. In the left column, list the organizational inhibitors to growth that led you to begin the redesign. In the right column, describe these same elements in your idealized organization of the future. In the center, list the design changes you intend to make and then ask yourself this question: Will each alteration in the middle help us to move from the specific weakness on the left to the ideal state on the right? If not, you should either scratch the change or ask yourself what other changes or adjustments you need to make to support it.

Iterating Change

Designing for implementability is always an iterative process and probably an endless one. To make progress, you must ask these questions at every step of the way:

1. What are we trying to achieve with this restructuring? Will each change advance this goal? Does each proposed change stand alone, or does it require supporting changes elsewhere in the business?

2. How does the organization actually work today? Are we proposing real-world changes or only changes to the paper structure?

3. Is the proposed change consistent with the core ideology and strategy of the organization?

4. Given that every change has advantages and disadvantages, how do we identify and prepare for the implicit trade-offs we are making as we restructure the organization? How can we use other elements of the design to mitigate the potential drawbacks? How can we manage these trade-offs day to day?

However you answer these questions, you must design the organization in explicit detail all the way from top to bottom and from side to side. You must design the links between your strategies and values and your business systems, and you must design the direction of team and individual interests. This doesn't mean that everything will have to change. But you will have to analyze all elements to make sure that they're internally consistent and directly support company goals.

Executing Fully

In our experience, companies that are otherwise thoughtful about change management can be very lackadaisical about carrying out a structural redesign. Even a thorough first-rate design for implementability will produce second-rate results if you fail to execute it fully. Full execution means the participation of every unit and individual without exemptions, boycotts, or pocket vetoes; it means scheduling every necessary change and completing the schedule; it means preventing the ten thousand small compromises that reduce change programs to nil. The best way to prevent confusion, build commitment, create motivation, and ensure that change actually reaches every required corner of the company is to make deliberate use of the principles of change management. During restructuring, the company should make a particular effort to do the following:

1. *Provide a context for the restructuring by building a clear, externally driven case to support the need for urgent change.* Many restructurings are the direct result of an environmental shift, so link the structural design to the new strategic reality. Reemphasizing basics—purpose, values, strategy, and objectives—is necessary to build commitment for change, reinforce new behaviors, and guide decision making.

2. *Create a vivid picture of the future.* It is hard for employees to grasp what a restructuring means at first glance. If you don't create the picture, employees will develop one of their own, based on fragmentary information. On one level, they want to know how the company will be different and how the redesign will contribute to company success. On another level, they want to know how the redesign will affect them and the people they work with. A vivid, compelling picture of the future is an opportunity to clarify, guide, and motivate.

3. *Communicate the new structure and the way it will actually work.* If you take our advice about the importance of a complete, detailed design, don't waste the advantage it gives you by failing to communicate what you've created. One of the best restructuring rollouts we've seen allocated its communication as follows: 30 percent on the context for change (from the outside in), 20 percent on the changes needed to become more competitive (from the employees' point of view), 30 percent on behavioral and process changes, and 20 percent on organizational charts and new assignments. We all know that rumors, misconceptions, and inaccuracies rush to fill any communication vacuum. You must provide a clear and consistent message across the entire organization and repeat it frequently. In evaluating change efforts, communication always tops the list of things that should have been done better.

4. *Manage the transition tightly.* Executives underestimate the amount of guidance, direction, and control required to get the organization operating as designed. An easy way to think about practical, "how will it work?" issues

is to ask yourself this question for each group or individual: "On Monday morning at 8:00 A.M., what do I expect this person or team to do *differently?*" Unless you have answers, your rollout is going to be bumpy. And the turmoil can turn into lasting problems if people begin implementing their own local answers to the question, erecting new barriers that may be hard to tear down later. Clear targets and tracking mechanisms are equally important. Emphasizing key measures, specific milestones, and a few ultrashort-term targets can help you to troubleshoot during the transition and keep the organization focused on its ultimate purpose and objectives.

5. *Give the new design time to work.* All redesigns take time even if they are tightly managed. Many executives find this frustrating, but put yourself in the shoes of someone standing at the intersection of several avenues of change. Now multiply that complexity by the number of divisions, teams, and external organizations that need transformation or creation, and you can readily see why it may take months to adjust. Do not fall into the trap of making additional changes before the original redesign has had a chance to work. You will be in that doom loop forever.

Tomorrow's Structures

As the pace and urgency of change increase, the life cycles of corporate and business-unit strategies grow shorter. Many companies have instituted continuous strategy development as opposed to the two-to five-year process common a few years ago. If this trend continues—if what the future holds is continuous strategic adjustment—then we can make several firm predictions about the organizations of the future.

First, few organizations will survive into the future unless they develop the capacity to implement rapid strategic changes without stress or dysfunction. Second, companies will continue to modify or totally redesign their structures as one means of achieving these course alterations. Third, the structures they adopt will include most of those we see today plus a range of new ones, some of them startlingly novel and some of them real breakthroughs. Fourth, their satisfaction with these new structures will continue to depend less on the structures themselves than on how thoroughly they design and how fully they execute the new designs and the mechanisms that support them.

7

IAIN SOMERVILLE
JOHN EDWIN MROZ

New Competencies for a New World

Iain Somerville is founder and managing partner of the Andersen Consulting Center for Thought Leadership, which engages in research and innovation on issues of concern to top executives. As a management consultant and educator, he has for two decades served the world's leading private, public, and social sector organizations. John Edwin Mroz is founder and president of the Institute for EastWest Studies, a pioneering global thought and action organization that brings together the private, public, and social sectors to solve public policy problems. As an adviser to heads of state, he has played a key role in the creation of market economies in Central Europe.

From the pre-Socratic physicists and ancient philosophers through Darwin, Marx, and Dewey, change has been a focus of inquiry that has evaded definition and measurement. Yet today's corporate leaders have no choice but to make decisions in a world where the pace and complexity of change have become nearly overwhelming, blurring accepted boundaries of time, geography, and language; of industries and markets; and of the public, private, and social sectors. Managers find themselves ill-prepared and increasingly frustrated in dealing with the changing rules of the game. Managing in the old way is not working, yet the new way is difficult to comprehend and operationalize.

Despite the need for breakthroughs in every dimension of performance, many of our formerly great private and public sector organizations appear unwilling or unable to do what it takes. They do not want to give up control, forge new alliances, share knowledge, dismantle their bureaucracies, or abandon traditional ways of doing business. They cling desperately to the ways of the past, like the so-called most powerful nations, the G-7, who no longer speak about leading global affairs, but rather of coping with immediate crises. Corporate leaders cannot afford the luxury of such avoidance.

Chief executives and their leadership teams, like their political counterparts in the public sector, need new maps to help them chart a course through the stormy seas of change. They and their organizations will require a more sophisticated understanding of the scope of the transformation that is sweeping our world and the new core competencies that will be needed to navigate change and to prosper into the next century. Organizational competence will be based not on past principles of ownership, stability, and control, but rather on the emerging principles of interdependence, flexibility, and partnership. Such competencies include ways to engage and inspire people, to evolve teams and partnerships, and to acquire and use knowledge.

Our experience with a wide variety of organizations from around the globe suggests that leaders are successfully developing new core competencies that enable them to be highly competitive and valuable today and that bode well for the longer-term future. From Hewlett-Packard and British Petroleum to the Santa Fe Institute and the U.S. Army, new ways of doing business are being developed and inculcated into the culture of the organization. Although solutions differ by industry and enterprise and there is no silver bullet, some new organizational competencies appear to go beyond traditional forms and get to the essence of what it takes to be a continually evolving marketplace leader. They stand the test of continuing relevance in a world of accelerating, increasingly uncertain, and boundaryless change.

This chapter presents our initial thinking on seven specific areas of new competence that are emerging and some simple indicators, drawn from cutting-edge enterprises, with which corporate leaders can begin to evaluate how their own organizations are doing. Although our research on new competencies is a work in progress and this list is not exhaustive, it does offer some criteria with which you can assess how well you are organized for this new world (see Figure 7.1). The process of assessment should stimulate your thinking about priorities for investment and action.

Commit to a Higher Purpose

Most organizations have made some top-management attempt to define a mission statement that sits in a picture frame or on a T-shirt, or to create visions that are heralded in annual reports but forgotten in the daily rush. Such efforts are often time-wasting distractions, because the ideas so rarely make a difference in the workplace or the marketplace. However, a few organizations have instilled a true sense of purpose that has become a hallmark of why they exist. They have transformed noble and lofty sentiments into a heartfelt response from their employees, customers, and other stakeholders. They have committed to a higher purpose that goes beyond ideas of mission and vision to the values and meaning that make people really want to get to work in the morning. When you talk with employees of the Ritz Carlton Hotels, Levi Strauss and Company, or the International Red Cross, you find that what many of them think about and do day to day is imbued with a personal sense of purpose that contributes to corporate excellence.

Capturing the hearts and minds of Generation X'ers and Z'ers will require an even greater commitment to worthwhile purposes. Organizations must forge a new relationship with their world that goes beyond competitiveness. They need to be purposeful in ways that resonate with the people they touch and to access levels of performance that go beyond the ordinary. This purpose is not so much a mission or goal as a commitment made visible in the day-to-day behavior of people throughout the organization. Also, this is not just an emotive phrase but a practical and businesslike way to be. At Herman Miller, Inc., renowned for quality furniture for work and health care environments, the aim is to "improve the quality of our customers' lives and become their reference point for quality and service." That is exactly what the company does.

Perhaps more important than the words is the process of instilling purpose, which demands openness and the involvement of people throughout

Figure 7.1. How Well Are You Organized for the New World?

Competence is rated from 0% (center of globe) to 100% (periphery).

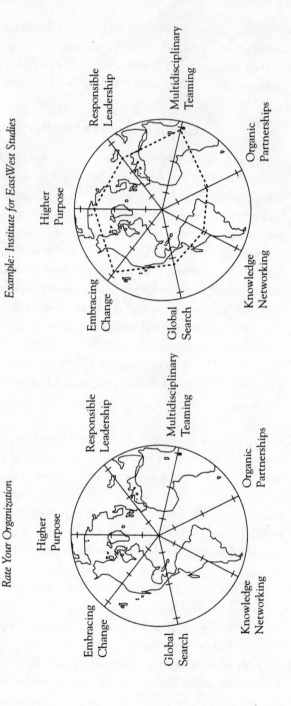

Rate Your Organization

Example: Institute for EastWest Studies

the organization, and engaging people so that they will choose to link their personal sense of purpose to the corporate purpose. If the world is unpredictable and chaotic for your organization, it is even more so for those you employ and serve. Corporate higher purpose can provide a point of stability and a motivational framework so that employees can bring their hearts as well as their minds to work. As Bob Haas, CEO of Levi Strauss, asserts: "We are not doing this because it makes us feel good, although it does. We are not doing this because it is politically correct. We are doing this because we believe in the interconnection between liberating the talents of our people and business success."

It is easy for top managers to forget a fundamental fourth-grade lesson, that the who, what, when, where, and why questions are less important than the remaining "so what?" Most people, whether they are customers or employees, are worried about the future for their children and the planet the next generation will inherit as much as they are about higher pay and promotions. What really inspires the people in your organization? What could be inspiring about the work you do? Where do personal and corporate intentions intersect? Do you have a carefully worded and dull mission statement hanging on your wall or, like the International Red Cross, do you have a clear, directional, lofty purpose—"to serve the most vulnerable"? As George Bernard Shaw said, "This is the true joy in life, the being used for a purpose recognized by yourself as a mighty one."

Instill Responsible Leadership

Much has been written about leadership. When we think about the kind of leadership that succeeds in our increasingly chaotic world, we focus not only on people in the traditional leadership roles but also on those throughout the organization who can make decisions worthy of a CEO. Where speed and flexibility of response are critical success factors, whether in an acute care hospital, a fashion store, an on-line bank, or a refugee camp, there is no time to refer to some remote corporate center or wait for a designated leader to turn up. Everyone needs to manifest leadership.

A battlefield at night provides a particularly relevant example. During recent U.S. Army tank battle exercises at Fort Irwin, California, a communication system failed, breaking the chain of command and leaving tank crews in confusion. A rout was in the making. Suddenly, a young tank commander, on his own initiative, took charge, rallied the armored squadron, and would have won the day, but for the senior officer getting back on-line and halting the initiative just long enough so that his forces were overwhelmed.

For people to take on leadership responsibility, they need support and encouragement, not controls and certainly not punishment. Growing responsible leadership means including everyone in the organization. If your leadership program is only for managers or executives, you are missing the point. Are your front-line employees capable of being leaders like those in coffee high performer Starbucks Corporation? Recently, when one of us was queuing for cappuccino and the cash register broke down, an employee simply announced free coffee. And he did it with enthusiasm. Guess where we'll be going for coffee from now on.

It is the responsibility of top executives to create the climate for responsible leadership. Although making decisions and taking action continue to be important, their focus should shift to coaching, mentoring, and being a role model of responsibility and accountability. One such role model is Sir Colin Marshall, chairman of British Airways, who, with Lord King, led the transformation of that company from a government-owned bureaucracy to "the world's favorite airline." When customers' baggage was delayed, he would take off his jacket and carry bags. He simply saw what needed to be done and did it, setting an example for others to follow.

Encourage Multidisciplinary Teaming

Most executives are well aware of the power of teams, whether in production lines at Honda Motor Company or product development at Sony Corporation, and the kinds of principles and models used to deliver high performance in team settings. What is not as well understood is the importance of creative composition in bringing about breakthroughs. We have found that teams constructed from diverse professional disciplines, life experiences, and cultural backgrounds (corporate, national, and others) are needed to address today's complex problems. The power lies in the extraordinary breadth of perspective they bring.

For example, acute care hospitals such as Lee Memorial in Fort Myers, Florida, and St. Vincent's in Melbourne, Australia, have adopted care delivery models through which multidisciplinary teams—including physicians, nurses, laboratory technicians, radiologists, and pharmacists—are organized around the needs of their patients and the families, rather than the convenience of their departments. Using principles from industrial manufacturing, these hospitals have created treatment-specific cells or "focused care units" to treat most of a patient's needs, from admission to discharge. Patients are no longer being wheeled around from department to department and waiting interminably in corridors for procedures and tests. Instead, the teams have the tools and resources they need to provide total care for the patient. Despite initial concerns about functional inefficiency and loss of control, the results have been dramatic: a substantial reduction in operating costs; greatly increased satisfaction for physicians, caregivers, and patients alike; and faster return to health for patients.

Organizations of the twenty-first century must find a way to make the spontaneous forming and re-forming of high-performing multidisciplinary teams a natural way of working. We are, in particular, thinking about teams whose membership extends beyond the sources that most executives consider. In a world where industry lines are blurring, competition is coming from nontraditional sources, and barriers to change arise from outside the private sector, multidisciplinary perspectives are essential, including those of customers, suppliers, and outside experts. Thus, the Keystone Center, headquartered in Colorado, has successfully linked rival stakeholders (corporations, environmental groups, citizens' organizations, public agencies, labor, and academia) to address the problems of toxic waste, starting from the notion that differences need not divide. The National Commission on Superfund reports that the consensus reached by these traditional adversaries will provide the basis for significant improvements over the current Superfund law. It will accelerate the actual cleanup process, involve communities in decisions that may affect their lives, reduce litigation, and address issues of environmental justice. These breakthrough solutions serve as a testament to the effectiveness of multidisciplinary teams.

If your organization is not yet a place where people from different functions and levels come together spontaneously to resolve interdepartmental issues, you have a long way to go. Multidisciplinary teaming requires what the Institute for EastWest Studies calls "thriving on diversity"—not just tolerating, not just appreciating, but thriving. Executives at all levels need to provide the personal and institutional support (including education, recognition, and rewards) necessary to encourage such radical thinking and teamwork. Easy to say; difficult to do. And this applies to the executive suite as well as to the front line. The results will be seen in extraordinary performance.

Forge Organic Partnerships

The teamwork ethic does, of course, need to extend beyond the traditional boundaries of the organization to the value chain of allied organizations and teams. Such alliance partners include product developers, suppliers, manufacturers, distributors, marketers, outsourcing partners, and even the customers themselves, who together embody the extended enterprise (or partnership) that serves the ultimate consumer. Recent Andersen Consulting surveys suggest that, in industries such as telecommunications and health care, over 85 percent and 95 percent, respectively, of their top executives believe that alliances are essential to their future. However, almost all of these same executives expect that their alliances will fail to deliver on the promised value, and the vast majority do fail and are dissolved.

The problems are often attributed to differing alliance partner agendas, unrealistic expectations, ownership battles, and cross-cultural conflicts. However the simple fact is that these supposed strategic alliances are not treated strategically. Partners need to learn how to partner in a mutually supportive, value-creating mode, bringing together their complementary competencies to create more value together than they could apart. They need to keep the lawyers and negotiators at bay and treat the alliance as a long-term, strategic relationship like that of Honda-Rover or Fuji-Xerox.

Although Wall Street has yet to wake up to the reality—witness the stock appreciation for recent megamergers that have little hope of repaying the purchase premium—our experience with 50–50 joint ventures suggests that they more often than not create more value than the 51–49 versions. The heart of value creation is trust, not ownership, the kind of mutual respect and synergistic behavior that occurs when all parties are pursuing a genuine win-win relationship.

Organizational competence in partnering begins by adopting a strategic approach to alliances. But that is just the first step. What we see evolving is a process of organic partnering, whereby a consulting partnership like Andersen Consulting or a pharmaceutical venture like Astra Merck or an oil company like British Petroleum continually forms, re-forms, learns from, and evolves alliance partnerships as a way of life, with the intention of retaining in-house only the core competencies that truly differentiate them in the marketplace. These organizations and their top executives have built competence not just in creating value from alliances but also in continuous "alliancing."

Promote Knowledge Networking

To cope with change, leading organizations are engaging in actively managing the knowledge they develop through their research, development, operations, logistics, marketing, customer service, and other day-to-day activities. The investment in knowledge goes beyond E-mail, Web pages, intranets, and groupware to the development and dissemination of experience and even wisdom, so that everyone in the organization—anywhere and at any time—can access the organization's knowledge capital and bring worldwide insights to his or her daily work.

The point is to build what Tom Peters has called "formal knowledge management structures" for capturing and managing knowledge as a strategic asset. For example, Andersen Consulting has built the Knowledge Xchange knowledge management system; it captures the lessons learned in its research and daily work and gives over thirty thousand consultants worldwide access to that knowledge twenty-four hours a day. The Knowledge Xchange is designed to enable consultants to both use and contribute to the firm's knowledge capital. Combining sophisticated user interfaces, discussion data bases, and paperless communication, the Knowledge Xchange makes the firm's knowledge capital available on demand.

The basics include building and maintaining a knowledge network infrastructure, including people and facilities as well as technology and systems, and applying the disciplines of library science to all stages of the knowledge life cycle, through acquisition, classification, valuation, storage, access, use, improvement, and retirement. If you have not yet seen the need for knowledge engineers to support your evolving communities of interest (both formal and informal), then you have barely started.

True knowledge networking involves the conscious creation of a knowledge marketplace within and beyond the organization, with the market disciplines and incentives needed to maximize the production and application of valued knowledge. In this increasingly knowledge-intensive world, where the half-life of ideas and experience is decreasing and the geographic applicability of knowledge (for example, the lessons learned from privatization) is increasing, the systematic acquisition, synthesis, and sharing of insight and experience is critical to the success of almost all organizations. The role of the top executive becomes that of the knowledge capitalist who creates a market that evaluates, recognizes, rewards— and thus shapes—the knowledge assets.

Foster Global Search

Even if they are impressed with the ideas of organizational learning, many private, public, and social sector executives find it difficult to make the concept a day-to-day reality that goes beyond incremental process improvement to the continual performance breakthroughs they hope for. Research departments can answer specific questions and pose alternative scenarios, but few are good at spotting the trend that hits from left field. Manufacturing and marketing departments can study best-of-class practices and even get underneath the data to surface valuable insights, but the study of best practice is about followership, not leadership. And so executives continue to rely on informal intelligence, such as peer networks, outside experts, and the media, to identify big issues and opportunities. There's truth in the refrain: "Its not what you know you don't know that will hurt you; its what you don't know you don't know."

Immediately after the collapse of Communism in Europe, a Polish official was shocked to hear that Europeanized Poland could learn something from Asia and Latin America about transitioning to a market economy and civil society. Today, the same Polish official writes that Europeans, Japanese, and Americans alike will soon discover that the Chilean model of pension reform is the one to emulate. Similarly, the Boeing Company has discovered that future generations of its aircraft are likely to be based on the work of poorly paid Russian scientists, who labored in an outmoded Moscow laboratory until Boeing acquired it after the Soviet Union's collapse.

Thus, a successful organization in the twenty-first century is one that will approach problem solving and decision making as a universal search to learn beyond internal and external boundaries. Global search means that all levels of the organization will embrace the effort to seek markets, competencies, and resources from the farthest corners of the globe. For to private, public, and social sector organizations alike, the search for ideas, expertise, and innovation in every pocket of the world will be paramount. Weaving this global search mentality into the fabric of the organization will demand instilling values and rewarding people for thinking globally, searching globally, and acting globally—even if the organization and its customers are all domestic. The ability to bring global power to a local problem will be one of the yardsticks of success in the organization of the future.

Embrace Change

The truth is that most change efforts fail. They are too costly, too risky, and too slow. Even when executives have truly understood the need for change, have communicated that need to their workforces through carefully orchestrated communications and meetings, and have put in place their well-thought-out programs of quality improvement, process reengineering, organizational restructuring, and other popular techniques, the organization and its culture usually thwart progress. The problem is that the world does not wait. In the months before its January 1991 bankruptcy, Pan American was engaged in companywide change efforts. In October 1989, desperate leaders of the German Democratic Republic daily gave away more and more freedoms to placate its citizens. Even then, it was too little too late.

Planned change is notoriously difficult to execute. On the one hand, the existing infrastructure (including systems, technologies, facilities, and organizational structures), built over decades at enormous cost, is usually not designed to support the new ways of working and needs to be replaced; this often requires major investments and years to complete. On the other hand, change is intrinsically unnerving to people at all levels, even to those who stand to benefit, and you can't change a culture directly. Cultures are emergent behavioral phenomena that arise over years, shaped by the stuff you can change—individuals, groups, measures, rewards, and so on. At the end of the 1980s, British Petroleum's global change program ("culture change, delayering, empowerment . . .") failed to change the culture, failed to address financial decline, and cost the CEO his job.

But there are success stories. Starting with the oil exploration business, British Petroleum's new CEO, John Browne, has focused managers on reaching for very challenging targets and has given them space and the support to question everything, to implement radical change, to really perform, and to be rewarded handsomely for their success. In the process, a new "performance culture" has emerged within a few short years and economic value has been created. The point is to address underlying causes, not superficial symptoms. Although we rightly admire a handful of success stories, such as British Airways' decadelong transformation from a poorly performing, government-owned, regional player to a highly profitable, privately held, global leader, the ability to implement large-scale change is only part of the solution. The challenge is finding ways to keep on doing it and building into the organization the capacity to continually transform itself.

By looking at industries such as investment banking, where change is pervasive, there are no periods of recuperation, and service reinvention is a daily activity, we begin to see what we mean by continual, radical change. Consider, for example, the experience of Goldman Sachs & Company, the banking powerhouse, when its profitability spiraled downward during the 1994 market slump. Fortunately, the firm's culture—forged over decades in turbulent markets where unique, high-value, high-risk deals are struck hourly—was able to sustain yet another rapid-fire change. The firm's managing partner withdrew in favor of Jon Corzine, who immediately began slashing costs, reining in the traders, and slowing the firm's breakneck pace of expansion while he pondered the firm's next move. Within weeks, a new firmwide governance structure was on the table that combined a streamlined executive committee, which ran the firm day to day, with broadened operating and partnership committees that engaged all functional and unit heads in critical decision making. In six months, the

Goldman partnership had given up a decadelong way of doing business and had institutionalized a fundamentally new management approach to restore its dominance; it is likely that in the future the firm can and will turn on a dime again.

Continual transformation demands a transformable infrastructure, including information systems and technology, such as the one that enabled MCI to offer the "Friends and Family" discount. Because AT&T's systems were not as flexible, it could not match that offer. Most important, a transformable infrastructure needs to include the kind of human resources management support, and other central services, that the business units need to bring about lasting behavioral change. For example, Motorola Semiconductor has redefined the role of the human resource professional—from hiring and firing to partnering with the business units and facilitating breakthrough change—and has recruited outsiders to inject the new skills. Motorola calls this process "continuously reinventing human resources."

A notable example of embracing change comes from Siemens-Nixdorf Information Systems, where Gerhard Schulmeyer led the turnaround of its ailing personal computer business, which had been losing hundreds of millions of dollars annually since 1991. One year after he took charge, Schulmeyer produced a profit, the first ever for the merged company. He publicly credited the turnaround to the creation of five thousand "change agents"—almost 15 percent of the workforce—drawn from the ranks of promising middle managers who volunteered to be engaged and trained, many while also performing their full-time jobs. Says Schulmeyer, "What is remarkable is that this has created a community of people in our organization who are mutually committed to change. . . . They internalized what they learned, welcomed change, and were prepared to take risks to lead their colleagues in pursuing the change agenda."

Conclusion

Developing these seven competencies will not be easy, nor will it be enough. Because the world is changing so fast and so many of the changes are likely to be unforeseen, the relative importance of these competencies will ebb and flow, and we can be sure that others will surface. Perhaps an organization's greatest challenge, and the one by which its top executives can truly measure success, will be its ability to continually recognize and develop the as-yet-unidentified competencies that our ever-changing world will demand. In the words of the great poet T. S. Eliot:

> We shall not cease from exploration
> And the end of all our exploring
> Will be to arrive where we started
> And know the place for the first time.

Part II

New Models for Working and Organizing

8 FRANCES HESSELBEIN

The Circular Organization

Frances Hesselbein is chairman of the board of governors of the Peter F. Drucker Foundation for Nonprofit Management. She served as founding president and CEO for nine years. She is editor in chief of the foundation's Leader to Leader journal and is coeditor of the Drucker Foundation Future Series. She received the Presidential Medal of Freedom, the United States' highest civilian honor, in 1998 in recognition of her leadership as CEO of Girl Scouts of the U.S.A. from 1976 to 1990 and her current national and international role in leading social sector organizations toward excellence in performance.

Five hundred years ago, Renaissance man discovered that the world was round. Three hundred fifty years later, organization man developed the practice of management. But as this practice evolved, he forgot that the world was round, and he built a management world of squares and boxes and pyramids. His world had a special language that matched its structure: the language of command and control, of order and predict, of climb the ladder, of top and bottom, up and down. In every large organization for the next hundred years, rank equaled authority. And for the most part, the old hierarchy that boxed people and functions in squares and rectangles, in rigid structures, worked well. It even developed the famous pyramid with the CEO sitting on the pointed top, looking down, as his workforce looked up.

And then a period of massive historic change began, of global competition and blurred boundaries, of old answers that did not fit the new realities. In all three sectors, in public, private, and social organizations, a new cynicism grew about our basic institutions. With government, corporations, and voluntary and social sector organizations trying to ride the winds of change, a different philosophy began to move across the landscape of organizations, and with it came a new language, a new approach, a new diversity of gender and ethnicity. In the 1970s and 1980s, some leaders in the private and voluntary sectors saw that the hierarchies of the past did not fit the present they were living or the future they envisioned, so they took people and functions out of the boxes; in doing so, they liberated the human spirit and transformed the organization.

Today we begin to see the new leaders, the leaders of the future, working in fluid and flexible management structures, and we hear a new language from these leaders, who understand the power of language:

"Organizations must be mission-focused, values-based, demographics-driven."

"Learn to lead people and not contain them."

"Management is a tool, not an end."

"Followership is trust."

We hear corporate leaders using more felicitous and inclusive language. For example, Jack Welch of General Electric Company, interviewed in the *Harvard Business Review*, said: "Ten years from now, we want magazines to write about GE as a place where people have the freedom to be creative, a place that brings out the best in everybody. An open, fair place where people have a sense that what they do matters, and where that sense of accomplishment is rewarded in both the pocketbook and the soul. That will be our report card." A corporate leader speaking of soul? Times *are* changing!

From my own experience in 1976, when I left the mountains of Western Pennsylvania to begin my work as CEO of the Girl Scouts of the

U.S.A., the largest organization for girls and women in the world, I knew that the old structures were not right for the next decade, let alone the next century. So volunteers and staff together unleashed our people through a flat, circular, fluid management system. In the new organizational structure, people and functions moved across three concentric circles, with the CEO in the middle looking out, not at the top looking down. Five minutes after this structure was presented, a colleague dubbed it "the bubble chart" and an observer called it "the wheel of fortune." Our people moved across the circles of the organization—we purged *up* and *down* from the vocabulary—and the result was high performance and high morale.

I am often asked by management students and middle managers in organizations I work with, "How can we free up the organization and make the changes you talk about if we are not at the top?" I reply, "You can begin where you are; whatever your job, you can bring a new insight, new leadership, to your team or your group." That advice applies equally, or especially, to senior executives. One place where they can affect change is in their own work groups and their everyday activities.

With the return of a more fluid, circular view of the world, the days of turf battles, the star system, and the Lone Ranger are over. The day of the partnership is upon us. Leaders who learn to work with other corporations, government agencies, and social sector organizations will find new energy, new impact, and new significance in their organization's work. But to manage effective partnerships, leaders will have to master three imperatives: managing for the mission, managing for innovation, and managing for diversity:

1. *Managing for the mission.* Understanding one's mission is the essence of effective strategy, for the small nonprofit enterprise or the Fortune 500 company. Consider the power of these questions, which Peter Drucker offers those who are formulating an organizational mission:

What is our business or mission?

Who is our customer?

What does the customer value?

A powerful, compelling mission will give people a clear and motivating reason for the organization's existence. Drucker observes that a mission statement should fit on a T-shirt. For example, "To serve the most vulnerable," the mission of the International Red Cross, satisfies both criteria and succeeds brilliantly; "To maximize shareholder value," the de facto mission of most corporations, satisfies only the first and fails miserably.

2. *Managing for innovation.* Peter Drucker defines innovation as "change that creates a new dimension of performance." If we build innovation into the way we structure the organization, lead the workforce, use teams, and plan how to work together, then innovation becomes a natural part of the culture, the work, the mindset, the "new dimension of performance." At the same time, we must practice "planned abandonment," as Drucker reminds us, and discard programs that may work today but will have little relevance in the future.

3. *Managing for diversity.* Perhaps the most critical question in today's world is, "How do we help people deal with their deepest differences?" Every leader must anticipate the impact of an aging, richly diverse population on the families, work organizations, services, and resources of every community. Headlines and TV tell us that governance amid diversity is the world's greatest challenge. Those headlines also remind us of the grinding reality that no single entity—whether public, private, or nonprofit—can restore our cities to health or create a healthy future for all our citizens. But in the emerging partnerships across all three sectors, we see remarkable openness and results. We need thousands more of these partnerships. All of us are learning from one another. Thousands of dedicated public sector employees overcome daunting odds every day to improve their corner of the world. A huge social sector, with over a million voluntary organizations in the United States and over twenty million worldwide, shows what dedicated people can do, even on woefully inadequate budgets. And the incredible resources, energy, and expertise of the private sector remind us that behind every problem there really *is* an opportunity. It is the leader's job to identify the critical issues with which his or her organization can make a difference, then build effective partnerships based on mission, innovation, and diversity to address those issues.

Not long ago, I was caught in New York traffic on the way to the airport for a conference with the staff of an international disaster relief agency. As I was thinking about how to open my session on leadership in a way that would connect with a rich mix of cultures, races, and ethnicity, I looked beside me at a bus that also was stalled in traffic, and on the side of the bus was a huge white placard with just four lines of text:

> To achieve greatness:
> start where you are,
> use what you have,
> do what you can.
> —*Arthur Ashe*

It was providential. I took this message from a distinguished American sportsman, humanitarian, and author at the tragic end of his life, dying of AIDS contracted through a blood transfusion, to people who deal every day with the most tragic human conditions and circumstances, often with massive needs, limited supplies, and too few workers.

His message was both inspiring and illuminating. It made profound change manageable and made personal change part of life. It is my hope that we can make change manageable with human dimensions—starting where we are, using what we have, doing what we can.

To be effective, leaders must see beyond the walls of the corporation, the university, the hospital, and the agency and work to build a cohesive community that embraces all its people, knowing that there is no hope for a productive enterprise within the walls if the community outside the walls cannot provide the healthy, energetic workforce essential in a competitive world.

9 JAY R. GALBRAITH

The Reconfigurable Organization

*Jay R. Galbraith is a faculty member at the International
Institute for Management Development in Lausanne, Switzer-
land. He is also a senior research scientist at the Center for
Effective Organizations at the University of Southern California.
His principal areas of research are strategy and organization at
the corporate, business unit, and international levels of analysis.
Galbraith is the author of* Competing with Flexible Lateral
Organizations *and coauthor of* Organizing for the Future
and Strategy Implementation: The Role of Structure and
Process. *He has also written numerous articles for professional
journals.*

It is an accepted fact today that change is constant. Change has become
the natural order of things. In the first volume of this series, a number
of authors saw leadership in the future as being "the management of
change." Indeed, an enormous amount of management's time and energy
is invested in changing, transforming, or revitalizing today's organizations.
This task can be made less difficult and less time-consuming by designing
organizations to be reconfigurable from the very beginning. If change is
constant, why not design our organizations to be constantly and easily
changeable? It is this easily changeable or reconfigurable organization that
I would like to describe in this chapter.

Competing with No Sustainable Advantage

Organizations have been created in order to execute business strategies. Different strategies have led to different organizations. The need for a reconfigurable organization arises from the decline in the sustainability of competitive advantages. When advantages do not last long, neither do the organizations that execute them. In the past, management crafted a winning business formula and erected barriers to entry to sustain this advantage. It then created an organizational structure around functions, products and services, markets, or geographies that was designed to deliver the success formula. To complete the integrity of the organization, planning and budgeting processes, information systems, new-product development processes, compensation systems, selection and promotion criteria, career paths, performance appraisals, and training and development sequences would all be designed and aligned with each other and with the organization's strategy and structure. Such an aligned organization would execute the strategy with as little friction as possible.

Today, in many industries, that model of organizational design is flawed. The reason is that success formulas do not last very long. The advantages around which the organization is designed are quickly copied or even surpassed by high-speed competitors. Therefore, to focus and align the organization is to become vulnerable. Some people have concluded that alignment is no longer a useful criterion for organizational design. Although I agree that alignment around a focused strategy can impede a change to a new strategy, it is the continued focus on a nonsustainable advantage that is the flaw, rather than too much alignment. On the other hand, misalignment of strategy, structure, and processes will cause activities to conflict, units to work at cross-purposes, and the organization to lose energy over many frictions. Instead, we need a new, aligned organizational design in which organizational structures and processes are easily reconfigured and realigned with a constantly changing strategy.

Thus, the challenge is to design organizations that can execute strategies when no sustainable competitive advantages are seen. When product advantages are not sustainable over time, the winners will be those who create a *series* of short-term, temporary advantages. Under this scenario, the leaders will be future-oriented and will continuously create capabilities that lead to customer value. They will move quickly to combine these capabilities so that they match and surpass current advantages (including their own). They will outmaneuver competitors by stringing together a series of moves and countermoves, as in a game of chess. The companies that have the capability of flexible responses and a variety of moves over the course of time will most likely win. The reconfigurable organization is the means of executing this continuous shifting of strategy.

The reconfigurable organization results from the skilled use of three capabilities. First, the organization reconfigures itself by forming teams across organizational departments. These lateral structures require an extensive internal networking capability. Second, the organization uses internal prices, markets, and marketlike devices to coordinate the complexity of multiple teams. And finally, the organization forms partnerships to secure capabilities that it does not have. These partnerships require an external networking capability. The three capabilities are best illustrated with an example.

An Example of the Reconfigurable Organization

A manufacturer of consumer baking products, like cookies and crackers, had competencies in brand management and distribution. It had a network of bakeries across North America and a logistics system that could deliver directly from the bakery to the retail store. Baking has always been a just-in-time business. This company's brands and its distribution systems had been its advantages and its barriers to entry. In the 1980s, these advantages came under attack. Retailers and their private-label suppliers could easily match the company's product quality at significantly lower prices. Also, the baker's products were high in fat and calories; hence, they were being avoided by both the budget-conscious and the health-conscious.

The company's resurgence began with its discovery of a low-fat ingredient that maintained the product's taste. After approval by the U.S. Food and Drug Administration, the company began reformulating its most popular brands and focused its promotions on the health segment. The new products flew off the shelves. The reformulation revived the brands and created an advantage that the private labels could not match. In order to capitalize further on the product's popularity, the company expanded into all possible distribution channels. However, different channels require different packaging, so the company created partnerships with independent manufacturers (called co-packers) to provide multiple packages. They now provide their products in enormous boxes for the discount club stores and in single-serving portions for vending machines and convenience stores.

Next, the company took the new ingredient into other categories where it could create an advantage, such as breakfast products and snacks. They joined with partners to create new products that were not baked, like granola bars. The expansion provided new business in different aisles of the grocery store. The new products could be kept fresh by using the company's existing delivery system. Other manufacturers of breakfast foods did not have either this capability or the low-fat ingredient.

The company also created partnerships (a system it called category management) with two of its larger customers. These customers turned the management of the entire cookie and cracker aisle over to the baking company. The baking company's skills in brand management, sophisticated analysis of bar code data, and knowledge of the cookie and cracker category allowed both the customers and the manufacturer to increase their profitability. By coordinating the product and cash flow from the bakery to the store, the company minimized its working capital. Groceries are now interested in packaging that is unique to them. Here again, the baking company, with its packaging flexibility, was able to meet its customers' needs.

In summary, the company in this example created an advantage through its development of a low-fat ingredient that maintains the product's taste. Using its existing capabilities in logistics and brand management, it successfully targeted and dominated the health segment. It created a multichannel, multipackage capability to enlarge the population it could reach. It used the ingredient and its logistics to enter the new category of breakfast products. The advantage of this ingredient will buy time for the company while it builds its knowledge in the new category. And finally, its enhanced reputation, brand management, logistics, and flexible packaging capabilities have made it an attractive partner for large retailers. The company has created a *series* of advantages by combining and recombining new capabilities with old ones to address new products, new segments, new distribution channels, and new customer relationships. It is a good example of the continuous creation of advantages. The baking company creates and implements an initiative that gives it an advantage. Then it quickly moves on to the next advantage. What is next? Perhaps some new segments like products for Asian or Hispanic tastes. But also coming is another new ingredient that is both low-fat and low-calorie (rather than just low-fat). The company will then repeat the sequence of advantages.

Creating Reconfigurability

The strategy of creating a series of short-term advantages can only be effective if the company has an organization that can execute it. Prior to the discovery of the low-fat ingredient, the company was organized functionally around research and development, operations, marketing, sales and distribution, finance, and human resources. It had reasonably good cross-functional relationships. Quite a few members of the top management group had cross-functional experience. In addition, for about five years, the company encouraged project management experience. Almost all managers had attended the project management course. Almost all had worked on cross-functional project teams. The company built on this base to implement the continuous strategy shifts.

The first organizational change was the creation of three cross-functional teams two levels below the level of the general manager. Each team was chaired by a full-time marketing vice president. Two teams were formed for the existing product lines: sweet products and salty products. Each function contributed a representative who spent at least 50 percent of her or his time on the team, had the authority to represent the function, and had information about the function that could be used in problem solving. The third team focused on the health segment in reformulating and relaunching the company's products. The new category was addressed by another cross-functional unit, chaired by a vice president of marketing. But this team was full-time and dedicated to the effort of breaking into a new category. Several salespeople worked exclusively for the unit and created a new sales approach for this category. This team reported directly to the chief executive to get the attention and focus that a new business requires.

A similar team was created for the new distribution channels. A vice president from marketing chaired the team but reported to the senior vice president for sales and distribution. All functions, except research and development, contributed a full-time, dedicated manager. Research and development were not represented because no new products were involved. The distribution channel team bought products from the factories and managed the relationships with the co-packers who packaged the products. Following these changes, two more dedicated cross-functional units were formed for the two customer partnerships. These units also consisted of full-time, dedicated people from all functions, again with the exception of research and development. The units were chaired by the account manager for the customer and reported to the senior vice president of sales and distribution.

In the meantime, the finance function was redesigning the accounting system. They implemented an activity-based cost system. At the same time, they installed enterprise software to automate the new system. The result is that profit-and-loss measurements can be applied to all of the strategic initiatives. The products, segments, categories, distribution channels, and customers are all measurable in terms of profit and loss. The human resources department is redesigning the reward systems to incorporate team-based rewards. Each of the teams is in fact a miniature business unit.

In this way, the company was configured and reconfigured itself from a functional structure with brand managers to a multistructure based on functions, products, segments, categories, distribution channels, and customers. It is a multiple profit-and-loss structure that can be flexibly changed to any dimension that will support the next strategic advantage. Although there is probably a limit to the number of miniature business units that can be in place at any one time, the company is creating the capability to organize any way it wants to. So instead of choosing to organize by function *or* product *or* market segment to implement a sustainable brand advantage, the company is organized by function *and* product *and* segment *and* distribution channel *and* customer to implement a series of constantly changing short-term advantages. In order to implement this reconfigurable organization, a company needs an aligned set of policies that permit it to form and re-form internal and external networks of capabilities. Two policy areas are particularly pivotal: information and goal-setting policies and human resource policies.

Information and Goal-Setting Policies

The power of the first policy area, information and goal-setting processes, to define an organization's capabilities is often overlooked and underestimated. The reconfigurable organization needs accounting systems, data structures, and planning processes that allow it to operate as a collection of miniature business units. As mentioned above, the costs and revenues must be assignable to products, segments, distribution channels, and so on in order to identify profitability. Policies for transfer prices need to accurately reflect market prices to coordinate resource allocations between the miniature business units themselves and with external partners. The same data and systems need to be used by all parties. The complex task of coordinating all of these miniature business units is made easier by the use of prices and markets. And, finally, a strong management team must be in place. There is really only one business and one profit-and-loss statement that counts: the company statement. However, shifting strategies and reconfiguring the organization requires that it be decomposed into many miniature business units. In this way, each unit can pursue different initiatives without disrupting the entire organization. Ensuring the interaction of all of these units is the task of the management team, which must set priorities, allocate resources, and resolve the inevitable conflicts.

Human Resource Policies

Equally important is the second policy area of human resources. Human resource policies must be aligned to create the behaviors and mindsets that support reconfigurability. Conflicts within a unit and between units over priorities and transfer prices can sap the energy from a company with miniature business units. The participants need to be cross-functionally skilled, have cross-unit interpersonal networks, identify with the company as a whole, and be part of a reconfigurable culture. Human resource policies are central to creating these skills, networks, and culture.

Human resource policies start with hiring practices that recruit and attract people who fit the organization, not just the job. The jobs will change and new skills will be learned, but the person's personality and the company's values and culture are much less likely to change. Hence, a person-organization fit is key to the reconfigurable organization. Personality tests, work simulations, and very extensive interviews are characteristic in hiring the person to fit the organization. The reconfigurable organization seeks people who like to work in teams, can solve problems and handle conflicts, and have the desire and potential to learn new skills. For example, the company described above uses a cross-functional interviewing process. Potential brand managers are interviewed by current brand managers and also by research scientists, manufacturing representatives, and sales managers with cross-functional experience. The company does not want a hotshot marketer whose sole interest is the fast track through brand management. The person must also be acceptable to research and development and manufacturing. The intensive interview process selects people who will be effective in cross-functional work. This process also sends a message—"Cross-function is the way we work"—and helps to build the reconfigurable culture.

Assignments and careers are also cross-functional for many managers. For example, research and development people often follow a new product they are working on into manufacturing and then into sales and distribution. At each step they learn new functional skills. They also learn the new-product development process as they move along it. But just as important are the relationships that they build and that add to their interpersonal network. The assignment process develops the individual and simultaneously develops the organization's network, building the social capital on which reconfigurability is based.

Training is continuous and targeted at cross-unit participants. Project management training, for example, is given to cross-functional teams prior to beginning new projects. Other subjects are delivered to cross-unit groups consisting of people who are working at key interfaces. The purpose is always to simultaneously build "know-how" and "know who." The reconfigurable organization sees all training events, and especially social events, as opportunities to build "know who." The events are investments in building the company's social capital.

Finally, the reward system needs to be equally flexible and reconfigurable, yet nothing turns a manager into a conservative faster than a recommendation to change the compensation system. Because of this conservatism, compensation systems are the greatest barriers to change and flexibility. At a time when pay plans need to be approximate, flexible, simple, and valid, they are instead precise, complex, quantitative, nonaligned, out of date, and rigid. It takes years to study a pay system, reevaluate the jobs, pilot the new plan, and introduce it unit by unit. Far more speed and flexibility are needed.

The new, nimble reward systems have three grades or bands, far fewer than the thirty pay grades of old. Salaries are based on a person's skills rather than on the job. Today we pay the person, not the job, because jobs change too quickly. So do the people, but the more they learn the more they earn. Often, skill-based pay is given as a one-time bonus for learning because skills also come and go. Fewer annuity-like additions are used; more often, on-time bonuses are substituted.

The appraisal process is also moving away from a boss's appraisal to a team-based appraisal or 360-degree feedback model. There is less ranking of all engineers along a single dimension and less complexity in the performance rating scales. Some organizations have an automated performance appraisal day, during which the whole process is done easily and quickly; the appraisal can be repeated often in quickly changing environments. Thus, pay systems are becoming more flexible by using more bonuses and fewer annuities, simpler scales and grades, pay for skills rather than jobs, and encouragement of faster changes and more experimentation.

Collectively, these human resource practices build cross-unit skills, cross-unit interpersonal networks, and, ultimately, a reconfigurable culture. They also build the skills and mindsets to link functions, both inside and outside the company, into a miniature business unit. In this manner, an organization is better positioned to capitalize on an opportunity and build a new capability. New capabilities can be combined and recombined in interesting ways to create the next advantage, but the lasting capability, and possibly a more sustainable source of advantage, is the capability of an organization to reconfigure itself.

What Happens to the Functional Organization?

The functional organization remains as a stable structure around which the reconfiguring takes place. The functions act as homerooms for people participating in projects and miniature business units. Functions are also the homes for experts and individual contributors. In the baking company described above, experts in food science, the chemistry of fats and oils, manufacturing process technology, and distribution system practices do not rotate across functions. They develop in-depth knowledge in their specialties that can become new capabilities to be combined and recombined.

The functions take on a long-term perspective. They become responsible for deciding on and building new capabilities, skills, and technologies. They build relationships with universities to develop new technologies and new graduates. The functions also benchmark the company's capabilities and evaluate potential partners. So while more and more business decisions move to project teams and miniature business units, the role of the functions is to build long-run capability.

The Cost of Reconfigurability

Reconfigurability, unlike quality, is not free. It takes time and resources to build information systems and human resource practices. A significant investment in recruiting and training is required, in addition to management's investment in coordinating work within and between miniature business units. It is a communication-intense form of organization.

The potential for problems also exists. Companies may not always be able to find people who can manage conflict and who desire growth and development. Everyone is looking for team players. In addition, there is a potential for unresolved conflict. Transfer price issues can consume enormous amounts of time. As in matrix-type organizations, discussions in a reconfigurable organization can degenerate into lengthy internal negotiations, leaving less time for customers. If all of the policies are not aligned, internal frictions can absorb the company's energy. However, these costs and risks must be weighed against not being able to adjust to a reconfigurable competitor.

Conclusion

The reconfigurable organization is the companion to the continually shifting strategy. When competitive advantage does not last very long, neither do organizations. Instead, competitive advantage results from a string of short-term advantages delivered through a reconfigurable organization. The reconfigurable organization consists of a functional structure around which projects and miniature business units are continually formed, combined, and disbanded. These units can focus on products, distribution channels, segments, customers, regions, suppliers, technologies, and so on. The company can literally and simultaneously organize any way it wants to. Reconfigurability rests on three capabilities:

1. *Extensive internal cross-unit networking.* This capability is built through aligned human resource policies. It attracts, holds, and develops the flexible people who create the flexible organization.

2. *Use of prices, markets, and marketlike devices to coordinate the multiple profit center units.* An accounting and information system that permits an accurate and flexible determination of profit and loss on any dimension is the central tool underlying this capability.

3. *External networking with partners to expand capabilities that can be combined to create new advantages.* The same behavioral skills of cooperation, conflict management, and influence without authority that are used in internal networking are indispensable in managing external networks.

The final element is a top-management team that sees its value in designing and supporting the organization's reconfigurability.

10 RON ASHKENAS

The Organization's New Clothes

Ron Ashkenas is a senior partner in Robert H. Schaffer &
Associates, a management consulting firm based in Stamford,
Connecticut. For many years, Ashkenas and his colleagues have
pioneered results-driven approaches to organizational transfor-
mation. He has written dozens of articles and book chapters and
is coauthor of The Boundaryless Organization: Breaking the
Chains of Organizational Structure. *His clients have included*
Motorola, SmithKline Beecham Pharmaceuticals, General Elec-
tric Company, the World Bank, and many other public and
private firms.

Like townsfolk who do not notice that the emperor has no clothes,
many leaders today are ignoring the fact that the organizational system they represent is no longer functional. The pace of change has accelerated beyond the capability of most organizations to respond, the
psychological contract between employees and employers has broken
down, and some of our most revered private and public institutions have
stumbled to the brink of disaster.

Note: Portions of this chapter are adapted from *The Boundaryless Organization: Breaking the*
Chains of Organizational Structure, by Ron Ashkenas, Dave Ulrich, Todd Jick, and Steve Kerr
(San Francisco: Jossey-Bass, 1995).

Yet despite these well-known and well-publicized sea changes, most organizations today do not look much different or operate much differently than those of twenty, thirty, or fifty years ago. The control-based hierarchy—with multiple levels, functional divisions, differentiated roles and rewards, and fragmented information—is still the prevalent organizational model. Despite years of total quality, reengineering, and dozens of other change prescriptions, fundamental transformation is still an illusion. The emperor has no clothes.

Why do so many organizations pretend that they are wearing the latest fashions even though their underlying patterns are still those of traditional dress? What will a new set of clothing look like for organizations of the twenty-first century? And what leadership actions should organizations take to begin reclothing themselves today?

The Past as Prologue

If the past is any indication of the future, we can be certain that the last half of the 1990s and the beginning of the twenty-first century will be turbulent and unpredictable. Only a decade ago, who would have imagined the stunning geopolitical shifts that we now accept as reality—the breakup of the Soviet Union, the end of Communism in Eastern Europe, a peace process in the Middle East, the demise of apartheid in South Africa, the economic emergence of the Pacific Rim? And who but a small band of futurists and technologists would have predicted the incredibly rapid commercialization and spread of new technologies such as fax machines, cellular and wireless communication, notebook computers, CD-ROMs, global positioning systems, digital cameras, multimedia workstations, interactive cable, the Internet's emergence as an electronic superhighway, and more?

Organizations, too, have been buffeted by a tidal wave of unimaginable change. Once-invincible companies such as IBM, General Motors Corporation, Sony Corporation, Eastman Kodak Company, Aetna Life & Casualty Company, and Apple Computer—previously unquestioned models of organizational excellence—have experienced severe performance problems and, in many cases, sudden shifts of leadership. At the same time, whole industries such as pharmaceuticals, entertainment, and financial services have been caught up in merger frenzies. And while some companies were racing to the altar, others, such as AT&T, ITT Corporation, the Dun & Bradstreet Corporation, 3M, and W. R. Grace & Company, were breaking themselves up. Even in the public sector, once-venerated institutions such as the World Bank and the United Nations have had their very existence questioned, while governments around the world, from the United States to the United Kingdom to the Philippines, have been reviewing, reinventing, downsizing, and privatizing their basic operations and services.

There is little doubt that this fast-track, kaleidoscopic pace of change will continue, or even accelerate. In fact, stories of organizations "hitting the wall" are becoming almost a routine feature of the business press. The question for organizations now is how to ride the crest of this tidal wave of change instead of being slammed into the rocks.

The Search for Magic Cures: Comfort in Old Clothes

As the pace of change has accelerated, organizational change efforts have also increased. In the past ten years, few organizations have avoided some major change program such as total quality, process redesign, customer focus, reengineering, rightsizing, or delayering. And although success stories have resulted from these powerful concepts and tools, all too often the returns have not matched the investments. What is even more disappointing is that even when some measurable gains have been achieved, the fundamental capacity of many organizations to deal with accelerated change has not been strengthened. Thus we have seen hundreds of companies fall prey to "serial programs"—one change effort after another, each one promising to accomplish what the previous one could not.

These change efforts have not paid off for two major reasons, both related to senior executives' discomfort at doffing the old set of organizational clothes and donning really new ones.

Moving the Boxes Around: The Illusion of Change

First, even though the aim of most change efforts is fundamental transformation, the outcome is often only a rearrangement of the existing organization. Boxes are moved around, cross-functional teams are ceremoniously launched, layers are removed, and support services are consolidated or distributed, but the fundamental dynamics of the business remain unchanged. It is simply too threatening for managers to question their basic business assumptions, to turn their backs on what is successful today in order to build for tomorrow. Thus, as Gary Hamel and C. K. Prahalad point out in *Competing for the Future*, most reengineering and other change efforts focus on making companies better at what they are currently doing, but not different. And in the long run (and increasingly in the short run as well), being better in an industry and an economy that are radically changing is not enough.

For example, a struggling group health division of a major insurance company spent several years reengineering its sales and customer service processes. Based on customer interviews and compelling financial data, multiple field locations were combined into regional service centers with team-based operations, sales forces were consolidated and refocused, product materials were redesigned, and more. The organization that emerged from this effort had a significantly smaller budget and faster cycle times, but it did not have any fresh thinking about its business case. Its basic product offerings had not been changed, nor had its definition of who its customers were. And while this division had been preoccupied with reengineering, several competitors had been reshaping their offerings to better fit the new realities of managed care, customer choice, and other factors.

Using the Old Process: The Delusion of Change

What is even more debilitating about change efforts like these is that the process used to foster change unintentionally mimics and thus reinforces all the old organizational patterns that need to be transformed. The change is driven from the top with the assumption that the people at lower levels must change their behavior; staff groups and consultants play powerful technical roles, but do not transfer their know-how to the line organization; employees are often kept in the dark until a small, elite group announces the details of what will happen to them; customers and other constituents are asked their opinions, but are not really engaged in the give and take of generating alternative solutions. Even reengineering programs, which purport to foster employee involvement, have more often than not been run by small, sequestered teams that collect and analyze data in isolation from the rest of the organization. When this happens, the hierarchical, control-based organization is amplified rather than transformed.

In the group health organization, the reengineering effort was sponsored by the divisional president, who designated a senior staff person to be accountable for the change effort. The senior staff member hired a consulting firm that provided a structured methodology. A small group of internal people worked with the consultants full-time for over a year to collect the data, analyze the findings, and prepare a reengineering proposal. After the divisional president was convinced that the proposal was "right," he directed his management team to implement it. A year of arguments, false starts, and anxiety then ensued. Eventually, most employees came to view the effort as a Trojan horse for downsizing them out of a job. Morale plummeted, employee concerns rose, and customer service suffered. As a result, hundreds of talented people could not focus on customer service or innovation or change—the stated aims of the effort—but rather on whether they would survive.

CEOs and presidents certainly do not intend their change efforts to have these outcomes or consequences. However, they are very uncomfortable about changing patterns that have made them successful in the past. Thus, they hesitate to radically transform their basic business unless it is crumbling around them, and only the exceptional few understand and are willing to work on changing their own proclivities toward hierarchical direction and control. What is needed to break the logjam are two things: a model for a different kind of organization and a practical process to make it happen that does not rely totally on a single, enlightened CEO as the driver of change.

New Clothes: The Boundaryless Organization

Although the organization of the future might not look much different from today's, it will certainly act differently, in a way that we call "boundaryless." Specifically, behavior patterns that today are constrained and blocked by long-standing boundaries between organizational levels and functions, between suppliers and customers, and between geographic locations will be replaced by patterns of free movement across these boundaries. No longer will organizations use boundaries to separate people, tasks, processes, and places; instead the focus will be on how to permeate those boundaries— to quickly move ideas, information, decisions, talent, rewards, and actions to where they are most needed. It is this effervescence that will create and re-create the organization of the future.

This does not mean that such an organization will not have boundaries. On the contrary, boundaries are necessary to separate people, processes, and production; to keep things focused and distinct; to give the organization shape. Without them, organizations would be *disorganized*. People would not know what to do. There would be no differentiation of tasks, coordination of resources and skills, or clear sense of direction. However, instead of the relatively rigid boundaries that exist in most organizations today, the organization of the future will have permeable boundaries, like the flexible, movable membranes in a living, evolving organism.

Rigid boundaries evolved in most organizations as a means of ensuring organizational stability and order. To foster this stability, a host of tools and frameworks were developed that eventually shaped the nature of behavior in modern organizations. These included mission statements, job descriptions, job-grading (point) schemes, grievance procedures, span-of-control analyses, approval limits, organizational design criteria, career ladders, information access criteria, performance assessment systems, and many more. In essence, organizations fostered stability through an intricate and interrelated series of controls, usually administered by senior management and a variety of staff groups (personnel, finance, legal, quality, and others). Whenever performance or behavior began to oscillate outside of the normal range, these controls were used to dampen the waves and return the organization to its steady state.

In a relatively stable world, this organizational system was effective and, in fact, it led to decades of unprecedented prosperity and social progress. In today's world, however, the oscillations no longer are controllable, nor do we want them to be. Rather, the organization needs to be let loose to ride the riptides of change and move in new directions. It needs to be fast and flexible, able to change directions quickly and nimbly and to innovate continuously. To do this, four types of boundaries need to be made more permeable and flexible:

1. *Vertical—the boundaries between levels and ranks of people*. When vertical boundaries are made more permeable, position is less relevant than competence. This usually leads to faster and better decisions that are made closer to the action and more access to ideas from people anywhere in the organization. For example, when SmithKline Beecham wanted to improve its processes for managing clinical trial data, everyone in the affected organizations, at all levels, participated in a two-month dialogue about alternative ways to proceed. Through conferences, task forces, and electronic forums, dozens of new ideas were generated, which eventually led to significant cycle-time reductions in the drug development process.

2. *Horizontal—the boundaries between functions and disciplines*. By increasing the permeability of horizontal boundaries, battles over turf and territory are replaced by a focus on how to meet customer needs. In Fidelity Investment's retail business, for example, a collaboration between operations, marketing, systems, phones, and the branch organization helped the company to reposition itself around more segmented customer needs such as education and retirement planning. The collaboration also streamlined procedures and services for customers, leading to integrated statements, simplified application procedures, and more effective telephone response. And all of this was done without changing the basic organizational structure.

3. *External—the boundaries between the company and its suppliers, customers, and regulators*. Traditionally, organizations form "we-they" relationships with external constituents and do business through negotiating, haggling, using pressure tactics, withholding information, and playing off customers or suppliers against one another. When this food chain mentality is replaced by a focus on the "value chain," tremendous efficiencies and innovations can be introduced into the entire product or service supply system. For example, GE Lighting has formed partnerships with retail chains. In these arrangements, the companies operate almost as one organization: point-of-sale purchases are tracked by GE, sales trigger shipments directly to stores, and all financial transactions are done electronically. The savings are shared by the companies and passed on to customers—a win-win situation for everyone.

4. *Geographic—the boundaries between locations, cultures, and markets*. Often stemming from national pride, cultural differences, market

peculiarities, or worldwide logistics, these boundaries may isolate innova-tive ideas and lead to competition between headquarters and the field. When geographic boundaries are made more permeable, companies can more rapidly leverage global successes. For example, Price Waterhouse & Co. now uses a worldwide groupware system to create client proposals that can be enriched by input from twenty-six offices around the world.

Leadership to Make It Happen: Tailoring the New Set of Clothes

No matter what a company's size, structure, or strategy, when vertical, hor-izontal, external, and geographic boundaries are traversable, the company is better able to navigate rapid change and can continually engage its peo-ple and its partners in remaking themselves. When these four boundaries remain rigid and impenetrable, they create a slowness to respond and a lack of flexibility that keeps an organization locked into old and ultimately self-defeating patterns.

As we move toward the twenty-first century, the challenge for organi-zational leaders at any level—not just the CEOs—will be to create this boundaryless capability through change processes that are themselves boundaryless. They can take several steps to make this happen:

1. They should identify a significant "stretch" goal or opportunity that will make a difference to the business—and that can only be achieved through more effective crossing of one or more boundaries. A goal might be to bring a new product to market in half the nor-mal time, to collaborate with a customer to reduce servicing costs by 30 percent, to increase the speed of customer-order processing by 30 percent or more, or to experiment with new ways to go to market. To the extent that it is possible, these goals should have the ability to redefine and reinvent the business, as well as to just do the same business better.

2. They should commission a cross-boundary team to achieve the stretch goal and to do so by means that create boundary-crossing capability. They should encourage the team to engage people at all levels in the process, including customers and suppliers. This

team should be given whatever help and resources it needs to be successful.

3. They should learn from the experience and do it again, and again, and again.

Dressing the organization in new clothing is not an overnight program. It requires hard work, experimentation, persistence, and energy. And because it is not a controllable, predictable process, it also requires that the organization have the confidence to allow a variety of people, from inside and outside the organization, to shape and reshape the future. This process is the operationalization of Peter Drucker's famous dictum that the true job of the manager is to get out of the way. But for those leaders who are willing to foster this capability and create the space to let it thrive, it may be one of the most effective and exhilarating paths toward organizational renewal that they will ever experience.

11 JOEL A. BARKER

The Mondragon Model

A New Pathway for the Twenty-First Century

Joel A. Barker is a futurist who began popularizing the concept
of paradigm shifts and vision in 1975. He is the author of
Paradigms: The Business of Discovering the Future *and*
Future Edge, *which was listed as the most influential business*
book of 1992 by Library Journal. He is one of the most sought-
after speakers in the world on the topic of change and how to deal
with it. His best-selling videos, which are available in seven lan-
guages, have been called by Industry Week *one of the most*
influential series of programs in the business world.

In the last years of the twentieth century, capitalism and the marketplace
have regained global preeminence. Socialist and Communist economies
are considered failures, and based on their performance, that is as it should
be. However, what has begun to reemerge is an attitude toward jobs and
work that we have not seen since the Great Depression. Job security is
considered part of an old paradigm that is rapidly disappearing. Enormous
job cuts across the industrialized world are blamed on market forces that
require the "leaning down" of organizations.

Bill Gates, head of a twenty-first-century organization, has said that
the only security his employees have is their skills, and he supports their

education to maintain and improve those skills. President Bill Clinton has repeatedly stated a similar theme: we must educate our people so that they can be employed in well-paid jobs. But one need only look at the number of well-educated people in the United States who are severely underemployed or out of work completely to know that education alone is not and cannot be the sole solution. This dilemma is repeated throughout the world.

Somehow, the for-profit enterprises, those organizations that create the jobs from whose wealth all other jobs are derived, must not accept the prevailing paradigm of lack of job security. To assume that it is impossible to create job security in the twenty-first century is to set a boundary that I believe is illusory. At least one significant experiment already exists that suggests otherwise. I would like to share that experiment as a model. I have been following it for fifteen years, and the success it has enjoyed is, at least in part, the result of reversing one of the most important premises of capitalism. The old rule of business is this:

> *When you are faced with the choice of risking your capital to protect jobs or risking jobs to protect your capital, always protect your capital.*

The reversal is:

> *When you are faced with a choice of risking your capital to protect jobs or risking jobs to protect your capital, always protect your jobs!*

The organization that has reversed the old rule is the Mondragon Cooperative, located in the Basque region of northern Spain. Mondragon represents a paradigm shift for organizational structure and thinking. I believe that an understanding of its history, structure, and success offers a profound alternative to the singular corporate vision of the future that is now in ascendancy.

The History of Mondragon

The Mondragon Cooperative was started in 1954 by a Jesuit priest named Don José Maria Arizmendiarreta (I will refer to him as Don José from here on) and five young men. Don José was a fascinating man whose background shows courage and a willingness to stand up for his beliefs. Upon his ordination, he was sent to the Mondragon region to minister to the people. When he arrived in 1941 he found great unemployment, poor education, and no positive vision of the future. The assets of the region were few but important: industrious people who knew how to work hard, solidarity based on being treated badly by the Spanish government for hundreds of years, and a strong social structure.

Don José began the construction of his paradigm shift by starting an industrial apprentice school in the late 1940s. He also taught classes on ethics to young men who planned to start businesses someday. As the school grew, so too did the unemployment in the region, reaching 20 percent in the early 1950s. Don José had read the papal edict that said that work should be considered part of spiritual development, and he was deeply disturbed by the number of his parishioners who, because of their lack of a job, could not participate in that aspect of their own growth.

In 1955, he began to take action to change the future of Mondragon. He invited five young men who had been in his business ethics classes to go with him to raise money, in order to buy a business and bring it to Mondragon. They put out the word that they were looking for loans. They had no business plan; they didn't know what they were going to buy or what they would produce. Yet on the strength of their reputations plus their own personal financial commitment to the project, they raised $361,604! This in a community with high unemployment. In 1990 dollars, that would be about two million dollars.

With the money in hand, the five young men went shopping and purchased a small manufacturing company that made Aladdin kerosene heaters. One year after they purchased it, they moved it to Mondragon and the cooperative was born. They named it ULGOR after the first initials of the five principals' names. When they asked Don José what they were going to do next, he answered, "We will build the road as we travel."

In 1956, the company had 24 employees. In 1958, it had 149 employees. In 1990, the Mondragon Cooperative Complex, of which ULGOR was the first of many connected cooperatives, had 21,241 member employees. It consisted of a complex of more than one hundred enterprises and was worth more than $2.6 billion. In the last half of the twentieth century, Mondragon has grown and developed a unique worker democracy in which the employees own the enterprises, the capital-worker relationship has been inverted, and entrepreneurship flourishes at a rate of success unparalleled anywhere else in the world.

The Principles of Mondragon

Five guiding design principles have resulted in Mondragon's incredible record of job creation and community continuity. Although the Basque country has special conditions that helped Mondragon flourish, any organization anywhere in the world can learn from this half-a-century-long experiment.

Power Structure

The first principle of Mondragon is that of democracy. It is a cooperative; therefore, every worker has a vote. The workers elect the board of directors and the board of directors hires the managers. This has a positive effect on the workers, because the people they elect are the people who hire their supervisors. If they don't like what the management is doing, they can always vote out the board. Part of the democratic structure is a worker's congress where everyone has a vote. There is also a "watchdog" council of workers that watches upper management and a social council made up of representatives of teams of twenty to fifty workers. In short, everyone has a voice and a representative with a voice. Although unions also exist within the cooperative, they play a very different role than in most corporations because of the high quality of communication between management and the workers and the power balance that is already in place.

In short, the principle of democracy allows the workers to know that, if they wish, they can fundamentally restructure any or all of the Mondragon Cooperative Complex. They are the final decision makers.

Financial Structure

Worker democracies are unusual, but they are not unique. The financial structure of the Mondragon Cooperative Complex, however, has no parallel in the world. Let's take a look at the key pieces.

First, all workers must put some of their own money into the cooperative they are part of. The money accumulates interest but can only be removed upon retirement. It guarantees that everyone has something to lose if the enterprise fails; it also carries with it a reward at retirement if the enterprise is successful. Second, a bank was created within the cooperative structure that serves the cooperative and is itself a cooperative. It has a very clear mission, which is to fund new jobs so that all people who wish to work in the Mondragon area can do so. This mission is even more important than making the best return on investment, thus violating the prevailing paradigm of banking. Simply put, the Mondragon cooperative bank risks its capital to protect the job base of the community.

All workers and the Mondragon cooperatives must use this bank. It holds the savings and retirement funds of the workers and processes all the funds flowing through all the Mondragon enterprises. In exchange for this monopoly of money, it provides services no other bank in the world provides to its members:

- Strategic information and guidance for both old and new businesses
- Up-to-date marketing reports that suggest new products and services that are needed in the region and throughout Europe
- A staff of older executives ready to mentor new cooperatives
- A willingness to fund start-ups to create new jobs in the area

The Mondragon bank perceives itself not just as a guardian of the money it uses, but as a catalyst for creating new businesses within the Mondragon Cooperative Complex structure. It always has the welcome mat out for anyone who wishes to create more jobs. Because of this attitude and the great skills Mondragon has developed in nurturing start-ups, its entrepreneurial success rate has been 80 percent! That is the failure rate for the rest of the world!

By the 1980s, the cooperative's bank had funded over one hundred new cooperatives and only three had failed. One British economist studying Mondragon declared this rate of success to be so startling "as to be a miracle." Another researcher, Robert Oakeshott, wrote that if you measured the bank by the criteria of creating worthwhile jobs or mobilizing savings, "it is outstanding." So successful has this bank been that in the

1980s it had to petition the Spanish government to allow it to loan money beyond the legal limits set for it because it had more money than the cooperative could effectively utilize. In many ways, the bank has acted like the head office of a private holding company. The only difference is that it is owned by its customers.

The Education Connection

The third principle is linked to education. Remember that Don José had started a technical school back in the 1940s to serve the young people in the Mondragon region. That school evolved along with the cooperatives. The needs of the growing cooperatives were always connected to the curriculum of the school. Many of the students also worked at the co-ops, so they could see the direct connection between their preparation and their job. The school added students and increased the range of its curriculum. It added management and marketing departments and now is considered one of the best business schools in all of Europe. As of 1990, more than 6,500 students were enrolled in degree programs and 3,500 in other types of training courses. This direct connection to specific enterprises and jobs is rarely emulated in the United States except with such programs as the Motorola University in Schaumburg, Illinois. But here we are describing a complete community, with a commitment to sustain an educational system that reinforces the ability to keep jobs within the region.

By the way, those marketing studies the bank maintained for would-be co-op entrepreneurs? They were done, for the most part, as coursework for the marketing program at the school. What more powerful incentive could you give students than to know that their work might very well be the basis of a vigorous new enterprise just down the street?

Pay Scales and Equity

The fourth principle focuses on the concept of fair pay. This issue, symbolizing who is and is not important in a society, is becoming a trigger in the United States as CEOs take larger and larger pieces of the pay pie. The Mondragon Cooperative Complex had three things going for it: fairness as part of the culture, a distinctly Christian slant to its enterprise ethics, and the Basque hallmark of moderation. As a result, the cooperative could create an extraordinary set of payment relationships and make them work.

Specific pay ratios were set in 1955 and held until the 1980s. The person at the top could earn no more than six times the salary of the person at the bottom of the cooperative. If the boss wanted a raise, everyone got a raise. In the United States, in 1996, the ratio is about 115 to 1 in major corporations. Recently, the ratios at Mondragon have increased to 15 to 1, because the rest of Spain has recognized how good Mondragon's managers are and lures them away with higher salaries.

Raises within various sectors of each cooperative are determined by many standard measures of productivity and absenteeism, but they also include unusual measures such as "relational skills," or how well the worker gets along with other people. That measure, in particular, constitutes 20 percent of the pay raise decision. Salaries are called *anticipos*, payments in advance of profits. Workers who choose to leave their job can be penalized up to 30 percent of the accumulated profits in their retirement fund. If they are fired for a grave offense, significant penalties can be imposed. In case of job loss, workers are paid 80 percent of their salary plus 100 percent of their social and health insurance for twelve months. The Mondragon Cooperative Complex is self-insured for job loss, so that is the very last thing it wants to happen. In fact, a whole series of actions must occur before a worker loses his or her job.

For instance, before someone is laid off, any profits accumulated during the year in the specific cooperative would be used to pay for the job position. If that is not enough, then all wages in that cooperative are dropped to 85 percent of standard. If that still isn't enough to finance the continuation of the job, the worker is transferred to another of the co-ops in the Mondragon structure. And if that job pays less than the previous job, the unemployment fund makes up the difference. Finally, if all of these efforts fail, the worker goes on unemployment and immediately begins receiving educational benefits to acquire new skills as fast as possible.

How well does this program work? During the world recession of the early 1980s, the Basque region lost 150,000 jobs. At the same time, the Mondragon Cooperative Complex created an additional 4,200 jobs. The final result: only 104 of its workers, or six-tenths of 1 percent, ended up unemployed.

Retirement

The fifth and last principle centers on an equitable retirement plan. The Mondragon Cooperative Complex self-funds and fully funds its retirement package. Workers contribute 32 percent of their earnings and receive 60 percent of their final salary. The cooperative also paid for all workers' health care until the late 1980s, when the Basque government assumed most of the financing. One nice touch is that as part of the retirement package, the worker is given a vegetable garden plot if he or she doesn't already have one.

Conclusion

There are many more provocative details in the story of Mondragon. But let me conclude with these observations for organizations that are looking for alternatives to the twentieth-century paradigm:

- Worker democracy and ownership is a real and viable alternative to the stockholder paradigm.
- Education plus community vision plus a bank that is committed to job formation instead of capital formation can create a long-term community job base.
- There is another way to create entrepreneurial wealth.
- Workers themselves can reinvent their work if the right kind of support is available.
- The role of a bank can be profoundly positive and supportive for communities if it has the right paradigm.
- Self-capitalization can be a powerful tool.
- The power of a shared vision cannot be overestimated.

The Mondragon model is not perfect. It requires a long-term commitment to moderation instead of excess. For too many in the industrialized world, excess is considered success. The Mondragon model also requires a commitment to the community and the people of that community rather than to a quest for short-term profits. And it requires a new kind of banking paradigm.

Yet Mondragon also represents something very important:

- It is a noble forty-year experiment illustrating that the marketplace of competition contains a significant place for cooperation.

- It is a work community where religious values and ethical considerations of fairness and democracy thrive to the benefit of capital formation and significant profits.

- It is a place where fear really has been driven out of the workplace in many ways.

- It is a clear demonstration that only human beings can add value to capital. It is never the other way around!

If nothing else, Mondragon serves as a reminder to us all that more than one pathway to the future exists. We must never be afraid to search for the one that lies on the highest ground.

Note: For further information on the Mondragon Cooperative Concept, see Whyte, W. F., and Whyte, K. K. *Making Mondragon*. (2nd ed. rev.) Ithaca, N.Y.: ILR Press, 1991; Morris, D. "The Mondragon Cooperative Corporation." Research and report commissioned by Joel Barker. St. Paul, Minn.: Institute for Local Self-Reliance, 220 West King Street, St. Paul, MN 55107 (612) 228–1875, July 1992; Morrison, R. *We Build the Road as We Travel*. Philadelphia: New Society Publishers, 1991.

12 DOUG MILLER

The Future Organization

A Chameleon in All Its Glory

Doug Miller is president and chief executive officer of Norrell Corporation. He joined Norrell in 1979, became president of the Franchise Division in 1984, and was named president and CEO of Norrell Services, Inc., in 1990. He assumed his present position in 1993. He held positions at McDonnell Douglas Corporation and IBM before joining Norrell. He currently serves on the advisory board of Georgia Business Forum, the boards of directors of the Cystic Fibrosis Foundation and American Business Products, and the dean's advisory council for Emory University Business School.

To describe the organization of the future, we first need to consider the chameleon. The chameleon is not a beautiful animal except to naturalists and schoolchildren. With its crests, horns or spines, and bulging, independently rotating eyes, it looks like a cruel trick of nature. The trick, however, is on the chameleon's prey and predators, for the animal has all the equipment to ensure its survival. The chameleon has a laterally flattened body and its skin changes color in response to stimuli such as light, temperature, and emotion. In other words, the chameleon constantly adapts itself to its environment.

The organization of the future likewise will be an ultimately adaptable organism. Its shape and appearance will change as its environment and the demands placed on the organization change. At Norrell, we see the results of organizations adapting to the new realities every day. We strive to anticipate changes in the environment in which we do business. Our customers increasingly ask us to take on more responsibility for total results. Where once they would ask us for pieces of a solution, they now ask us to be an integrator. In fact, we have promised our customers, employees, and shareholders that we will continue to challenge and change the rules. Our view of the future is based on our experience with thousands of companies.

The chameleon organization has five critically important characteristics: great flexibility, commitment to the individual, superior use of teams, strong core competencies, and a taste for diversity. Although the ultimate chameleon doesn't yet exist, a few organizations currently exhibit some or even a majority of these characteristics.

Great Flexibility

The organization of the future builds itself on a premise of flexibility. It commits to moving, adapting, and changing as required by changes in its environment—and that certainly means changes in its customers. The chameleon organization does not feel threatened by change; it eagerly pursues change.

In Charles Handy's *Age of Unreason*, the underlying thought of which I much admire, he writes of the shamrock organization. One leaf of the shamrock is the essential core, the second leaf is work that is outsourced, and the third leaf is the flexible workforce. What is important to note as the real world of experience takes off on this theory is that even the essential core changes over time, and it changes more rapidly as the overall rate of change in business accelerates. In part, this means that whatever worked in the past—processes, organizations, structure—not only may not work in the present or the future, but in fact may be an impediment to success. Even successful companies can be encumbered by their own paradigms.

In my view, the changes in IBM over the past few years provide an illustrative example. For years, IBM failed to adapt to a changing business environment because its past success had contributed to an unyielding corporate culture. When the wakeup call came, first from customers, then from Wall Street, it was sharp, swift, and painful. Subsequently, IBM not only restructured and downsized, but changed its very core. After shedding tens of thousands of jobs, the company is now looking to fill ten thousand new jobs that require very different skills and mindsets—all of which serve to accelerate and deepen the change in the core.

The core itself has to reflect the outside business environment. This means that the trend toward outsourcing is likely to accelerate, especially as companies reorganize around their core competencies. Successful flexibility has to become part of the organizational culture. The organization must adapt. Inside the Norrell organization, autonomy and ownership were the rule in what we see now as the "old" organization. We are rapidly shifting to the elements of matrix management and team orientation so that we can remain as flexible as our changing business environment demands. Our customers require us to deliver services in a variety of configurations, sometimes in our own bricks and mortar, sometimes from the customer site, and sometimes off-site. We have to be prepared to move quickly to meet any customer need. Clearly, all of this happens only when individuals are passionately committed to flexibility as an organizational value. Yet all of us know that something dramatic has happened to the social contract that individuals have historically enjoyed with their organizations.

Commitment to the Individual

The traditional social contract, loosely defined, had at its heart the notion that individual work—loyal, consistent, and enduring over time—would be rewarded with steadily increasing pay, responsibility, and security. Although it was not universally applied, the social contract was a significant thread in the fabric of everyday work life in America. This contract has now been irrevocably broken. Over the past few years, businesses have eliminated hundreds of thousands of their jobs. Some did so analytically; some did so because it had become an accepted way of managing. The dislocation caused by downsizing and restructuring has been enormous. Like a phoenix from the ashes, however, a new contract has to emerge.

The new contract, as strange as it sounds, is centered on a commitment to the individual. Like any good contract, both sides, the organization and the individual, have to buy in to its provisions. The pervasiveness of the current social change in organizations has created the conditions that allow both sides to buy in. On the one hand, the organization has placed its bets on results rather than on work. On the other hand, the individual has said that what matters is meaningful work and growth, whether it occurs in a particular organization or a series of organizations. The chameleon organization will tap this powerful confluence of interests.

Studies have shown that young people don't expect, nor do they necessarily want, cradle-to-grave job security in a traditional hierarchy. What younger workers want is an environment in which they can grow, acquire skills, and increase the value of their work. From another perspective, people want to be in on the problem-solving work of their organization. The requirement of the organization, then, is to ensure that its people can do the work of problem solving. This means that the chameleon organization will invest heavily in the training and development of its people, especially those associated with its core. We already see indicators that this is the right direction in which to move. The American Management Association has found that in most cases, downsizing did not result in increased profits or productivity. Yet it also found that companies that followed layoffs with increased training budgets were twice as likely to show increased profits and productivity as firms that cut back on both workers and training.

Simply offering training programs is insufficient. Training and development will have to be actively managed. It is understood that many of the skills transferred to individuals by this training are portable. The organization trains its people for the problem solving at hand. Once the work changes, the organization, as we have already seen, also changes. Some of the trained people will stay with the organization; some will leave. The organization benefits from having well-trained people. The individuals benefit from adding skills to their tool kit. Invariably, customers benefit because their suppliers have a cadre of well-trained people.

Superior Use of Teams

Among the skills that the chameleon organization will impart to its people are those required for operating in teams. Such skills are critical because teams will play a greater role in performing the work of the organization. Certainly, the team concept has been sullied by its poor use in any number of organizations. We all know of teams that self-perpetuate, teams that find the lowest common denominator, and teams that cannot or will not deliver results. Yet it is the team that is going to prosper in the chameleon organization. The self-directed, self-managed team provides the muscle inside the flexible organization. As the business environment changes, the organization adapts, and internally the organizational structure is fluid in order to accommodate all the changes. Teams will form around a problem. Once the problem has been solved or redefined, some teams will disappear and new ones will form. Individuals on the teams may find themselves part of one, then another, and perhaps members of several at once. The teams will change as required.

The skills associated with a team approach are basic to successful operation of the teams. This means that the organization needs to equip its people with all the necessary skills. Depending on the situation, people will find themselves as the leader on one team, a peer on another, and a subordinate on a third, the roles being defined by the nature of the work. Superior individual effort is still necessary and desirable, but only as it contributes to the output of the team. Functioning in these different roles requires a whole new set of skills from those acquired in a traditional organization. This kind of training is not often delivered by our schools; therefore, it is incumbent upon the organization to provide it.

I had the opportunity to visit an organization in the Northeast that illustrated the value of self-directed, self-managed teams. The people operated out of a rambling structure with no offices, partitions, or hierarchy. There were numerous tables and desks, in no particular order, with a great number of laptop computers. A lounge area was included, but nobody was lounging. Instead, about seventy-five people were working in what could only be described as organized chaos. They were responsible for new-product introductions for a major company. Their work included presentation development, identification of the top fifty markets and the top fifty clients or prospects in each market, local market training, product promotion events, and a rollout schedule that called for implementation within fifteen weeks. As if this were not enough, three new-product launches were going simultaneously. They were flexible, focused, driven, and totally reliant on working in teams.

Strong Core Competencies

The chameleon organization's strength lies in its core competencies—the knowledge of what the organization knows how to do best. Core competencies are different from core businesses. A core competency is built on knowledge and expertise, as opposed to a core business, which is built on tasks. The difference is a major one. James Collins and Jerry Porras, in *Built to Last*, say that the organizations that endure master the "and." They define their strong suit, their core competencies, and then organize around them while remaining alert to new opportunities. In fact, in all likelihood, the chameleon organization will pull together a shopping basket of competencies, organize them, and deliver results as needed by the customer in the marketplace. Noncore functions will be outsourced. The organization understands that it has neither the time nor the resources to invest in noncore functions. This cannot happen with a hierarchy—it's much too threatening.

At Norrell, we've identified one of our core competencies as our relationship skills—our ability to adopt our customers' perspective in order to deliver innovative, customized solutions to their problems, whether they are organizational, technological, or structural. We see different solutions all related to human resources—the management of work and workers. We've also become convinced that relationship skills are absolutely essential to the future organization. Businesses must include this kind of training in their own portfolio or outsource it to another party. It is critically important. Increasingly, Norrell is taking on more responsibility for total results, by helping our customers define their problems and providing the total solution to those problems through supplemental staff or a flexible workforce. Our customers' change from asking for pieces of the solution to asking us to be an integrator is, I believe, a reflection of our core competency.

A Taste for Diversity

The chameleon organization, prizing the value of the individual as it does, has a taste for diversity among its workforce and its supplier cadre. Diversity is prized not on a racial, gender, religious, or ethnic basis, but rather for the competencies and perspectives it brings to the solution of customer problems. The organization of the future pursues diversity, which may also include accepting a longer or shorter work week and dividing the total hours expended differently from week to week depending on the requirements of the work.

Finally, a note of caution: the greatest impediments to change and the greatest obstacles to an organization's success lie within the organization itself. The test for senior management is how to eliminate the impediments and the obstacles. Give everyone the opportunity to buy in to change. Provide a reasonable amount of time and training to effect the change, yet be willing to experience some pain by, for example, removing stars within the organization who refuse to change their behaviors.

In other words, to change an organization, start with behaviors, and especially with senior management's modeling of desired behaviors. Understand also that changing the attitudes beneath behaviors takes much longer. The future belongs to the chameleon organization—an organism so attuned to its environment that it can quickly adapt. The fact that it does so almost effortlessly is all the more amazing.

13 GLENN R. JONES

Creating a Leadership Organization with a Learning Mission

Glenn R. Jones is chairman of Jones Education Networks, Inc., and chairman and CEO of Jones Intercable, Inc., and Jones International, Ltd. His company has become one of the ten largest cable television operators in the United States and has been the springboard for Jones's creation of a number of innovative enterprises, among them Mind Extension University: The Education Network.* He is a member of the board of directors and the executive committee for the National Cable Television Association, the board of governors for the American Society for Training and Development, and the board and Education Council of the National Alliance of Business.

Leadership organizations are made, not born. This may sound trite because the "made, not born" description is currently in vogue when describing leaders themselves. It's also easy for the presence of top performers with some leadership abilities to be confused with evidence of a leadership organization, especially as those individuals champion short-term causes and often win small battles and an occasional campaign. The far greater challenge is to put their collective innovation and talent into

---

*Mind Extension University® and The Education Network™ are registered marks of Jones International, Limited.

a cohesive form that truly represents a leadership organization for the future. Today it's convenient to talk the talk of leadership and entrepreneurship, and this type of talk flows freely within most corporate hierarchies. "Walking the talk" is another matter. Deploying the results of "walking the talk" inevitably brings chaos throughout all types of corporate structures.

The real-life model of the twenty-first-century leadership organization does not yet exist. Vestiges of it are appearing on the horizon, but given the rapidity of business change, it will likely only appear after the fact as a case study for dissection and critique in business school seminars. My own view of that hypothetical model might be considered frivolous, save for the fact that a multitude of organizations, for-profit and nonprofit alike, are now straining to define the shape of the mold. I predict that the leadership organization of the twenty-first century will be part technology-based, part customer-service-oriented, and part adult schoolhouse. Indeed, its most distinguishable trait will be a culture of continuous learning for all of its associates, a term I prefer over *employees* and one that applies to mailroom clerks and CEOs alike.

The output of the learning-based leadership organization will be information-rich products and services distributed through draconian warfare in the marketplace. I expect the feverish battles for market share already in progress to only intensify. I leave them for the elite strategists in their cellular command posts and for other book titles devoted to them. What I want to relate here is a view of some of the aspects of learning-based leadership organizations and the principles of leadership they must reflect as their leaders prepare them for the challenges of the next millennium. It is my own interpretive blueprint of leadership organizations that have already been transformed or that are in the process, gleaned from the experience of my own company and many more that I have observed over the past thirty years.

Luminaries as Leaders and Mavericks

In these days of Goliath-sized technology and media enterprises, we often forget that such luminaries as Gordon Moore of Intel Corporation, Ted Turner of Turner Broadcasting System, Bill Hewlett and David Packard of

Hewlett-Packard Company, and Bob Magness and John Malone of Tele-Communications, Inc. (TCI), began their companies in garages and tiny warehouses, fought fierce battles with competitors and investors, more than once faced the prospect of losing control of their own enterprises, and, in some cases, approached outright personal financial ruin. Examples exist in the public sector as well. In 1907, Maria Montessori outraged traditional educators by opening her school for "uneducable" poor children in Rome and revolutionized early childhood education in the twentieth century.

These leaders, all branded as mavericks, simply wanted to accomplish objectives that required them to operate beyond the norms of conventional wisdom. As I have become acquainted with some of these leaders over the years, it has struck me that all of them were considered heretics for pursuing unproved ideas and were the subject of ridicule by some of their peers during the early stages of forming their enterprises. To persevere, they employed three key strengths:

1. They honored the integrity of their dream and their accompanying instincts.

2. They had a strong aptitude for attracting other risk takers to their side.

3. All of them became students as well as mentors, learning from their followers, their mistakes, and their adversaries.

A Personal Journey

As a young naval officer on a troopship making its way to Korea in 1954, I had my first lesson in the relevance of education and of learning from those around me. During the long, tedious journey, I asked some of the young Marines and soldiers on board why they were willing to go to another country and possibly lay down their lives for people who shared neither their culture nor their language. Most could speak in simple terms of defending freedom, but none of them were well equipped to explain exactly what freedom was or meant to them. I found this deeply troubling. These men were the products of one of the world's most advanced educational systems, but I was at a loss for a remedy that would have supplied them with the words and concepts that they could not verbalize.

Years later, during my first visit to the Vietnam Memorial in Washington, D.C., where I watched veterans and loved ones tenderly touch names etched on black granite, the same quandary came vividly to mind again. This time it was an obvious dilemma to which I might offer a remedy, if not an outright solution, through education. People will rise to meet seemingly insurmountable obstacles and challenges if they understand the worthiness of their personal sacrifices and effort. Supporting that understanding must be mentors who provide leadership; without both ingredients, a cause will go unrealized and a mission is likely to fail.

What We Learned with Mind Extension University

When we started out to create Mind Extension University (ME/U), both our internal studies and various education and technology experts indicated little prospect of success. Our first task was to convince our own associates that this was a worthy goal, outside detractors in both education and television programming notwithstanding. This included communicating a sense of mission and passion about the idea that distance education (delivering educational content to students who are geographically removed from the site of origin) was not just an adjunct to traditional education, but an area worthy of its own discipline and of a large commitment of resources from Jones International, ME/U's parent organization.

Today, college-level courses from thirty different universities, plus original course content produced by Jones, are delivered to over ten thousand enrollees annually in the United States, with enrollments increasing in Europe and Asia. Whereas ten years ago one in six students was an adult learner, today, in the United States, four out of six college-level students are taking courses after completing a normal degree program or while holding a full-time job. It was a trend we could sense, but no one could foretell the shifts that technology, political liberalization, and global economics would bring to the education marketplace.

We started out to educate the world, and along the way we became students ourselves. To date, 1,124 of Jones's 4,000 associates have taken ME/U and other college-level courses while holding down full-time jobs with the organization. Some 200 have earned associate's, bachelor's, and master's degrees while filling their positions here, in fields ranging from education and health sciences to business communication and history. Our associates now take principles of accounting, advanced languages, computer science, and Western civilization courses through our system.

One of the reasons we have become such ardent practitioners of adult distance education is that we have learned that you cannot communicate or attempt to offer others what you have not experienced. As we designed the curriculum in the late 1980s, we had to experiment to find the right ways to make it happen and to make it appealing and effective. Certainly, much of this took place as we pursued a grand vision and master plan. But as is the case with many successful learning and leadership experiences, it was also a voyage of serendipity and discovery, a process that must be recognized as highly valuable in true leadership organizations. Again, it's easy to pay lip service to such concepts, but much harder to integrate them into the bottom-line realities of organizations striving to map out a five-year strategic plan.

The Lesson of History

Most organizations fail when it comes to such integration, and they will continue to come up short as they try to prepare for a schizophrenic future in a disembodied world. I offer this view based not on futuristic musings or any sense of cavalier prognostication in reaction to accelerating trends in our technology-driven world. Rather, my convictions emanate from simple personal experience and from reflecting on the five-hundred-year development of capitalism and entrepreneurship, which have their roots in the European development and proliferation of the movable-type printing press in the mid 1400s. This lesson of history is worth considering as a backdrop to what is happening today in the world of technology and education.

The fifteenth century was the dawn of the Age of Discovery, as documented in Daniel J. Boorstin's authoritative work, *The Discoverers: A History of Man's Search to Know His World and Himself.* In its own chaotic way, it was also the beginning of the end of education exclusively for the elite, meaning those who were conversant in Latin, the only language of university education. It was the beginning of the proliferation of literacy throughout the social classes, thanks in large part to the printing press.

The parallel between what happened with Johannes Gutenberg's wonderful device, which probably was an adaptation of Chinese and Japanese technology, and our access to information via telecommunications in the late twentieth century is inescapable. The printing press was pursued as a remarkable commercial opportunity. Thousands of Bibles, other books, illustrations, and maps were reproduced because the technology was at hand to do so. Publications in languages other than Latin were all at once feasible, so these materials were translated. The technology itself was quickly overshadowed by applications and content.

Although the world of international commerce was controlled by European nation-states through their navies and shipping fleets, the printing press helped to cause this monopoly to begin to fragment, thanks to one primary product: the map. Varying tremendously in perspective and accuracy, maps in Latin, Dutch, French, Portuguese, and Spanish were available by the early sixteenth century and seemed to offer the key to riches to those who could read. Perhaps the first mass-produced business strategic plan was a navigation map that an entrepreneur adventurer, predating Balboa and Magellan, purchased on the cheap and followed to a watery grave.

How Technology Stimulates Education

Printing technology may have been the product of enlightened humankind, but in turn it heightened the incentives for literacy and more education. Trading companies such as the Dutch East India Company kept their maps, charts, and captains' logs under lock and key, but literate sailors from their crews would readily sell their own unofficial versions of documents, which were quickly mass-produced. Today, as it was almost five hundred years ago, technology has proved a catalyst. The need and role for a learning organization is simply accelerated by the tools at hand.

The industry that has provided the foundation for the Jones companies is the cable TV business. Cable TV is less than fifty years old, younger than some of my midcareer managers, younger than the computer industry, and younger still than the Apollo 7 astronauts. Cable TV, I suspect, is also a prescient example that in today's arena of rapid change, relative youth is no guarantee of longevity. I do not expect cable TV to pass much beyond its fiftieth birthday in a form that its pioneers, most of whom are still living, will recognize.

Many of the companies that lead cable TV today and control its enormous revenue flows—in the multibillion-dollar league—are rapidly being transformed into or absorbed by new telecommunications giants. The TCIs, Time-Warners, and Bell Atlantic Corporations will undoubtedly recreate themselves several times by the early 2000s as the full force of free-market telecommunications opportunities unfolds around the globe.

Departing from the Cable TV Model

I chose a somewhat different path for Jones International because of personal conviction and also the lessons of experience. This path has made my organization the object of intense scrutiny and more than a little ostracism from industry pundits over the past ten years, since I first began redirecting the company to a mission as a technology-based, knowledge-driven learning organization; thus some explanation is instructive.

It has been my experience that an organization is only as strong as the continuing education of its principal managers and leaders. This is a somewhat different view from that of organizations that tally their management firepower in terms of the number of PhDs, JDs, and MBAs on the company roster. I do not demean these credentials in any way, but they are only half of the learning organization equation. All viable organizations allow for continuing education and training of their more junior associates but, as often as not, the demands of the executive team allow insufficient time for the education of those who are expected to lead. By education, I am referring to an overall ongoing education in the liberal arts, business management, and technology. Education within a leadership organization is a multilegged stool; in my experience, a solid education in only the engineering sciences, management, or law is well and good, but it leaves the practitioner with at least two weak legs. Likewise, an education derived solely in liberal arts and the humanities does not prepare the student for the multidisciplinary demands of today's world, in either the community or the workplace.

A great deal is being said and written about the knowledge worker of today, about a workplace with workers who constantly shift among employers, are continually being retrained, or have to upgrade their skills on their own. Although much of this is true, the popular view tends to treat the new workforce as a one-dimensional entity and obscures the subtleties and complex demands of the work world. At Jones, we started out virtually stringing TV cable between customers' homes, becoming sort of high-tech cowboys in the 1960s and 1970s. We learned about the new technology in the field as it became available and had to be installed.

Today, formal schooling is available for cable technicians and engineers, our field trials focus on high-speed cable modems, and the research and development work involves technology-delivered college classes that cater to Internet-literate customers. On the market-skills side, managers at all levels must be able to work directly with international partners and clients, as well as listening and responding to customers who have just lost their TV reception in the midst of the NBA playoffs.

The Invisible Hand of Leadership

Organizational leaders who want to truly restructure and steer organizations—as opposed to acting as stewards to a previously defined or industry-defined course—must immerse themselves both in history and in the fabric of their organization. Despite the anticorporate rhetoric that is popular today, successful organizations in many ways are living, dynamic organisms that attach themselves to their associates and leaders. To continue their evolution and avoid the path to extinction, they must nurture, channel, and provide what I call an "invisible hand of leadership" for those who work with them. This leadership can be demonstrated in many ways in their relationships with their customers, members, or other constituents, but it is best demonstrated within the relationships the organization builds with its associates.

It does not require leadership to follow a board-approved strategic plan. Vigorous management and discipline, yes, but not true leadership. Bona fide leadership emerges in evolving organizations where frustration, surprise, and outright failure loom constantly on the horizon. This leadership must nurture the troops and offer them hope when all of the product development groups report failure, when the market tests don't even register on the audience response meters, or when a contract award just went to the same leading competitor for the third time in a row. When leadership emerges under these conditions, it becomes a fundamental part of the organization's DNA.

Does the blueprint transfer readily to another organization? No. The test and charge of the leadership organization is to find its own design and its own path, to eschew "Shake and Bake" formulas and find its own way. Although dynamic internal leaders may emerge from the ranks of an organization and can come in any number of model types, one essential characteristic is difficult to teach. Finding responsible but willing risk takers is one of the greatest challenges for corporate leaders. No matter who the architects of a blueprint are or what the noblesse oblige is of those who will employ it, leadership organizations will be hard-pressed to succeed if they do not have risk takers at all levels who contribute to the design and feel a passionate stake in it.

As the leadership organization of the twenty-first century looks ahead to define its course, its next most valuable undertaking will be the identification of associates who are willing to become lifelong learners. Once these choices and internal leaders are known, the path to mission fulfillment will begin to define itself.

Part III

Organizing for Strategic Advantage

14 ROSABETH MOSS KANTER

Restoring People to the Heart of the Organization of the Future

*Rosabeth Moss Kanter holds the MBA Class of 1960 Chair as
professor of management at Harvard Business School. An adviser
and consultant to leading organizations worldwide about the
management of change, she was a cofounder of the Boston-based
consulting firm Goodmeasure and serves on many public interest
boards and government commissions. Her latest book is* World
Class: Thriving Locally in the Global Economy. *Among her
other best-selling, award-winning books are* When Giants Learn
to Dance, The Change Masters, *and* Men and Women of the
Corporation.

T he characteristics of the organization of the future are largely known
today. What is missing, however, is the "social contract of the future"
that will motivate people to work in it.

Many organizations seek problem-solving, initiative-taking associates
who go the extra mile for the customer. But companies are not going the
extra mile to invest in employees and their future. Because of the unpredictability of even the most benign restructuring, managers are less able to
guarantee a particular job—or any job at all—no matter what a person's

performance level. A reduction in hierarchical levels curtails a manager's ability to promise promotion, and managers therefore have less power to influence careers. Cross-functional and cross-company teams can rob managers of their right to direct or even understand the work their so-called subordinates do. Partnerships and joint ventures put lower-level people in direct contact with each other across departmental and company boundaries.

A shift from manual work, which was amenable to oversight, to "knowledge" work, which often is not, makes the worker's own commitment more important, but organizations in the midst of reengineering are eliminating the means for building commitment. Many managers can no longer even give their people clear job standards and easily mastered procedural rules. And the complexities of work in the new organization—projects and relationships clamoring for attention in every direction—exacerbate a feeling of overload on the part of many workers. Downsizing often reduces the number of people without reducing the number of tasks.

Thus, it is critical to examine the impact of organizational change on the people who staff organizations. Six important shifts of emphasis are shaping the organization of the future, and each has significant human implications.

1. *From fat to lean: the new staffing principle.* Employment assumptions have moved away from "big is better" to "smaller is beautiful"—and more flexible. Increasingly, the desire for "fat" organizations, which relied on redundancy, encouraged overstaffing, and could afford to waste people on nonessential tasks, has been replaced by a preference for "lean" organizations with focused efforts. Such organizations rely on outsourcing and external suppliers for internal services and impose overtime and overload on existing staff before adding others. This makes the organizations more flexible and cost-efficient, but it also strains people's endurance, and it undermines their security by eliminating career paths or increasing contingent jobs.

2. *From vertical to horizontal: the new organization.* The hierarchical emphasis in traditional American corporations was orderly, at least in theory. Information flowed down a vertical chain of command; that chain also ranked people in terms of their status, compensation, authority, and influence. Today more work is being done in cross-functional or cross-

departmental project teams. People are encouraged to look horizontally across the organization for influence and collaboration, rather than upward to their bosses.

3. *From homogeneity to diversity: the new workforce*. As women and minorities have increasingly gained access to positions in which they were formerly rare, and professional labor markets have gradually globalized, occupational segregation by sex has started to decline. The workplace increasingly contains teams of people from many different social and cultural categories. Instead of using affirmative action to recruit individuals, the managerial priority in more enlightened companies (such as Xerox Corporation, Hewlett-Packard Company, or Bank of Boston Corporation) has shifted to managing groups characterized by diversity.

4. *From status and command rights to expertise and relationships: the new power source*. Power in organizations has always stemmed from both the characteristics of the job and the nature of relationships. But now, as hierarchies are deemphasized, the formal authority derived from hierarchies is less important than professional expertise in gaining the respect required for influence and leadership. And the balance between job-related power and network-derived power is shifting toward the value people bring to organizations from their relationships, not just from their ability to accomplish a task.

5. *From company to project: the new loyalty*. In the traditional corporation, commitment was a matter of the bond between a person and the company; people were expected to be loyal to their employers. But the new organization is characterized by weaker attachments to the company and stronger attachments to one's own profession or project team. Professionals work hard, project by project, and maintain high standards, but they also take their sense of worth from their field, not from their bond with a particular company.

6. *From organizational capital to reputational capital: the career asset*. Careers in the traditional corporation were institutionally derived; they were composed of a sequence of steps up the rung of a job ladder. Along the way, people accumulated "organizational capital"—the experience and contacts that helped them move up in a particular company. Today, people rely primarily on their human capital. They need portable career assets—skills and a reputation that can be applied anywhere.

For the workforce as a whole, these changes increase the uncertainty of careers and widen the arena for power seeking. Some groups benefit from the weakening of hierarchy and bureaucracy. For women, the new organization opens opportunities—it makes them less dependent on a single boss, provides a variety of team relationships, and creates greater variety in career paths that no longer go in lockstep up a ladder—as long as they can demonstrate clear expertise and take initiative. Women are already finding their greatest opportunities in the professions and through entrepreneurship. Even women in the female service army of clerical workers, nurses, flight attendants, and hotel clerks might gradually gain greater professionalism in their work in the companies that acknowledge the need to empower front-line service workers to compete effectively for customer loyalty.

But that's the sunny view. The rise of the new organization and new careers also has a dark side. The weakening of traditional organizational career structures creates new anxieties. Self-reliance sounds good only when there is work to be found. The new context underlines the uncertainty of careers and increases the likelihood of involuntary displacement and fluctuating fortunes. Within many workplaces, tensions are rising, morale is shaky, and sexual harassment is far from suppressed. Greater workplace diversity adds strain; men and women and members of different ethnic or racial groups are still learning how to work together as peers. Men accustomed to security do not welcome more competitors for fewer, less secure positions. Career uncertainty and workplace demands are rising at the same time that the new workforce struggles to juggle out-of-work responsibilities, turning family issues into public issues.

Toward Renewed Investments in People

The organization of the future requires a focus on new human resource policies. Organizations must help people gain the skills and self-reliance to master the new environment, to find security and support when they can no longer count on large employers to provide it automatically. And companies must see that revaluing human capital and emphasizing team collaboration are the best ways to create workplaces and workforces capable of addressing the challenges of the global economy. To compete effectively, businesses must attract, retain, motivate, and utilize effectively the most talented people they can find. Some recognize this, at least in rhetoric, giving lip service to the importance of human capital. "Our most important assets walk out the door every day," some executives say. Those human assets are walking out the door, all right. And in many cases—because of downsizing, workplace tensions, or lack of commitment—they are not coming back. People do not want to invest their talents without feeling that they are getting enough in return.

New approaches are required. Assumptions and policies that derive from the corporatist model of the twentieth century are an inadequate basis for the social contract of the twenty-first century. For many people in the second half of the twentieth century, careers were constituted by large institutions. Large employers in the public and private sector were expected to provide—and guarantee—jobs, benefits, and upward mobility. Long-term employment was considered to be a central component of high-commitment, high-productivity work systems. And corporate entitlements, from health benefits to pensions, were based on an assumption of longevity, especially in the United States, where employers were expected to offer benefits like those provided by governments in other countries. Now sweeping industrial transformations are forcing large companies to downsize—a euphemism that masks the human turmoil involved. Even in Japan, the bastion of lifetime employment in big businesses, where nearly three-quarters of the country's sixty million workers have stayed with one employer throughout their working life, cutbacks and layoffs beginning in 1992 have been shaking the social contract.

The United States has been fortunate in not depending solely on large enterprises. America has a vibrant entrepreneurial economy, a small business sector that creates a higher proportion of jobs than are similarly created in European nations. But employment in smaller organizations is inherently less secure, especially given the high failure rate of new small businesses, and such jobs often come without the benefits and safeguards mandated for companies with more than fifty employees. Americans count on entrepreneurs to pull the country out of the economic doldrums when large companies sputter and downsize. But an entrepreneurial economy is full of churning and displacement, and the fate of small companies is often linked to the fate of big ones that they supply and service.

Thus, traditional values are eroding, including long-term employment security and the loyalty of employer to employee and employee to employer. Some wonder how we can sustain productivity, quality, and innovation under these circumstances; don't they stem from the mutual commitment of employer and employee? Others wonder about the human consequences of the inevitable displacement, the social costs that must be borne when people are left to wonder about uncertain organizational futures.

New policies must reflect new forms of security while embracing the merging realities of flexibility, mobility, and change. If security no longer comes from being *employed*, it must come from being *employable*. Employability security—the knowledge that today's work will enhance a person's value in terms of future opportunities—is a promise that can be made and kept. Employability security comes from the chance to accumulate the human capital of skills and reputation that can be invested in new opportunities as they arise. No matter what changes take place, people whose pool of intellectual capital or expertise is high are in a better position to find gainful employment, with their current company, with another company, or on their own. For example, a senior executive developing new ventures for a materials company offered no guarantees of continued employment to the people he recruited, promising instead, "If you give the new business a whirl, you will be a better and more salable person for it." The proof of his proposition? He left three years later to join a rapidly growing venture capital firm.

In many high-tech firms, people already acknowledge the new reality. They bet their future on continuing hard work and growth in skills that match changes in the industry, finding security in their own ability to generate income, perhaps as entrepreneurs themselves. Companies come and go, but technical know-how and learning opportunities—chances for people to grow in skills, to prove and improve their capacity—enhance their ability to stay employable. Challenging jobs on significant projects are more important, in this calculation, than promises about the future or benefits programs contingent on long service. In software, for example, many people feel that they work for the industry rather than their current employer, they are motivated by the excitement of the technology and the challenge of learning, and they dream about starting their own company someday. (Of course, software is a growth industry full of young people.)

Even in cases in which employment security is promised, this guarantee is only possible because of programs aimed at ensuring employability. Companies can offer to invest in retraining and career counseling to continually upgrade people's skills so that they will always be employable, though specific jobs might disappear and employees might have to prove their ability to contribute to the company over and over again throughout their careers. Continuing to upgrade skills and pursuing new opportunities is a lifelong proposition even inside a single corporation, an essential part of the corporate fitness regime for global competition. And in the wake of restructuring and downsizing, when large employers shed jobs in bundles of ten thousand, the same proposition needs to be extended outside the corporation: social safety nets must be extended to help people upgrade skills and deal with the costs of transition as they seek new jobs or plan new businesses. Helping men and women succeed as mobile professionals is a matter of public self-interest.

A society that encourages investment in human capital through continuing education, training, and support for the creation of new ventures can help people to feel secure even when they move across companies or invent their own jobs.

The New Motivational Tools

With the old motivational tool kit depleted, leaders need new ways to encourage high performance and build commitment. Human resource policies should center around the things people value that help them build their own futures and reap rewards for present contributions.

1. *Mission*. Helping people believe in the importance of their work is essential, especially when other forms of certainty and security have disappeared. Good leaders can inspire others with the power and excitement of their vision and give people a sense of purpose and pride in their work. Pride is often a better source of motivation than the traditional corporate career ladder and the promotion-based reward system. Technical professionals, for example, are often motivated most effectively by the desire to see their work contribute to an excellent final product.

2. *Control of the agenda*. As career paths lose their certainty and the future of companies grows less predictable, people can at least be in charge

of their own professional lives. More and more professionals are passing up jobs with glamour and prestige in favor of jobs that give them greater control over their own activities and direction. Leaders give their subordinates this opportunity when they give them release time to work on pet projects, emphasize results instead of procedures, and delegate work and decisions about how to do it. Being able to choose their next project is a potent reward for people who perform well.

3. *Learning.* The chance to learn new skills or apply them in new arenas is an important motivator in a turbulent environment because it's oriented toward securing the future. "The learning organization" promises to become a business buzzword in the 1990s as companies seek to learn from their experiences more systematically and to encourage continuous learning for their people. In the world of high technology, where people understand uncertainty, the attractiveness of any company often lies in its capacity to provide learning and experience. By this calculation, access to training, mentoring, and challenging projects is more important than pay or benefits. Some prominent companies—General Electric Company, for example—have been able to attract top talent even when they could not promise upward mobility, because people see them as a training ground, a good place to learn, and a valuable addition to a résumé.

4. *Reputation.* Reputation is a key resource in professional careers, and the chance to enhance it can be an outstanding motivator. The professional's reliance on reputation stands in marked contrast to the bureaucrat's anonymity. Professionals have to make a name for themselves, while traditional corporate managers and employees have stayed behind the scenes. Indeed, the accumulation of reputational "capital" provides not only an immediate ego boost but also the kind of publicity that can bring other rewards, even other job offers. Managers can enhance their reputations—and improve motivation—by creating stars, providing abundant public recognition and visible awards, crediting the authors of innovation, publicizing people outside their own departments, and plugging people into organizational and professional networks.

5. *Share of value creation.* Entrepreneurial incentives that give teams a piece of the action are highly appropriate in collaborative companies. Because extra rewards are based only on measurable results, this approach also conserves resources. Innovative companies are experimenting with incentives such as phantom stock for the development of new ventures

and other strategic achievements, equity participation in project returns, and bonuses pegged to key performance targets. Given the cross-functional nature of many projects today, rewards of this kind must sometimes be sys-temwide, but individual managers can also ask for a bonus pool for their own areas, contingent, of course, on meeting performance goals. And everyone can share the kinds of rewards that are abundant and free—awards and recognition.

The best organizations will base jobs and careers on flexible work assignments, not on fixed job responsibilities. To promote innovation and responsiveness, two of today's competitive imperatives, managers need to see the new organization as a cluster of activity sets, not as a rigid struc-ture. The work of leadership in this new corporation will be to organize both sequential and synchronous projects of varying lengths and breadths, through which varying combinations of people will move, depending on the tasks, challenges, and opportunities facing the area and its partners at any given moment.

Leaders need to carve out projects with tangible accomplishments, milestones, and completion dates and then delegate responsibility for these projects to the people who flesh them out. Clearly delimited projects can counter overload by focusing effort and can provide short-term motivation when the fate of the long-term mission is uncertain. Project responsibility leads to ownership of the results and sometimes sub-stitutes for other forms of rewards. In companies where product develop-ment teams define and run their own projects, members commonly say that the greatest compensation they get is seeing the advertisements for their products. One engineer told me that he trumpeted to his family, "Hey, that's mine! I did that!" the first time he saw a commercial for his group's innovation.

This sense of ownership, along with a definite time frame, can spur higher levels of effort. Whenever people are engaged in creative or problem-solving projects that will have tangible results by a given dead-line, they tend to come in at all hours, to think about the project in their spare time, to invest the vast sums of physical and emotional energy that are needed. Knowing that the project will end and that completion will be an occasion for reward and recognition makes it possible to work much harder.

Revaluing Human Capital

The rhetoric about valuing human capital is increasingly in place. Leaders speak of "core competence," of "competing on capabilities," or of their desire to become a "learning organization." But accounting systems have not caught up with the shift that is needed from measuring only the use of financial capital to measuring the building of human capital. Financial measures can swamp other measures of performance and value and claim disproportionate time and attention, even when accounting is a poor indicator of company health because measures are focused on short-term profits rather than on the building of long-term capabilities.

In the 1980s, debt lost its traditional moral sting, and money became too easily detached from purpose. But both business and society are endangered when people see themselves as making money rather than products, or as growing rich from speculation rather than labor. Some Japanese worry that too many of their compatriots are obsessed with money technology— *zaitek*—instead of real technology. Holders of financial capital are praised on ubiquitous lists of the world's richest companies and the world's richest people. Builders of human capital are not. How often do we see lists of companies that have created the most jobs or trained the most employees to build future capabilities? Even the few indicators of social value that are starting to appear (like the "most admired companies" list) are published only once a year. Stock prices are available by the minute, every minute. It is too easy for managers to lose sight of their business purpose because of the seduction of following price movements.

Finding ways to value and measure human capital—skills, capabilities, and know-how—is an important step in focusing managers' attention on the centrality of their people to their success. Skandia, a Swedish insurance service company expanding rapidly in international markets, has begun issuing an annual report on its "intellectual capital" in parallel with its financial reports.

Writing the New Social Contract

It is time for a new social contract based on the new realities. This "contract" should show people what the company is willing to do to help them build their own futures. It should be an explicit statement of how much people are valued. And it should be a commitment to specific actions and specific investments in people.

Imagine an agreement, which every manager would sign and give to every person in the company, that would read something like this:

> Our company faces competitive world markets and rapidly changing technology. We need the flexibility to add or delete products, open or close facilities, and redeploy the workforce. Although we cannot guarantee tenure in any particular job or even future employment, we will work to ensure that all our people are fully employable—sought out for new jobs here and elsewhere.
>
> We promise to increase opportunity and power for our diverse workforce. We will:
>
> - Recruit for the potential to increase in competence, not simply for narrow skills to fill today's slots
>
> - Offer ample learning opportunities, from formal training to lunchtime seminars, the equivalent of three weeks a year
>
> - Provide challenging jobs and rotating assignments that allow growth in skills even without promotion to higher jobs
>
> - Measure performance beyond accounting numbers and share the data to allow learning by doing and continuous improvement, turning everyone into a self-guided professional
>
> - Retrain employees as soon as jobs become obsolete
>
> - Emphasize team building, to help our diverse workforce appreciate and utilize fully each other's skills
>
> - Recognize and reward individual and team achievements, thereby building external reputations and offering tangible indicators of value
>
> - Provide educational sabbaticals, external internships, or personal time-outs at regular intervals
>
> - Find growth opportunities in our network of suppliers, customers, and venture partners
>
> - Ensure that pensions and benefits are portable, so that people have safety nets for the future even if they seek employment elsewhere

- Help people to be productive while carrying family responsibilities, through flex-time, provision for sick children, and renewal breaks between major assignments

- Measure the building of human capital and the capabilities of our people as thoroughly and frequently as we measure the building and use of financial capital

- Encourage entrepreneurship—new ventures within our company or outside it that help our people start businesses and create alternative sources of employment

- Offer opportunities for meaningful community service through the company, including community service in our leadership training and team development

- Tap our people's ideas to develop innovations that lower costs, serve customers, and create new markets, as the best foundation for business growth and continuing employment and as a source of funds to reinvest in continuous learning

Policies like these can renew loyalty, commitment, and productivity for all men and women, in organizations both large and small, as they struggle to create jobs, wealth, and well-being in the global economy.

15 PHILIP KOTLER

Competitiveness and Civic Character

Philip Kotler is the S. C. Johnson & Son Distinguished Professor
of International Marketing at the Kellogg Graduate School of
Management at Northwestern University. He has consulted for
such companies as IBM, Apple Computer, General Electric,
Ford, AT&T, Motorola, Merck, Ciba-Geigy, J. P. Morgan,
Merrill Lynch, and others in the areas of marketing strategy and
planning, marketing organization, and international marketing.
He is the author of Marketing Management: Analysis,
Planning, Implementation, and Control, *the most widely*
used marketing book in graduate business schools; Principles of
Marketing; Strategic Marketing for Nonprofit Organizations;
and Marketing Places: Attracting Investment, Industry and
Tourism to Cities, States and Nations.

Given a world beset by myriad social problems—hunger, homelessness, crime, AIDS, environmental degradation—the question may be posed: Does it make sense for a company to visibly adopt one or more of these problems as a company concern? We are not talking about turning the problem into a business opportunity. This will happen anyway: companies can make money fighting pollution, building houses for the poor, inventing wonder drugs, and so on. Let's reframe the question: Should the company actively contribute money and employee time to ameliorate a social problem? Is it right to preempt some money that would have otherwise gone to the stockholders and spend it on good social works? And there is a second question: Does a company win consumer preference when it builds a reputation for being a "good citizen"?

Consider the following extreme example:

In 1976, Anita Roddick opened her first store, The Body Shop, in Brighton, England. Today, Body Shop International operates 1,366 stores in forty-six countries. Last year, The Body Shop's profits rose 13 percent, to $53 million, on sales of $349 million. The Body Shop manufactures and sells natural ingredient–based cosmetics in simple and appealing recyclable packaging. The ingredients are largely plant-based and are often obtained from developing countries to aid in their economic development. All the products are formulated without any animal testing. Roddick's company donates a certain percentage of profits each year to animal rights groups, homeless shelters, Amnesty International, Save the Rainforest, and other social causes. Many customers patronize The Body Shop because they share these social concerns. Her employees and franchise owners are also very dedicated to social causes. According to Roddick: "I thought it was very important that my business concern itself not just with hair and skin preparations, but also with the community, the environment, and the big wide world beyond cosmetics."

Anita Roddick and The Body Shop stand at one extreme in the debate on whether companies should devote some energy to ameliorating social problems. Roddick actually flaunts her causes, voicing strong political statements on their behalf, and even has occasionally led a boycott or a march on behalf of a cause. She organized 250 members of her staff to march on the Brazilian embassy in London to protest the burning of the Brazilian forests. On another occasion, her company put up an enormous electronic sign across the street from a Shell station, blaring: "STEER CLEAR OF SHELL—BOYCOTT NOW." When considering whether to grant franchises, she spends time interviewing each applicant to make sure that the applicant is a caring person and would hire other caring people. She openly flaunts the commercial side of her industry, suggesting that her cosmetics industry competitors manipulate their public with ads of beautiful women, implying that their products will increase the customer's desirableness and making similar exaggerated claims.

Not surprisingly, Anita Roddick's critics charge that it is she who is manipulative, and that she has built her business by exploiting the innocence and idealism of her customers. They charge her with being a blatant publicist and exaggerating her own social dedication. In the September 1994 issue of *Business Ethics,* Jon Entine wrote an article charging Anita Roddick with hypocrisy about The Body Shop's claims of doing no animal testing, its charitable contributions, and its purchases of materials from the Third World. Yet most people believe that Anita Roddick is genuinely passionate about her causes and that she has raised public consciousness about these issues as no other person has. Whether her products and practices fully match the company's claims is for its consumers to decide.

One slight notch below The Body Shop's record for social activism is Ben & Jerry's:

In the late 1970s, two guys from Vermont—Ben Cohen and Jerry Greenfield—formed a company to produce a superpremium ice cream that they branded Ben & Jerry's Homemade. Their sales, which were $9.8 million in 1985, climbed to $97 million by 1991. Their share of the superpremium ice cream category is now 36 percent and climbing further. Why the appeal? First, they are masters at creating innovative "mix-in" ice cream flavors, such as Rainforest Crunch, Blueberry Cheesecake, and Chocolate Chip Cookie Dough. Second, they espouse a concept of "fair pay," holding down their top executive's pay to seven times the average for their workers. (Recently, they made an exception to this in order to hire a very talented new CEO whose "market price" was much higher.) Third, they believe in contributing a percentage of their profits to alleviate social and environmental problems. Their corporate concept is that of "caring capitalism," which focuses equally on a product mission, a social mission, and an economic mission. Although it is hard to tell how much customer loyalty arises from their super-rich ice cream and now much from their social cause advocacy, there is no doubt that Ben & Jerry's customers are extraordinarily loyal.

The reason we put Ben & Jerry's a slight notch lower on the social responsibility scale is that although they have set up a foundation and give

7 percent of their profits to good causes, they are less strident than The Body Shop about these causes. They don't place pamphlets in their ice cream shops urging customers to give money to the homeless or to save the whales or to boycott some company. Nor do their ice cream containers in the frozen-food sections of supermarkets contain any advertisements of their good works. They are simply "good guys" (some might call them "bleeding hearts") who want to pay something back to society for their good fortune.

Along with Ben & Jerry's and The Body Shop, four hundred other similarly disposed companies are members of an association called The Social Venture Network. All of these companies give active support to social causes and make noteworthy charitable contributions. Two other socially conscious associations of business firms are Business for Social Responsibility and Co-op America Business Network. Also, many writings on business character appear in *Business Ethics: The Magazine of Socially Responsible Business*.

Now we can step down another slight notch in the social responsibility scale and cite companies that are generous in supporting good causes, though they don't make a big thing out of it or give away more than a tiny percentage of their profits. McDonald's Corporation provides a good example:

> Almost everyone likes McDonald's, whether they eat there or not. McDonald's runs a clean fast-food operation that offers value for the money, and its employees are generally friendly and responsive. Kids love McDonald's and McDonald's has added play equipment next to several of its outlets. Beyond this, McDonald's has carried out a number of worthwhile social initiatives: it has given money to several hospitals devoted to children's care, it has produced educational materials for elementary and high schools to help teach standard courses better, it has given financial support to high school bands and music programs, and it has urged its franchisees to get involved in the local community and contribute to local causes.

Again, every company has its critics. A cynic might say that McDonald's takes these steps to build a bank of "public goodwill" to protect itself against charges that its foods are not healthy—that its fatty and high-calorie hamburgers, fries, and pies are going to put a lot of people into hospitals. Every day, twenty-seven million people eat at McDonald's, many doing it several times a week, and this can give rise to vocal calls to break the McDonald's habit.

Let's examine another generous company—IBM:

> IBM is a "soft touch" when it comes to supporting standard charities. It is especially active in supporting the arts, specifically traveling art shows, concerts, dance groups, and so on.

The cynic in this case will note that IBM is a very rich company (in spite of its problems in the last few years) and that it chooses its causes carefully, concentrating on those that appeal to its normal customers, who are more educated and affluent. Thus it might be charged that IBM's support of the arts is simply part of its marketing budget that is aimed at building preference among its natural clientele.

Many generous companies may be headed by idealistic executives. Their generosity may also have a pragmatic side in that good-citizen companies are more likely to motivate their employees, avoid lawsuits and fines, gain favorable publicity, and attract customers who look for value and values.

Next we have a range of companies that don't cultivate a visible "charitable character" but deserve commendation for their products and business practices. They pay good wages, set up good working conditions and health plans for their employees, produce good-quality products, and treat their customers fairly. They make contributions to local charities when solicited but otherwise see themselves as commercial enterprises, not social institutions. Even then, sometimes the impact of their products may make a greater social contribution to the lives of people than the charitable contributions of the preceding companies. Consider Mary Kay Cosmetics:

> Mary Kay Ash runs a major multilevel, direct-selling cosmetics company with $1 billion of estimated retail sales and net company sales of $624 million as of 1992. The company sells a range of skin care, personal care, and cosmetic products through approximately 275,000 independent salespeople known as beauty consultants. They purchase the products and resell them at skin care classes or facials, held

in homes, that are attended by several women who have been invited. Beauty consultants also get a commission on the sales of any new beauty consultants they recruit. Mary Kay Cosmetics defines its mission as promoting business opportunities for women so that they can earn an independent income and gain self-confidence.

Ironically, one can argue that Mary Kay's organization has done more to raise the esteem and income independence of women than Anita Roddick has ever done just selling cosmetics in Body Shop stores. To Mary Kay Cosmetics might be added all the companies that invented the time-saving appliances such as microwave ovens, electric dishwashers, and laundry machines that have liberated women from their homes and have given them the time to develop careers.

Another group of companies deserves commendation for manifesting social responsibility, not because the companies sought it but because they rose to the occasion during a crisis. Any company might suddenly find itself facing a product crisis: its car is called unsafe, its food made some people sick, its drug had an unexpected side effect. Companies respond quite differently to these crises. Some respond immediately, even though it may be at great cost; this was the case with Johnson & Johnson when someone criminally laced its Tylenol capsules with cyanide. Some procrastinate, as was the case when Chrysler Corporation's minivans were charged with having poor rear-door locks. And some present stubborn denials, like the cigarette companies that still claim that cigarette smoking is harmless. We need to commend the companies that act swiftly to rectify situations in which their product or activity appears to present a public danger.

We next move further down the social responsibility scale to companies that advertise a record of social concern that they have greatly exaggerated. Some years ago, an oil company was found to spend two million dollars on conservation activities and four million dollars on advertising them. There is something profoundly hypocritical and manipulative in spending so much money to advertise a company's virtue on such a slim base of good deeds.

At the next level are a countless number of companies that engage in no civic activity. These companies see no reason why they should connect their economic enterprise with any social purpose. The Nobel Prize–winning economist Milton Friedman has put forth the most persuasive defense of these companies, saying that the marketplace will be more efficient and grow more wealth if companies focus on maximizing their self-interest. Successful companies will be able to pay higher wages in order to attract the best employees, and stockholders will be free to distribute their wealth to whatever charitable causes they deem deserving. Friedman would rather see a company take the money that it would have given to charitable causes and reinvest it in the business to produce more wealth.

Finally, a large number of companies define the extreme negative pole on the social responsibility scale: their activities actually hurt the social interest. We are not only speaking about companies that engage in criminal activities. We include those that pay poor wages, employ child labor, pollute the environment, produce poor-quality products, and so on.

Having defined the extremes of social responsibility and social irresponsibility, and the several levels between, we can address the question that we raised at the beginning: Does a company win consumer preference when it builds a reputation for being a "good citizen"? Put another way, does a company's good character bolster company sales? We do believe that the public has some awareness of good-citizen companies. If people are shown a list of well-known companies and asked to rank them according to their civic character, they probably will give a higher ranking to Johnson & Johnson than to General Motors Corporation, to McDonald's than to Exxon Corporation, and so on. But does this awareness influence their purchase choices?

The answer is not a simple yes or no. Clearly, some people will be influenced in their choices of products and services by the civic reputations of the supplying companies. Although many people buy Body Shop products for their perceived value, many others are also attracted by The Body Shop's causes. Most people buy Ben & Jerry's ice cream for its intrinsic taste, but many others confess to having a stronger feeling about Ben & Jerry's as a company than, say, its rival Häagen-Dazs. In every country, some citizens will be found who care deeply about social problems: they join environmental protection groups, give money to the homeless, and so on. In one country, this might be 5 percent of the population; in another country, 20 percent. These are the people who might factor in the company's civic image in deciding from whom they will buy.

The argument in favor of a company's investing in its civic reputation may also be strengthened by another phenomenon. Today, the products of many competing companies are seen as similar. People may see little difference between a Coke and a Pepsi, between a Hyatt hotel and a Westin hotel, between a General Electric refrigerator and a Whirlpool. It is getting harder for a company to differentiate itself, because any differentiating element that works well tends to draw imitators. If more buyers start insisting on buying a safe car, more auto companies will start building in more safety features and will compete more directly with Volvo.

So how can a company achieve more sustainable differentiation in the public's mind? I would argue that one fairly sustainable basis for differentiation is the company's civic character. McDonald's has spent over fifty years building up its civic character, and it is not easy for its competitors to duplicate this. Company images tend to persist for a long time. These images will often carry strong emotional charges that may create customer bonding or, in the opposite case, repel customers. Harley-Davidson is an excellent example of how a strong company image may drive customers' choice of products. Its motorcycles may not be the best, but tens of thousands of people will choose motorcycles, leather jackets, beer, cigarettes, and restaurants that have the Harley-Davidson brand because these customers have bonded with the firm. Can't the same thing happen when the bonding image is one of company social concern rather than macho motorcycles? We are saying that of the many images a company can acquire, one is a civic image. And it may well be that in the future, as company products grow more alike, a company's civic image may be one of the most potent customer preference builders.

16 C. K. PRAHALAD

The Work of New Age Managers in the Emerging Competitive Landscape

C. K. Prahalad, Harvey C. Fruehauf Professor of Business Administration at the University of Michigan Business School in Ann Arbor, specializes in corporate strategy and the role of top management in large, diversified, multinational corporations. He has been a visiting research fellow at Harvard University, a professor at the Indian Institute of Management, and a visiting professor at the European Institute of Business Administration. He coauthored The Multinational Mission: Balancing Local Demands and Global Vision *and* Competing for the Future. *Many of his articles have won awards.* Business Week *called him "a brilliant teacher," possibly "the most influential thinker on corporate strategy today." In 1995, he received the American Society for Competitiveness Award for his outstanding academic contribution to competitiveness.*

The last decade was one of turmoil in management thought, concepts, and tools. From total quality to reengineering, cycle time, empowerment, transformational leadership, boundaryless behavior and values, teams, networks, and alliances, this agitation represents an ongoing search for ways to cope with significant competitive discontinuities. Although each initiative may contain important insights, as yet, no consensus has emerged about the changing nature of managerial work. The only conclusion that is not in dispute is that managerial work *will be different.* I will attempt, in this chapter, to outline the major competitive discontinuities and to derive a tentative specification for the work of the New Age manager.

The Nature of the Competitive Landscape

All industries are in a state of flux influenced by a subset of the discontinuities described below:

1. *From cozy to competitive.* Around the world, the pressure to privatize and to deregulate represents major discontinuities for industries, such as utilities, telecommunications, airlines, the health care industry, financial services, and education. Managers are forced to cope with an unprecedented transformation in skills, attitudes, managerial processes, and economic models. The era of managing supply levels, prices, profits, investments, and patterns of technological evolution on the basis of secretive negotiations between managers and bureaucrats is giving way to a healthy respect for the voice of consumers and the marketplace. This transformation is not about seeking efficiency in the existing game; it is about inventing a new game and becoming efficient at it—it is about becoming *different*. The task of reinventing businesses with long traditions in a short period of time—often within five to ten years—compounds the problem. Rapidly (and selectively) forgetting the past and learning the new is a challenge.

2. *From local to global.* Increasingly, customers, competitors, and opportunities are becoming global. Global opportunities create new asymmetries for established firms. Rapid growth in Asia coupled with low or no growth in Western Europe, and a sudden burst of new knowledge businesses in the United States, create geographic asymmetries in opportunities. As a result, the geographic deployment of a firm's resources will change markedly during the next decade. For example, most Western and Japanese firms may find that Asia represents more than 50 percent of their assets and revenues. Resource redeployment on such a scale will change the "center of gravity" for most traditional multinational corporations (MNCs).

Even businesses that until recently were considered purely local, such as cleaning services, will be subject to global competition. International Service Systems (ISS) from Denmark and ServiceMaster are examples of global firms in the cleaning business. Further, globalization will not be the concern only of very large, investment-intensive businesses. For example, smaller software firms are discovering that they can be global with revenues as low as two to three million dollars. They can sell around the world and often can outsource part of their work—developing code—worldwide. Multinational businesses of all sizes will be created, from large to micro. Increasingly, globalization defies the nature of business and the size of the firm.

3. *From "like me" to "like whom"?* The competitive dynamics in most industries are changing dramatically. For example, for over twenty years, many industries were characterized by a few established global competitors. The last big change in the "club of global firms" was a result of the emergence of Japanese competitors during the late 1960s and the 1970s. Today new competitors from South Korea and Taiwan are breaking into this club. More will follow. Also, competition is not just between "incumbents" and "challengers"; it exists between established and emerging businesses as well. Consider the picture today. In the high-volume consumer electronics industry, we can identify four clusters of competitors, as shown in Figure 16.1.

From 1968 to 1988, traditional MNCs, such as Philips NV and Matsushita Electric Industrial Company, competed among themselves in traditional consumer electronics (CE) businesses, such as color televisions, high-fidelity components, and VCRs. They are currently challenged by new MNCs, such as the Samsung Group and Daewoo Corporation. In fact, Samsung has wrested the first, second, and third positions in a wide variety of traditional CE businesses. During the next decade, Indian and Chinese firms are likely to be challengers in these businesses as well. Further, in the evolving, new, high-volume electronics (HVE) businesses, such as personal computers, PC-TVS, cellular phones, printers, and personal digital assistants, new MNCs, such as Nokia Corporation and the Acer Group of Taiwan, compete vigorously with L. M. Ericsson or NEC Corporation, as well as with Philips and Matsushita.

Traditional computer firms like IBM are also trying to compete for a consumer franchise at home. The need for growth and a desire to manage the evolution of their traditional products, such as the PC's transformation into a TV or a household appliance, forces these firms into an unfamiliar

Figure 16.1. The Evolving Pattern of Global Competition.

New Multinational Corporations	Nokia (c) Motorola Acer	Samsung (b) Daewoo Goldstar
Traditional Multinational Corporations	IBM (d) NEC Ericsson	Philips (a) Thomson Matsushita

New
High-Volume
Electronics
Business

Traditional
Consumer
Electronics
Business

battlefield. This complex competitive battle between incumbents and challengers in old and new industries brings familiar and unfamiliar foes to the battleground. Consumer business is as unfamiliar to Ericsson and IBM as PC business is to Philips and Matsushita. Each cluster of firms brings different sources of advantages; everyone recognizes that this game is not just about "competing with folks like us"—it's also about competing with "folks who are different."

4. *From clear to indeterminate industry boundaries.* In many businesses, the traditional boundaries are becoming irrelevant. Traditional boundaries, such as professional and consumer business, leisure, fun and work, home and work, communication, entertainment, education, and computing, are no longer valid. The evolving digital technology makes a mockery of these traditional boundaries. Consider, for example, the ubiquitous personal computer. Is this a professional or a consumer product? Is it used for work or play, education or entertainment? Although traditional industry boundaries are rapidly collapsing, the contours of the new industries are still indeterminate. For example, traditional telecommunications firms and software companies are competing (and collaborating) to create businesses that will combine the functionalities of a home computer, television, home controller, and communicator. Given this commingling of functionalities,

firms tend to compete as much for migration paths to these new opportunities as they do to define new businesses. This competition is complex, vigorous, and different from competition for end products and services.

5. *From stability to volatility.* Given the indeterminateness of industry boundaries and migration paths and the uncertainties surrounding customer expectations, firms must experiment with new products and services. These market experiments go through uncertain lives. A product may be a smashing success or a total failure. A smashing success can be replaced by a new product in a very short space of time. Consider the resulting volatility—problems of scaling up (or down) and speed of new product introduction—with products such as desktop printers. The managerial demands of volatility in evolving businesses are significantly different from those in stable businesses such as producers of chainsaws or beverages.

6. *From intermediaries to direct access.* A systematic process appears to be afoot to reduce the number of layers between manufacturers and end users. With Quicken in banking, the Charles Schwab Corporation in brokerage, Dell Computer Corporation in distribution and service, and the Internet in electronic commerce, the focus is on removing the inefficiencies and the costs involved in the delivery of goods and services from the manufacturer to the end user. This trend will accelerate with the proliferation of the Internet and the World Wide Web. The capacity to directly connect manufacturers with consumers reduces the barriers to entry for new players, dramatically altering the cost structure and the business model for existing players. Inevitably, the pace and rhythm of businesses will change. Logistics is increasingly taking a center stage in competitive strategy.

7. *From vertical integration to specialists.* Henry Ford, George Eastman, and the Du Ponts took pride in their vertically integrated empires. During the past decade, firms have been busy breaking from their past and outsourcing "noncritical" activities. Now they are confronted with two interesting trends. First, suppliers of components are often competitors in end-product markets. American Airlines supplies the reservation system used by other airlines with which it competes for customers. Toshiba supplies LCD panels to its competitors in the laptop business. Competitors often trade core components and subsystems among themselves. This creates a new competitive dimension: the technological trade balance between competitors who trade among themselves. Trade balance among

competitors may be as important a dimension of competition as trade balance across nations.

The other trend is the evolution of core-product specialists, such as Intel Corporation. Having access to the core-product supply base is critical for anyone who aspires to be a viable end-product competitor. Take the case of PCs. The value chain in the PC business is both geographically and legally fragmented. The specialists (for example, those who supply microprocessors, LCDs, and monitors) and those with manufacturing expertise are geographically dispersed. The United States, Japan, Taiwan, Singapore, and Malaysia have emerged as the geographic nodes. Further, most of this geographic dispersion is not contained within the same firm. Each firm is a distinct legal entity. As a result, coordination in the PC business of product development, logistics, production volume, timing of product release, and pricing must cut across geographies and a network of legally independent but strategically dependent firms.

8. *From a single to a multiple intellectual heritage.* The convergence of multiple technologies creates a new demand on managers in established firms. The integration of chemical technology with electronics and software (for example, the Eastman Kodak Company), mechanical technology with electronics (for example, the Ford Motor Company), and pharmaceutical technology with fashion (for example, Revlon) is forcing managers not just to accept a new intellectual heritage, but to actively work toward integrating it with the traditional historical expertise of the company. In the same vein, traditional professional (engineering) business-oriented firms are becoming consumer marketers (for example, Hewlett-Packard Company). The need for integration and the development of hybrid products and services, such as Photo CD at Kodak, creates a new challenge: managers have to learn, adapt to, and exploit basically different reasoning processes.

We can easily add other equally demanding, radical shifts—the fight for industry standards in most industries, environmental demands, and competition for capital. The purpose is not to be exhaustive, but to indicate that the changes taking place are not gradual trends, but are instead discontinuities.

The Work of New Age Managers

The emerging competitive landscape suggests that managerial demands in the future will be very different. At a minimum, managers will have to recognize that they must create the capabilities in their organizations to:

1. *Conceive and execute complex strategies.* Strategies today are focused, not just on market share and profits, but also on influencing the evolution of industry standards, migration paths, and entrance into nontraditional markets. Strategies are pursued alone, as a firm, and with suppliers, customers, collaborators, and competitors as a constellation. Strategic thinking must incorporate collaborative arrangements of all types. As a result, the degrees of freedom available to any one management group to act autonomously are greatly reduced. However, if they are wisely used, these relationships can enhance considerably the resources and influence available to a firm in its competitive battles.

2. *Share and protect intellectual property.* Unlike traditional manufacturing businesses, today's businesses are based on "invisible assets"—competencies, patent portfolios, brands, logistics, and reputation. Protecting intellectual property is more difficult than protecting knowledge embedded in physical assets.

3. *Manage the public-private interface.* Although deregulation and privatization are moving apace, governments still can influence industry direction. Further, consumers, environmentalists, human rights activists, investors, and employees demand more transparency and accountability of managers. The current controversy about human rights violations and working conditions in sweatshops in Honduras and China that are plaguing corporations in the textile and shoe businesses is an indicator of the broadening view of the accountability of senior managers.

4. *Provide intellectual and administrative leadership.* In an era of major discontinuities, employees, customers, and investors are eager for a source of intellectual leadership. Managers are expected to provide foresight and a compelling view of the future. This can become the beacon that motivates and energizes the organization and the industry. Simultaneously, they must demonstrate the administrative savvy needed to quickly shepherd

the organization through dramatic changes in skills, attitudes, behaviors, and business models.

We can easily recognize that business will be global, operating in multiple locations and multiple cultures and requiring multiple skills and perspectives. Learning new concepts, tools, technologies, and markets will be crucial; however, accomplishing this may involve a wide variety of collaborative arrangements, so sharing and learning from others must coexist with protecting one's core skills. Speed will also be a major issue, in product development, competence building, and exploitation of new opportunities and, most important, in effecting basic changes in the orientation of the organization.

During the next decade, the critical work of managers who are confronted with these competitive discontinuities will be to:

1. *Create a shared competitive agenda for the entire organization.* This agenda will be shared with employees, current and potential customers, suppliers, collaborators, and investors. The view of the future must be compelling, directional, and motivating. As the organization starts to share an overall competitive agenda, senior managers can afford to decentralize decision making. Distributed, networked intelligence needs an overarching architecture to work together. Senior managers must define the "sandbox" but not every game that is to be played within it. Lower-level managers, who are closer to customers and competitors, can define the appropriate product-market strategies.

2. *Focus on changing the industry dynamics and leveraging the resources of the company.* The goal is to reshape existing industries, as well as to create new ones. In order to accomplish this goal, the organization must focus on resource accumulation and resource leverage more than on resource allocation per se (the current preoccupation of managers). Managers must stretch beyond the resources available to them within their firms to creatively exploit resources that are available from suppliers, partners, competitors, and customers. These then become multipliers of the resources available within the firm.

3. *Create a flexible system that can reconfigure resources to address emerging opportunities.* In most firms the organization becomes an impediment

to proactive and rapid response to the marketplace. The ability to conserve and redeploy resources rapidly is a critical capacity for the future. This means learning fast, forgetting even faster, becoming boundaryless, and focusing on winning in the marketplace.

4. *Develop a global capability.* This means that the organization can think and act globally or locally and access customers, suppliers, and talent worldwide. The organization must become a color-blind meritocracy.

The New Age Manager

These goals are unlikely to be achieved if the New Age manager does not rise to the surface. The New Age manager, at a minimum, must have the following characteristics:

1. *Systems thinking.* In an age of discontinuities, the capacity to conceptualize and synthesize the whole, to see the connections between parts and be able to imagine the future, can be crucial. The New Age manager must harmonize the hard and soft information, combine analysis and intuition, and balance private and public interest.

2. *Intercultural competence.* As firms become part of the global marketplace and increase their dependence on other cultures (markets, suppliers, employees, and investors), intercultural competence becomes a significant advantage. Managers must migrate from preoccupations with personal competence to interpersonal and then intercultural competence. The recognition that other cultures do not necessarily share the same values and beliefs as one's own is a critical asset. Multiple language skills and a deep understanding of history, religion, and art facilitate the development of intercultural competence.

3. *Extensive and continuous training.* The knowledge explosion, coupled with discontinuities and globalization, suggests that managers must continuously be exposed to new ideas, technologies, business practices, and cultures. The "half-life" of what we know is embarrassingly short. Managers must seek opportunities for continuous education.

4. *Personal standards and standards of behavior.* No dispersed, global organization with continuous pressure for change can survive without clearly spelled-out standards of behavior. Managers must create a system

that establishes minimum standards of values and behaviors for the global organization—but, more important, they must hold themselves accountable to even higher personal standards of excellence. Excellence relates to substantive knowledge of the business, commitment to performance and accountability, concern for due process, interpersonal and intercultural sensitivity, and the development of others.

The New Age manager will not just be a *doer*; she or he will be a *thinker* as well. In an important sense, the manager will be "half yogi and half commissar."

Conclusion

An integrated view of the work of the New Age manager is hard to develop without a point of view about the nature of competitive discontinuities. They provide a basis for identifying the new demands that will be imposed on firms and managers as they struggle to create wealth. The specifications for the New Age manager are derived from this understanding. The next decade will be full of opportunities for those who are willing to challenge themselves, to learn, to share, and to change. Those who resist change will be left behind and will totally miss the excitement of creating the future.

17 MARTIN E. HANAKA
BILL HAWKINS

Organizing for Endless Winning

*Martin E. Hanaka is president and COO of Staples, Inc., a
nationwide chain of office supply stores. He spent more than
twenty years with Sears, Roebuck & Company, where he ended
as vice president of the Home Appliances, Home Electronics,
and Office Centers Division at Sears Brand Central. He also
served as president and CEO of Lechmere, Inc., a leading
consumer electronics chain. Bill Hawkins is a principal of Keilty,
Goldsmith & Company, an international consulting firm based
in San Diego, California. An active consultant for over eight
years, he specializes in leadership development and organizational
change and has worked with more than twenty Fortune 500
companies on five continents. He has donated his services to the
International Red Cross, the New York Association for New
Americans, and the Girls Scouts of the U.S.A.*

As one of only nine companies in history to reach three billion dollars
in sales in its first decade, it might seem logical for Staples to just
keep doing what has made it so successful. As the original office superstore,
Staples has expanded to include mail order and contract commercial sales
divisions. As we look to the future—even the relatively near future of the
next two or three years—it is clear that winning organizations like Staples
must be prepared to compete in a world that is vastly different from today's.

In the future, competitive advantage, which often was expressed in the past simply as low-price leadership, instead will come to those who focus on understanding and serving customers' needs. To address these changing needs efficiently, winning companies will need to find ways to design flexibility into their organization. They will need to utilize networks for effective communication and decision making in multilingual, multicultural, multichannel, and multicurrency environments. The future also will see competitive advantage in the form of joint ventures as the rule, not the exception. Organizations that continue to operate just as product resellers are going to lose.

Stress in the Organization

Businesses selling to businesses will find their market increasing in complexity, brought on by a mix of economic, demographic, and technological trends. We recently have witnessed the economy pushing more dual heads of households into the workplace. More people want to start their own home-based business or feel compelled to do so. Increasingly, more people are working at home or bringing their work home. As a result, more and more homes now include an office complete with fax, copier, personal computer, and related products like printers and scanners. A fax machine that would have cost a thousand dollars only a few years ago can be purchased for half that now, and with more features. These machines are so affordable that even a part-time business needn't function without one. Many people with home businesses are going on-line as well, plugging into the information highway. When these people shop for their business needs, we, as retailers, need to be on our toes. They also represent new business opportunities, for example, in the areas of school supplies, PC accessories, and storage items.

This shift in business culture has resulted in a surge of new and different customers, many with competing requirements. Therefore, both marketing and product offerings must be different from the formulas that were successful in the past. Staples has expanded its product line by 40 percent and added exclusive brand-name products to appeal to this new, broader base. Although this evolution places tremendous stress on an organization, much of that stress can be reduced, eliminated, or turned to the organization's advantage by focusing on the customer mission and engineering a supportive corporate culture.

Build Around the Customer

The challenge for the winning organization of the future is to accurately predict and respond to the rate and breadth of the market changes that will inevitably cut across customer groups. To do this, the new organization should not be built around traditional structures like lowest cost, product groupings, incumbents, or geography but, rather, around the customer. This new model of successful business will be based on understanding specific customers, their requirements, and their expectations.

Staples has committed itself to serving every end-user segment efficiently and economically. To win, we know we need to serve customers in the methods *they* choose, whether they are in the store, on the phone, or ordering electronically. Why? We are experiencing a time famine. The average work week is eight to ten hours longer and discretionary off-the-job time has been reduced by the same amount, just since the 1980s. The winning organization must not be just low-cost but also efficient in methods of operation that save the customer time as well as money.

At the functional level, Staples has entered new sales channels over the past two years, moving from a consumer-oriented business to one targeting small businesses and on to mail-order operations. More recently, a strategic move was made into the contract commercial business that serves medium-sized and large organizations through contracted relationships. Though these various customer groups may want similar (in some cases, identical) products, the highly valued, highly satisfied repeat customer in each group has very different requirements in packaging, quantity, and selection. This may mean that we offer the same 3M tape in different package sizes and different packaging, or perhaps even on a large-scale bid basis to government and other large customers. The organization that focuses on understanding specific customers and moves to meet their unique needs will be in a position to be in front on inevitable changes in taste and expectations.

In theory, according to one popular model in the 1980s, organizations with the lowest cost structure are the most competitive. They should have the most room to compete and win on an economic basis. An example of businesses organized on this basis are the wholesale warehouse clubs. In fact, much of the initial success at Staples was based on having the right products in stock at the lowest price. The truth of the matter is that the cost advantages enjoyed by a company over its competition are usually only sustainable for a brief time. The sophisticated information technology needed to efficiently order and manage inventory is readily available to everyone—and at ever more affordable prices. Cost is important, but organizing around price alone is not the best long-term strategic solution.

The shift in focus from operations and low-cost pricing to servicing the customer leads to an entirely different makeup—an organizational structure that allows service to multiple groups with targeted sales and marketing processes that are extremely efficient.

Partnerships

To win in the future, organizations must evaluate the types of relationships they develop with both their suppliers and their major customers. Staples has established four tiers of supplier relationships, ranging from those that are strategic and global in nature to purely opportunistic ones. A global relationship means that wherever Staples chooses to do business, our suppliers (and, to a large extent, our multinational customers) will follow. These relationships are managed at the highest level and can include guarantees of shelf space, advertising, training, and minimum inventory levels.

Another example of strategic partnership is an ongoing industry study on activity-based costing, launched together with Georgia-Pacific Corporation, ACCO World Corporation, Global Furniture Company, and Hewlett-Packard Company, which looks specifically into the cost of serving us as a customer and generally into the cost of channels of distribution. It proves to the partners that each is committed to changing methods of operation, reducing mutual costs, and reinvesting in future growth together.

The future will see retail organizations increasingly involved in product development partnerships as a way of differentiating themselves from the competition. Contract manufacturing will allow the retail organization to have truly unique, distinguishable products that can be targeted to very specific customers and to create value by taking some of the cost out. Another dimension will be our willingness to guarantee distribution in exchange for favorable lower-cost terms overall. A corollary is the critical need to differentiate product offerings. Our product development people work overtime to develop licenses whereby Staples is the exclusive supplier of certain products, such as AT&T-brand diskettes and calculators, thus making our stores unique. The concept is much like the President's Choice labels used at Loblaw's, the Canadian grocery chain. Further, in partnerships with manufacturers of private labels, retail organizations like Staples can drop-ship to its own stores or distribution centers, cutting out shipping and warehousing costs.

Taken together, contract manufacturing, product development, and central distribution will give us a lasting advantage in the marketplace. The organization of the future will need to pursue optimal flexibility in selling products, certainly, but that flexibility will have to be coupled with the most efficient channels and methods of distribution for the product, thus producing the *value* for the customer. If you sell only national brands, your value position can never be an endlessly winning one.

Creating a Culture

The organization's mission and value system provide an anchor in the face of change, thus keeping stress on the organization in check. The mission keeps the focus on doing the right thing. The values define a clear culture that helps to attract the right people and guide their day-to-day behavior on the job. The organization of the future needs people who bring more to the job than required skills. We also need a profile of the "type" of person who will be successful in our culture.

Traditional practices allow us to understand someone's skills, experience, expertise, knowledge, education, and accomplishments, but what about intangible qualities? Southwest Airlines, for example, has created a profile for new employees that goes beyond job skills and looks to the issue of compatible "personality." Southwest wants to know: Is this the kind of person who can have fun and be fun on the job? The company hires only 3 percent of the job applicants, who go through a series of interviews, including interviews with customers.

At Staples we know that the type of person who will be successful in our environment needs to be a risk taker who can handle the complexity of fast-paced expansion across boundaries and channels. It is also important for candidates to be willing to share their knowledge. To help find these people, we have developed, with Tom Reed of TDR International, behavior-related competencies. These competencies allow the company to make better-informed hiring decisions by profiling how a candidate approaches unfamiliar and risk-taking situations. Using such guides, we can place candidates in real-life decision-making situations. We want to know what framework is used to make a decision, what the trade-offs are, how criticism is managed, and if any aversions to risk are present. At the core of the behavioral competencies are questions about the candidates' values, how they solve problems, whether they are adept learners, and if they can handle contention and stress.

Staples is a company growing at warp speed. We set aggressive targets. We want people who find fast-paced, complex change exhilarating. Under traditional methods, it would be difficult to make this assessment during interviews. The organization of the future can't afford to find out after the hire that the skill level was fine but the person was wrong for the job and therefore could not contribute to the organization's mission. Instead, the organization will need to establish a culture, with a mission and values, and better match its needs to specific behavioral competencies. Abandoning tradition, organizations will need to use behavioral tools and pressure testing. The most successful organizations will pay a lot of attention to who is hired and not just put a body in place.

Empowerment and Communication

Once the right person has been hired and trained, it is critical to leverage the new talent. Staples has traditionally been a purely top-down, finance-driven, and operations-driven company with just a few people making virtually every decision. It has become clear, however, that if we are focused on the customer, the customer defines the market, and Staples must respond. Quickly. The challenge of organizational effectiveness has been to recognize a needed shift from the financial and operations culture to a service-driven one. The only way this can happen is with an empowered workforce where decisions are made at the appropriate level. In reality this means that the organizational pyramid is turned upside down, with the customer at the top. It also means that the thousands of Staples associates who are the closest to the customers must be empowered to make decisions that will run the company on a daily basis. We have to allow people to make decisions that affect the customer and service to the customer without having to check for approval first.

To make this happen, senior management must not only be willing to let go of day-to-day decision making, but also to make sure that the appropriate people at appropriate levels have access to all the information needed to make informed decisions. The key to the future is communication. At Staples, we have made the mistake a lot of corporations in America have made by not effectively communicating with our associates. Too many ended up with information overload, buried by analysis and levels of detail that were important to a few, interesting to some, and needless to most. Effective communication for the future, if it is to be efficient and therefore profitable, will be timely and have an appropriate level of detail.

Part of the complexity referred to earlier involves leveraging technology within the organization to make appropriate communications "happen" more effectively than they did in the past. Empowered associates of the future will be pressed for time. Only the information that is critical needs to be communicated. People will be on the go. They need portable electronics and mobile communication. What we are seeing today with E-mail and laptops is that this trend is going to accelerate. Additionally, the organization of the future will need more sophisticated tools, many of which are just emerging, like the Internet and the intranet (used for sharing knowledge internally). Staples has a twofold interest in the technology of information and communication. We will not only use this technology to run the business; selling it will also spawn new sales opportunities for us.

The Final Challenge

It is not enough to put the right structure together, not enough to get the right talent on board, not enough to have the right communication processes. To be able to make decisions at the proper level in a fast-growing and complex environment, we must share the knowledge base that we have attracted through the hiring process and inherited through acquisition. The winners will take knowledge that doesn't show up on the balance sheet and find ways to share it throughout the whole organization.

So, in the final step, we need to set a winning environment that allows dissent to take place while ensuring that people support and are aligned with the overall mission. We will be measured by how the values and principles on which Staples was built prosper and perpetuate a healthy culture. To be sure, Staples will be measured by financial performance, but the ultimate test is whether people continue to recommend Staples as a place to work for family and friends. This is the highest compliment any organization can receive. Our shareholders deserve it.

18 STEPHANIE PACE MARSHALL

Creating Sustainable Learning Communities for the Twenty-First Century

Stephanie Pace Marshall is the founding executive director of the Illinois Mathematics and Science Academy in Aurora, Illinois. Prior to this, she served as the superintendent of schools in Batavia, Illinois, and as a member of the graduate faculty at Loyola University. In 1991, she was elected to head the Association for Supervision and Curriculum Development (ASCD), an international educational leadership association committed to the success of all learners. In April 1992, she became its president. In February 1984, and again in 1990, she was selected by Executive Educator magazine and the National School Board Association as one of North America's one hundred top school executives.

Building on discoveries in fields as diverse as quantum physics, chaos mathematics, evolutionary biology, neuroscience, cognitive science, and systems theory, revolutionary insights about the universe, the natural world, and human learning have all converged into a new understanding of how human systems continue to grow, evolve, and learn (or change). Although these disciplines seem either remote from or irrelevant to designing and leading twenty-first-century organizations, the new learning they provide allows us to reconceptualize the language and professional discourse of organizational learning and leadership and to discard the cause-and-effect mental models that have grounded them in the past.

Behavioral algorithms do not govern the dynamics of organic living systems.

To prevail in the face of the *dis*ease and *dis*organization of the twentieth-century workplace requires new organizational forms, new visions of leadership, and new metaphors for organizational growth and change that are grounded in the hopeful and enduring characteristics of the natural world, the human spirit, and the brain itself. Although this chapter focuses on the principles and conditions governing the creation of robust, resilient, and dynamically sustainable learning communities within the structures currently called schools and classrooms, they apply to *any* learning enterprise. Every organization must become a generative learning and teaching community if it desires to enhance the fullness and diversity of human capacities.

All around us, we see evidence that we are in the midst of a cultural transformation, fueled by the recognition that the competition, independence, and isolationism of the past cannot elevate the capacities of the human spirit that will energize and guide us in the next phase of our development as we create new ways of being together in the world. Human interdependence, not independence, will be the foundation for a new global civilization, one that will require new mental models and structures for learning.

The Crisis in Learning

For well over a decade we have been barraged with reports and rhetoric about the crisis in public education. It is my belief, however, that the espoused crisis in public education is predominantly a crisis about learning and that it is fundamentally grounded in the dynamic integration of two new domains of inquiry:

1. The paradigm shift from a machine-based "clockwork" conception of the universe to a complex adaptive system perspective

2. The paradigm shift from understanding the brain as a computer to be programmed and learning as a linear process of information accumulation to understanding the brain as a dynamic, self-organizing neural network and learning as a natural, active, and messy process of pattern formulation and constructed meaning

Inherent in the old mental models are three mechanistic metaphors that have historically contextualized our view of schooling and learning: universe as clock, brain as computer, and learning as tabula rasa (blank slate). The insights of complex adaptive system theory and learning theory have fundamentally altered these metaphors and have radically reframed the discourse on learning and schooling; in place of machine-based metaphors are fluid, organic, and biological metaphors that place current schooling structures in dynamic opposition to our new knowledge.

The Creation of Clockwork Organizations and Schools

The way that scientists view the dynamics, patterns, and relationships of the universe and natural world has profound implications for the way we construct our world. As a consequence, we shape, organize, and direct our institutions according to the science of our times. For three centuries, the dominant scientific worldview was the image of a static, repetitive, predictable, linear, and clockwork universe. This Newtonian worldview seemed to create an obsession with linear thinking and encouraged the escalation of an almost exclusively rational trajectory that has controlled and defined almost every dimension of our cultural and organizational life, including our schools.

As leaders, we focused on predictive cause-and-effect models of human learning; we became preoccupied with things and efficiently managed our organizations and our schools by reducing them to discrete, observable, and measurable parts. Deriving our insight from Newtonian science, we behaved as if we actually believed that by understanding the parts we would discern the behavior of the whole, and that analysis would inevitably lead to synthesis. We may have thought that the structure of our current educational system was derived from the principles of Frederick Winslow Taylor and Adam Smith and the needs of the nineteenth-century industrial revolution; however, it is even more fundamentally rooted in seventeenth-century science and false conceptions of how the brain works and learning occurs.

In alignment with the clockwork, mechanistic metaphor of schooling, we embraced an erroneous and dysfunctional paradigm of learning based on the following assumptions:

- Education is passive and incremental, not dynamic and developmental.

- Learning is acquired information, not constructed meaning.

- Intelligence is a fixed capacity and is not learnable.

- Potential and capability are finite and are not capable of being enhanced.

- Learning is defined by the calendar and the amount of time one stays on task and not by demonstrations and what David Perkins calls "performances of understanding."

- Content coverage and reproduction are more important than genuine understanding.

- Rote memory is "better" than spatial memory.

- Prior knowledge is unimportant to future understanding.

- Content segmentation is more highly valued than concept integration.

- Reliable evaluation can only be objective and external, not qualitative and self-adjusting.

- Competition is a far more powerful motivator than cooperation.

By design, we constructed and operated our Newtonian schools as we understood our world, and this produced iatrogenic and learning-disabled institutions that have suppressed reflective thought, creativity, and the innate and inexhaustible human capacity for lifelong growth. The unexamined application of Newtonian laws to complex adaptive social systems diminished our capacity for continuous growth and change because it diminished our capacity to "grow" the individual and collective intelligence, energy, spirit, and hope of the whole system.

We had designed a linear system based upon predictive models of change and a belief that learning was incremental, when in fact human systems, like most of nature, are not predictable; change is nonlinear and learning is dynamic and patterned. Human beings do not follow the logic of cause and effect. We crave connectedness and meaning, we seek lasting and deep relationships, we grow by sharing and not by keeping secrets, and we need to trust and be trusted in order to feel safe enough to dare. If we want to create learning communities that continuously renew and reintegrate themselves toward higher levels of complexity, we must ground our organizational transformation and our leadership in the science of our times and we must create conditions for the purposeful and soulful engagement of people in their work.

A New Learning Covenant

The turn of the twentieth century brought the linear and mechanistic worldview to an end and heralded the conception of an ecological universe—a holistic, dynamic, and inextricably connected system in which everything seems to affect everything else. Furthermore, the last two decades have produced revolutionary new insights about how human beings learn and how we can best create environments that accelerate our natural learning processes. These new insights come at a time when we are beginning to experience some of the transformational power of information and communication technologies.

Because knowledge is doubling at a remarkable rate, the structures (schools) and strategies historically used to deliver that knowledge in prescriptive and linear ways are now being challenged by knowledge-based institutions that recognize the need for continuous workplace learning. According to Stan Davis and Jim Botkin in their fascinating book *The Monster Under the Bed,* "Lifelong learning is the norm that is augmenting and in some cases displacing school-age education" (p. 16). Consequently, "the schoolhouse of the future may be neither school nor house" (p. 23). We must prepare our children for the learning workplace they will encounter. The foundation for growth and sustainability in this new learning environment is the continuous generation and exchange of knowledge, a process made possible by our inherent desire and capacity for new learning.

The old "educational efficiency" contract for the nineteenth-century school prescribed a "one size fits all" delivery system that accepted erroneous proxies like class time and course credits as indicators of genuine understanding. As a result, we created brain- and learning-antagonistic environments that actually inhibited integrative learning, distorted the learner's identity and his or her competence as a learner, and discouraged inventiveness, inquiry, and complex cognition. The new personalized learning covenant for the twenty-first century must continuously build individual capacity by stimulating natural learning, and it must be established and built upon a foundation of connection, coherence, mutually created meaning and purpose, dynamic relationships, and the evolutionary nature of the human experience itself.

What all this means is that we must transform the mechanistic paradigm of schooling into an integrated, holistic, and systemic vision of a sustainable learning community. How might we do this?

A Pattern Language

In a remarkable book titled *The Timeless Way of Building*, architect Christopher Alexander describes the essence of creating alive and dynamic space. According to Alexander, the structures we build (buildings or organizations) are created through a "system of patterns which function as a language" (p. 178). He says, "All acts of building are governed by a pattern language . . . and the patterns in the world are there entirely because they are created by the language that people use" (p. 193). As we explore the principles and conditions necessary to create sustainable learning communities, we must recognize that our new understandings about the universe, the natural world, and learning are enabling us to create a new pattern language for conceiving and describing learning environments.

We have moved from a linear language to a living language, from machine-based metaphors to ecology-based metaphors, and from rigid structures to mutable environments. Because, as Alexander asserts, "patterns are not things, but are complex and potent fields" (p. 223), we must acknowledge that the natural world itself is trying to draw us closer to a new way of seeing and being in the world, and this has profound implications for the creation of learning communities. When we acknowledge that the brain is a complex, self-adjusting, living system and *not* a computer, when we understand that learning is a goal-directed and internally mediated process of constructing meaning and *not* an information accumulation process, and when we recognize that human systems are dynamic and organic and *not* linear and predictive, we are compelled to use this new understanding to create new language, new patterns, and new environments that support and celebrate the nature of learning itself.

The reason our society must create a new language for learning communities that transcends school and classroom walls is that the dominance, attraction, and power of the current machine-based language of schooling is not capable of generating the organic patterns of the global learning community we now require. The very nature of the language, the potency of its field, and the meaning it constructs preempt its capacity to generate living patterns; only a living language can create living patterns and only living patterns can create living environments. We have excelled in the language of schooling. We must now become fluent in the language of learning and life.

If our language is prescriptive, our schools cannot be generative. If our language is static, our schools cannot be dynamic. If our language is linear and algorithmic, our schools cannot be playful and creative. If our language is controlled, our schools cannot be mutable. A school cannot come alive and cannot become a sustainable learning community without a living language that creates living patterns of interaction and relationships; the language of nature and the new learning technologies provide such a lexicon. The creation of ecological learning communities is, therefore, inextricably connected to the language of learning itself.

We need to create learning and teaching communities that enable learners to direct their own learning toward greater rigor, coherence, and complexity; to increase their intellectual, social, and emotional engagement with others; and to foster collaborative and dynamic approaches to learning that enable them to develop thoughtful and integrative ways of knowing. We must create a learning culture that provides a forum for risk, novelty, experimentation, and challenge and that redirects and personalizes learning. We must create learning communities for learners of all ages that can give power, time, and voice to their inquiry and their creativity.

Such a community is governed by the principles of learning, not schooling, and is:

- Personalized, flexible, and coherent (learning is connected to real-life issues)

- Internally and externally networked and not bounded by physical, geographic, or temporal space
- Invitational, with students engaged in meaningful research and serious inquiry
- Accountable to the learner to provide adaptive instructional environments
- Rich in information and learning experiences for all learners
- Open to emergent and generative knowledge
- Self-organized around core principles, beliefs, and a shared and mutually created purpose
- Intergenerational in the configuration of learning experience
- Flexible, diverse, and innovative
- Interconnected and collaborative, fostering interorganizational linkages
- Engaged in authentic dialogue with members of the internal and external community
- Focused on inquiry, complex cognition, problem finding, and problem resolution
- Committed to increasing what David Perkins, in *Outsmarting IQ*, calls the "learnable intelligences" of every individual
- Comfortable with ambiguity and paradox
- Playful
- Trusting
- Responsible
- Lovable

If we are truly going to create learning communities for the twenty-first century, we must view our schools as dynamic, adaptive, self-organizing systems, not only capable but inherently designed to renew themselves and to grow and change.

Leaders' New Work

Although my focus has been on the creation of sustainable learning communities to replace the linear and depersonalized delivery system of schools, the sustainability of *all* human systems lies in their evolution to learning and teaching communities. It is for this reason that the current context of organizations must be reframed so that self-organizing complex adaptive systems can emerge. Leaders, therefore, will need to understand their systems' natural desire for self-organization.

What creates self-organization in living systems? In *Leadership and the New Science*, Margaret Wheatley has made it clear that self-organization in natural systems will emerge from the webbed and dynamic interconnectedness of three domains: *identity, information,* and *relationships*. If we want to build the resiliency and adaptive capacity of everyone in the organization; if we want the organization to increase its collective intelligence, potential for relatedness, and shared sense of meaning; and if we want to ensure long-term sustainability, leaders must be engaged in new work—they must create the conditions whereby identity, information, and relationships are dynamically connected around the system's larger purpose. What are the conditions that leaders must create?

Identity

Identity is the principle that is most fundamental to all self-organizing systems. It encompasses the organization's meaning, purpose, and intentionality and provides the coherence around which system stability emerges. Identity facilitates order and transformation even in turbulent environments because it provides a constant frame of reference for organizational integrity and renewal. Organizations and people have the capacity for self-reference when the organization's identity, purpose, and meaning are clear and when leaders create the following conditions:

- They bring the system together to think about itself and to make decisions for itself *as a system*.
- They involve the expertise and experience of everyone in the system in creating the organization's fundamental beliefs,

values, and shared purpose (mission) and encourage people to organize around them.

- They clearly and continuously identify the patterns in the organization, what the organization is trying to accomplish, and how each individual is connected to its future.

- They promote an organizational consciousness and a sense of belongingness to a larger purpose.

- They make decisions at the local level based upon a strong sense of organizational self (identity).

- They promote individual and organizational freedom and efficacy.

Information

Information is both the medium of exchange for generative organizational learning and its source of power. Within self-organizing systems, information is not a thing; it is the dynamic center of organizational life that allows continual growth and defines what is essential for sustainability. Without the constant flow of informational energy to both excite and serve the system, the system will become closed and isolated. Leaders can create the following conditions to ensure its robustness:

- They create open and multiple pathways for communication.

- They infuse the organization with abundant information by explicitly bringing the environment's voice into the system.

- They move information everywhere in the system.

- They continuously generate and share new knowledge.

- They promote honest dialogue, feedback, and interaction.

- They keep rules simple for detecting, processing, and integrating information.

- They seek out information that is complex, ambiguous, and paradoxical and encourage people to publicly discuss and use it.

- They encourage frequent and rapid experimentation.

Relationships

Relationships represent the neural network of the organization; they establish the organization's capacity for participation, engagement, and interconnectedness. Unless we feel connected to the organization and its members, we cannot identify with this purpose or generate and use its information for growth. Within this context, leaders must create the following conditions:

- They create networks and webs of dialogue, interaction, and generative communication.
- They establish open access to everyone in the system.
- They promote diversity of all kinds.
- They seek opportunities to engage as many people as possible in dialogue to reinforce their interdependence, connectedness, and sense of shared intention about the purpose and meaning of their work.
- They distribute power throughout the system.
- They encourage people to act simultaneously and to coordinate their actions with each other.
- They establish strategic internal and external alliances and partnerships.
- They cultivate mutual interdependence.
- They build capacity for reflective, collective inquiry and collaborative accountability.
- They make the organizational boundaries permeable and flexible.
- They cultivate organizational coherence while building capacity to adjust to discontinuous change.
- They avoid neatness, tolerate messiness, and enable relationships to be redundant and overlapping.

Our attention to the connectedness of the physical world and to what Kevin Kelly, in *Out of Control*, calls the "bio-logic" of the natural world is revealing new insights into the nature of learning organizations and lead-ership. These new insights negate the mechanistic command-and-control principles of the past, dispel the concept of the single positional leader as the source of organizational identity, nurture the individual learner, and affirm the covenantal nature of organizational life.

Through the paradigm of the new sciences, we are coming to under-stand that the essence of leadership is to create the conditions that enable the intentional integration of the three domains of self-organizing systems found in the natural world: identity, information, and relationship. It is this integration that will enable system synergy to emerge. As a result, we need courageous leaders who can think and act in integrative, systemic, and soulful ways and who are not afraid to create transformational com-munities that learn their way into the future by inviting, engaging, and developing the fullness of human capacities.

19 DAVE ULRICH

Organizing Around Capabilities

Dave Ulrich is professor of business administration at the School of Business at the University of Michigan. He is coauthor of Organizational Capability: Competing from the Inside Out, Human Resources as a Competitive Advantage: An Empirical Assessment of HR Competencies and Practices in Global Firms, The Boundaryless Organization: Breaking the Chains of Organization Structure, *and* Human Resource Champions: The Next Agenda for Adding Value and Delivering Results. *He has been listed by* Business Week *as one of the world's "top ten educators" in management and the top educator in human resources.*

Stop people on the street and ask them what comes to mind when they think of an organization. Most answers will probably reflect an implicit image of the hierarchical nature of organizations:

- Roles (organizations give people status and titles)
- Rules (organizations have procedures and processes for getting things done)
- Chain of command (organizations tell people who is in charge and who is not)
- Accountabilities (organizations make people responsible)
- Specializations (organizations divide up how work is done)

Reframing the Organization
from Pyramid to Network

For the last century, the pyramid has been the organizational symbol for structure, control, status, and bureaucracy. More recently, organizational symbols have shifted to networks and cobwebs, with descriptors such as high-performing or ad hoc teams, horizontal processes, and virtual, bound-aryless, and chaotic systems. The shifting image of the organization, how-ever, is found less in morphology and structure and more in the concept of capabilities.

Capabilities represent the skills, abilities, and expertise within an orga-nization. They describe what organizations are able to do and how they are able to do it. They are collections of individual competencies turned into organizational ones. Gary Hamel and C. K. Prahalad, in *Competing for the Future,* described capabilities as core competencies, focusing pri-marily on the technological expertise resident within a firm—for exam-ple, Honda Motor Company knows how to make engines. Organizational capabilities go beyond technology; they characterize the identity or per-sonality of the organization. As organizations become flatter, capabilities must also change. The hierarchy was established to preserve a set of cher-ished capabilities: clear accountability, legitimate authority, established routines, division of labor, and specialization. In a world of unpredictable change, globalization, dynamic technologies, and educated employees and consumers, these capabilities will not work.

Figure 19.1 describes a common trap of organizations facing change. Most managers want to do the right work well. Unfortunately, once we learn how to get work done, we often fail to adapt and fall into the dan-gerous trap of doing the wrong work, but doing it very well. This is where organizations fail to respond and decline. For example, for years, General Motors Corporation (and other car companies) had the capabilities of assembly-line manufacturing. They were able to produce cars in lots of 100,000 more efficiently than had ever been dreamed about. However, with changing markets, long assembly lines become the wrong way to build cars. Even though General Motors did long assemblies well, it was the wrong thing to do. Doing the wrong thing well is dangerous because the company becomes dependent on traditional capabilities (how we do

Figure 19.1. Impact of Change.

		Is the Organization Focusing on the Right Work?	
		Right	*Wrong*
How Well Do We Get Work Done?	*Well*	We do the right work well.	We do the wrong work well.
	Poorly	We do the right work poorly.	We do the wrong work poorly.

things) and fails to adapt (do the right thing). A capability focus on organization helps managers to do the right work well.

Capabilities Needed to Win

As organizations are expected to change what they do, they are also going
to be expected to change how they do it. The capabilities of the past will
not be those of the future. A new set of capabilities must emerge. Let me
propose five critical capabilities for this future organization.

Establish a Shared Mindset

A shared mindset represents a firm's identity in the minds of employees,
customers, and investors. In *Built to Last*, their work on companies that
have been successful over time, James Collins and Jerry Porras report that
these visionary companies have a core ideology that defines what they
stand for. In my own work on creating culture, I have drawn on research
from cognitive psychology to identify what companies are known for. Having a unique identity in the minds of employees, customers, and investors
creates value for all three stakeholders.

The utility industry in the United States is undergoing dramatic change,
from a regulated world where performance was contingent upon relationships with the utility commission to a competitive world where survival depends on responsiveness, flexibility, and speed. In this competitive

environment, the Southern Company has set bold, aggressive goals to become America's best diversified utility. To do so, their executives have explicitly stated that a new mindset focused on empowerment must permeate the company, a mindset where people closest to the work own responsibility and accountability for improving quality and efficiency. They believe that if they can establish this mindset among all employees inside the company, customers outside the company will be better served. They hope to increase empowerment by sharing information from top to bottom, ensuring competence by developing employees and pushing down decision making and accountability, and sharing rewards. The payback of this mindset will be lower costs because less direct supervision will be needed and higher quality because more competence will be closer to the actual decisions.

In the organization of the future, employees must become more autonomous, self-directed, and self-motivated. When individuals share a common mindset about the company's identity, their personal strengths merge to form a stronger whole. This shared mindset is created when employees know what the company is trying to accomplish, why the company is headed in one direction over another, and what each individual contributes to the overall goal.

Reengage Employees

Recently a Japanese consulting firm visited with a leading U.S. consulting firm to review its reengineering products and services. At the end of the week, the Japanese consultants were convinced that reengineering could achieve the 20 percent productivity gains it promised, but they opted *not* to take the ideas to Japan. Their reasoning was that the strife and stress on employees after reengineering would, over time, far outweigh the benefits of short-term process improvements. Similar concerns are beginning to come from firms that have been through the wave of downsizing, consolidation, and reengineering. Employees are beginning to wonder what's in it for them.

At Sears, Roebuck & Company, executives have realized that associates in the stores who interface with customers are the most critical link in the firm-customer relationship. (The argument that employees on the front line are key interface contacts comes from *The Real Heroes of Business and Not a CEO Among Them,* by Bill Fromm and Len Schlesinger.)

To engage these employees, Sears has begun a series of town hall meetings where employees take ownership for the changes they must make to serve customers better. In these meetings, employees identify practices that they might stop, start, or simplify to improve customer service. As a result of the meetings, Sears has also reengaged employees by providing services that help them, such as economic literacy courses, day care, and improved benefits.

The organization of the future must learn to capture the intellectual capital of its employees. Intellectual capital must be the most appreciable asset in the firm. To capture this asset, the firm must find ways to engage employees so that their hearts, minds, and souls are committed to the goals of the firm. Intellectual capital is earned, not declared.

Become Boundaryless

As organizations grow, categories are often created to differentiate individuals. Levels (manager versus employee), functional specialties (marketing versus manufacturing), and scope (corporate versus field) are examples of boundaries that classify individuals. Removing boundaries means paying less attention to the category in which the individual works than to the competencies he or she possesses. In a boundaryless organization, talented individuals provide expertise regardless of hierarchy, function, or position.

General Electric Company has systematically worked to reduce boundaries. It encourages town hall meetings where employees can share ideas with their managers, who respond on the spot. It has cross-functional teams that are focused on serving similar customers. It involves customers and suppliers in training programs and shares information, authority, competence, and rewards throughout the organization.

Boundaryless capabilities are important for the organization of the future. As boundaries are removed, organizations can make decisions faster and better. Customers and suppliers are engaged in one continuous work process. Employees at all levels and functions of the organization are focused on serving customers.

Create Capacity for Change

The future is unpredictable. Rather than spending enormous amounts of resources creating strategies that may or may not succeed in an uncertain future, firms are becoming more successful by creating a capacity for change. The capacity for change focuses on agility, flexibility, and speed. Both losers and winners will face uncertain futures. While losers are forming teams and task forces to study change, winners will already have adapted. Organizations have varying degrees of capacity for change. Some organizations seem to have become rigid, inflexible, and unable to change; others have a built-in capacity to shift, move, and adapt quickly to changing conditions.

The computer industry is a rapidly changing, dynamic industry. The industry is littered with companies where good products became single events, where rapidly changing events overshadowed new products. At Sun Microsystems, Scott McNealy, the chairman, CEO, and president, claims that 85 to 90 percent of what Sun ships in a given year was created within the previous twelve months. He believes that few computer firms will survive the ongoing industry shakeout because most of them cannot adapt to a rapidly changing technology. Strategies in his world are visions and images of the future, not elaborate mathematical projections that are already outdated by the time they are refined. Similarly, Bill Gates, founder and CEO of Microsoft Corporation, expresses fear that complacency and arrogance will replace commitment and action. Creating the capacity for change keeps organizations alive and fresh.

In the organization of the future, the inability to know the future will not create fear *if* the organization can quickly, nimbly, and cleverly change and adapt. Being able to change processes, pricing, brands, products, and services more quickly than a competitor becomes a predictor of success.

Master Rapid Learning

Learning is the ability of an organization to generate and generalize ideas with impact. Rapid learning differentiates organizations by the speed with which they create and disseminate ideas. It occurs when ideas in one part of an organization are codified and shared throughout the organization so that mistakes are not repeated and successes are replicated.

The Coca-Cola Company is working to create a rapid learning capability. It is placing in each geographic area and product line talented individuals who have the responsibility of synthesizing keys to winning and sharing this information throughout the company. Rapid knowledge transfer through technology, forums, best-practice studies, and workshops will help executives to leverage Coca-Cola's global position. They believe that if they can move good ideas from one region of the world to another faster than their competitors, they will gain market share.

The organization of the future needs to be seen as an ongoing learning sandbox where thoughtful managers make informed decisions, then share insights with each other. When rapid learning becomes an accepted part of an organization, not only will innovation occur within an organizational unit, but the innovation will be quickly disseminated throughout the enterprise.

Summary

Are these the right, empirically defined capabilities of the competitive organization of the future? Not necessarily. My intent is to shift the focus in organizational thinking away from structure, forms, rules, roles, and accountabilities and into a debate on capability. What will it take to sustain the winning organization of the future? Experience and evidence suggest that if organizations possess and master *a shared mindset, engaged employees, boundaryless behavior, capacity for change,* and *rapid learning,* they will be more likely to win.

Executive Implications of a Focus on Capability

Before people on the street can be expected to think about organizations as bundles of capabilities, executives need to capture this focus. With a focus on capability, executives would do the following:

- Spend less time on formal planning and more time on making things happen
- Be worried less about organizational charts and structures and more about how to get work done regardless of the structure
- Be concerned about how results were achieved as well as about the results themselves
- Be measured by the extent to which they create unique and definitive capabilities within their organization

- Look for leaders who not only have personal charisma, but also the ability to create sustainable capabilities
- Constantly ask what capabilities will be required to anticipate customer expectations

A focus on capability shifts business strategy from a two-step dance to a three-step. In the old two-step, strategies were formed, then implemented. In the new dance, strategies are formed and capabilities created, which leads to sustained implementation, as shown here.

Toward a Theory of Capability

Traditional Theory of Strategy (without capability)	*Emerging Theory of Strategy (with capability)*
Strategic intent	Strategic intent
	Capability
Management practices	Management practices
Organizational processes	Organizational processes
Individual action	Individual action

Part IV

Working and Organizing in a Wired World

20

ANTHONY F. SMITH
TIM KELLY

Human Capital in the Digital Economy

Anthony F. Smith is a director of Keilty, Goldsmith & Company, an international consulting firm headquartered in La Jolla, California. He has worked with a wide range of clients, including McKinsey & Company, the Coca-Cola Company, General Electric Company, ESPN, and the National Geographic Society. He has served on the faculties of several universities, including the University of California and the European School of Management at Oxford. Tim Kelly is president of National Geographic Television. He has been with the National Geographic Society for twelve years, where he began as coexecutive producer of the critically acclaimed Explorer series. Under his leadership, the division has amassed over three hundred awards, including numerous Emmy and Ace awards. The division was converted to a for-profit subsidiary of the National Geographic Society in 1996.

Considering the rapid and voluminous changes affecting today's organizations, it is both difficult and risky to identify the "core" building block for any organization, not to mention the organization of the future. From market strategy and information technology to global and strategic alliances, the art of forecasting has become far more complicated and uncertain than it was in the past. For instance, in the agricultural era, land was the core building block to establishing strategic and economic advantage. Quite simply, those who controlled land were those with the

199

economic advantage. With the advent of the industrial revolution, economic advantage shifted to those who controlled and occupied the main power source of the time, the engine—first the steam engine and later the internal combustion and electric engines. However, the transition to the future will require a far different power source, an asset much more challenging to cultivate and manage than land: human capital, or what Lester Thurow calls skills, education, and knowledge. Another Nobel Prize–winning economist, Gary S. Becker, stated in *Business Week,* that "human capital is as much a part of the wealth of nations as are factories, housing, machinery, and other physical capital."

To be sure, dimensions such as technology, strategy, global alliances, and innovation are all critical components that will affect competitive advantage in the future. However, each of these areas is still dependent on and driven by human talent. Therefore, we believe that future economic and strategic advantage will rest with the organizations that can most effectively *attract, develop,* and *retain* a diverse group of the best and the brightest human talent in the marketplace. With this premise in mind, this chapter will expand on these three core processes as well as providing some final thoughts on building the organization of the future.

Attracting the Best

Although we have separated the three core organizational processes, we have done so only for purposes of explanation and clarification. We fundamentally believe that organizations whose environment fosters continuous human development will simultaneously attract and retain their human capital.

Attracting the best begins with an organization's ability to understand the psychological predisposition of those entering the workforce. This, by the way, is no simple task. A *Time* magazine cover story on the twenty-something generation stated that they have only a "hazy sense" of their own identity. In interviews, respondents struggled with trying to define themselves and their generation. Complicating the matter is the fact that they are not about to let the older generation define and clarify for them who they are and what they want. Current research would suggest, however, that some trends are beginning to emerge. It is becoming clear that although employees no longer expect lifelong employment, they do expect employability, an experience that allows them to develop their portfolio of transferable skills. It is also apparent that top talents will have a far better understanding of their own market value and will thus be quite demanding concerning their rewards (tangible and psychic) and compensation (money and opportunity). Unlike past generations, they will operate from a quid pro quo perspective in which they will demand value received for value given. Finally, we believe that employees in the future will expect comprehensive disclosure from their prospective employers.

Now, while these *absolute* demands, desires, and expectations seem obvious as well as consistent with today's workforce, we believe that, in the future, the relative *degree* of skill development, recognition, and disclosure required will greatly increase as will the intensity and vibrato of the demands. Let us expand on each of these points, beginning with what we call corporate candor, followed by recognition and compensation, and ending with employability.

Corporate Candor

Clearly, the best and brightest talents will be an enlightened body of people. They will not only have access to tremendous amounts of information through such resources as the Internet, but they will also have experienced corporate disloyalty, manifested through significant downsizing, restructuring, and expanding executive and shareholder compensation. A recent study reported in *Business Week* confirms these perceptions. In analyzing trends from 1990 to 1995, it was discovered that CEOs' pay increased by 92 percent and corporate profits increased by 75 percent, whereas workers' pay increased by only 16 percent and worker layoffs increased by 39 percent. Given such trends, the skepticism and cynicism of those entering the workforce in the future will be even greater than that of people who are entering today.

Therefore, any organization hoping to attract top talents must be prepared to fully disclose such things as executive compensation, hours involved in an average work week, the probability and speed of advancement, and the *real* mission and values of the organization. In essence, the tables will turn when it comes to the interviewing process. Just as *job* hunters in the past traditionally prepared to answer a multitude of tough questions, *employee* hunters in the future can expect to experience the same phenomenon. There is no question that top talents will follow a course of due diligence in finding out about potential employers. Through computer networking, job seekers not only will have at their fingertips all the facts and figures about a prospective employer; they will also have the capability of interviewing employees about the actual realities of working in the organization. For example, the cultural elements of the company that were traditionally known only to tenured employees will become accessible to the new job hunters. As a result, organizations, in their disclosure, must be willing to reveal how each employee will be evaluated and what the organization is willing to do in terms of recognition and rewards, as well as the programs and opportunities for skill development that are available.

Recognition and Compensation

Current trends would suggest that top talents will demand to be rewarded based on the merits of their own performance. At present, organizations are rapidly departing from compensation systems that reflect simply good work, loyalty, and seniority. Unfortunately, a significant segment of the current workforce entered their organizations with the expectation that as long as they did a good job and remained loyal to the company, the company, in turn, would continue to reward them and provide advancement opportunity. As a result, organizations are still struggling with balancing the expectations of the tenured workforce and creating incentives for new workers. When not managed effectively, the new workers will justifiably feel that they will be at a disadvantage when competing with their tenured counterparts. To most high achievers, a level playing field is always a prerequisite to engaging in any type of work relationship. To be sure, seniority and loyalty will be recognized by organizations in the future, but only to the extent that an individual's committed years can translate into competitive knowledge and/or the security of valued customer relations. It is clear that organizations with credible performance-based compensation systems will be at an advantage in attempting to attract and retain top talent.

Perhaps the most complicated issue for an organization in the future will be meeting the psychic demands of its workforce, such as their desire for self-determination, an opportunity for leadership and advancement, and the meaningfulness (significance) of their work. The only way for an organization to meet such demands will be to embrace aggressive planned growth, entrepreneurship, and decentralization, all of which create the need to rapidly build skills within the workforce.

Employability

Although we will cover this topic in greater depth in the next section, let us state here that it is now widely known that investing in employees can yield significant returns if the organization is clear on its core competencies and if the training systems in place are effective and aligned with the company's strategy. A recent article by Frank Lalli in *Money* magazine titled "Why You Should Invest in Companies That Invest in Their Workers" reported that an American Management Association study found that organizations that increased their training budgets, particularly after announcing layoffs, were twice as likely to report improved profits and productivity as the firms that did not increase their investment in training. Among those that increased training, "an impressive 79 percent boosted profits long-term and 70 percent raised productivity."

Most organizations today, regardless of whether they have downsized, are involved with some form of training and development. From ad hoc weekend workshops to highly systematic and elaborate approaches, today's organizations have clearly embraced the view that traditional on-the-job learning is insufficient. Organizations that can develop methods for increasing the need for and impact of learning will clearly have a competitive advantage, not just in terms of advanced human capital, but also in their ability to attract the best and brightest. Figure 20.1 illustrates the difference between traditional and futuristic organizations and the speed of learning. As the figure indicates, the organization of the future will learn and develop its human capital far more rapidly and significantly than organizations of the past and present. We believe that the strategy for "raising the S curve," achieving higher impact in less time, will occur through systematic training and development—the key to developing the best.

Developing the Best

Systematic training and development involves four key elements: induction and socialization, working in teams, real-time feedback and coaching, and accountable follow-up.

Figure 20.1. Speed of Organizational Learning.

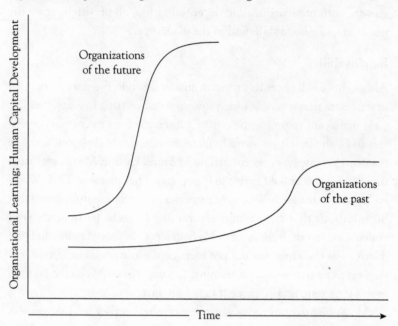

Induction and Socialization

Every organization has its own distinctive culture, the unprinted rules, styles, and codes that directly affect one's ability to thrive, if not survive, in the organization. Traditionally, new employees simply learned the culture of the organization by trial and error. As in any culture, people learn by receiving negative reinforcement for violations of cultural codes and positive reinforcement for supporting and behaving in accordance with the cultural codes. In the past, such learning was considered to be "paying your dues" or "natural barriers to entry." In fact, many tenured employees reveled in observing new employees "learn the ropes" the way they had. Although such fraternal behavior is predictable, it does impede performance by distracting the focus and energy of employees. However, in the future, competitive organizations will no longer be able to afford such slow learning. Learning a culture through traditional means can also cause undue anxiety, resulting in myriad unwanted consequences, including suboptimal human performance. Therefore, organizations in the future must be extremely thoughtful about how they induct and socialize their new talent. By developing an effective, comprehensive orientation program, organizations can both speed up cultural learning and send a message to new employees that the organizations genuinely care for these employees and are doing all that they can to ensure success—a powerful message in attracting top talent.

Working in Teams

Although some brilliant performers prefer to work independently, we believe that "Lone Rangers" will have limited opportunities in the organization of the future. Teams, when they are led effectively, are truly the most powerful and productive means for accomplishing work. To be sure, certain tasks are more efficiently accomplished individually, but for complex and sophisticated work, shared knowledge, support, and accountability are significant drivers to high performers. Just as important, perhaps, is the fact that most top talents desire to work with other top talents. They know that working in teams provides accelerated learning, not to mention being more enjoyable. Giving employees the opportunity to work in teams greatly enhances an organization's recruiting power by providing enjoyable work and accelerated development.

Real-Time Feedback and Coaching

Peter Senge has eloquently and convincingly described the organization of the future as being a learning organization. We could not agree more with this premise. In fact, we would argue that in order for individuals to learn at the current rate of organizational change, the feedback and coaching they receive must be thoughtful, useful, and, most important, real-time. Now as much of a buzzword as "real-time feedback" may be, it does accurately capture the nature of the feedback that is necessary to rapidly develop the human capital within an organization. Casual feedback, coming in the form of "Good job!" and "Keep working at it," and even formal feedback, such as performance reviews that occur every quarter—or, worse yet, every six to twelve months—quickly become a joke even in today's organizations.

Formal training will always serve a valuable role in developing human capital in that it is the most effective and efficient means for disseminating best practices and new knowledge. However, real-time feedback and coaching, delivered in the spirit of true apprenticeship, will be a far more powerful vehicle for changing human behavior and building human capital.

Accountable Follow-Up

One trend that has clearly emerged over the years is a decrease in the length of formal training along with an increase in the frequency of systematic feedback and follow-up. Given what has emerged in the research, we believe that this trend will only continue. For example, Marshall Goldsmith reported in *The Leader of the Future* that the perceived effectiveness of leaders is directly correlated to the feedback they receive and how often they follow up with the individuals they work with. Again, it is clear that feedback and follow-up are critical components in building human capital. Figure 20.2 describes and illustrates these core components of developing the best. As the figure illustrates, all these components are connected and essentially drive one another in a circular fashion. Even formal training should be driven by the collective themes that emerge from an ongoing feedback and coaching process, which is also known as accountable apprenticeship.

Clearly feedback, coaching, and follow-up are effective, but not sufficient, means for human development. A great deal of truth lies in such statements as "We treasure what we measure" and "We do what we are paid and reinforced to do." The organization of the future must contain systems that track and monitor human development for the purpose of holding both apprentice *and* master accountable. If the organization has no consequences for nondevelopment and no recognition for development, development will not take place and the survival of the organization will be jeopardized.

Retaining the Best

As we stated at the beginning of this chapter, ensuring continued human development is perhaps the most effective means for retaining talent; it is not, however, the only means. In exploring additional factors, we would like to refer to "The Puzzles of Leadership," by Steven Bornstein and Anthony Smith, in *The Leader of the Future*. The authors argue that in order for leaders to be effective in the future, they must first be perceived as credible by their potential followership. Credibility, they claim, is based on six dimensions: conviction, character, care, courage, composure, and competence. The reason we believe that the credibility model is applicable in this context is twofold. First, if the collective leadership of an organization is not credible to the employees, the best will certainly begin searching and, ultimately, fleeing the organization. *Working for,* not to mention *following,* individuals who are significantly lacking in any one of the "six C's," and thus who have lost their credibility, is not a very compelling proposition for high-performing talent. Remember, talented performers will always have, and be knowledgeable about, their options. Moreover, credible people tend not to follow those who are not credible. Second, the credibility model is useful in describing the core dimensions of an organization's credibility. Character, competence, and care are particularly applicable in attempting to understand how organizations attract and retain their best people.

Few would argue that organizations such as McKinsey & Company, the Walt Disney Company, Microsoft Corporation, Goldman Sachs, and, yes, the National Geographic Society have a competitive advantage in attracting and retaining top talent. In fact, these organizations are sought out by the best in the industry. We believe the reason is that they all are seen as very *credible* organizations in their respective fields. They all are extremely *competent* at what they do; in fact, in most cases, they are setting the pace and are benchmarks for other organizations in their industry group. They are also seen as organizations with *character*—maintaining integrity, value-driven, professional, and committed to excellence. In these times of corporate scandals and inside deals, these organizations have created cultures based on core values that have enabled them to avoid such character blunders. Last, these organizations *care* for their employees, their clients and customers, and their communities. Just as it is with leadership credibility, organizational credibility is based on many interdependent dimensions; being perceived as great in only one or two dimensions will result in lost *overall* credibility. Furthermore, we can never forget that credibility is a perceived phenomenon. It is those whom the organization is attempting to attract, develop, and retain who will ultimately determine if the organization is credible.

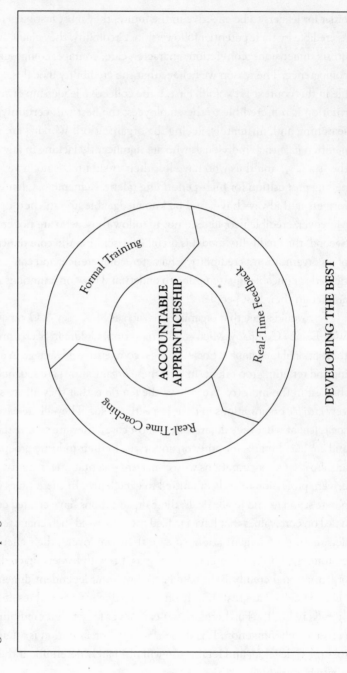

Figure 20.2. Developing the Best.

ACCOUNTABLE
APPRENTICESHIP

Formal Training

Real-Time Feedback

Real-Time Coaching

DEVELOPING THE BEST

Formal Training

Disseminating best practices, frameworks, and new knowledge

Practicing skills and receiving professional feedback

Networking, sharing, reflecting, and encouraging

Being driven by ongoing feedback that is received and analyzed

Real-Time Feedback

Sharing observations of an individual's work or performance

Sharing suggestions for change and development

Ensuring that individuals have the wherewithal and ability to correct and change on their own

Reinforcing frameworks and best practices disseminated in formal training

Real-Time Coaching

Assuming that individuals do not have the wherewithal and ability to correct and change on their own

Providing suggestions and resources for change

Periodically following up with individuals to supervise progress and offer continuing support and suggestions

Encouraging individuals to develop through continued feedback and formal training

Accountable Apprenticeship

A process whereby individuals learn a set of skills under a master teacher who, in turn, has conditional responsibility over the learners

A covenant, not a contract, is made for accountability measures, clarifying rewards and consequences

Conditional responsibility and accountability for skill development, career development, and fulfillment

Conclusion

Much of what we have described and prescribed here has been said before in some form or fashion. The crystal ball is full of exciting and challenging vignettes of the future. Depending on your point of view, any of the organizational variables we have described here have the potential of becoming a core building block of the organization of the future. Technology, global strategy, lifestyle, meaningfulness of work, and global alliances are obviously important factors. Perhaps the only unique and bold claim we have made is that human capital, above and beyond all other variables, will be *the* core building block for the organization of the future. Organizations of today would be wise to critically evaluate their current systems and practices for attracting, developing, and retaining human capital. Although we had no intention of being comprehensive in this chapter, we will present just a few additional considerations for thinking about the three core processes of building human capital.

In *attracting* the best, keep in mind that top talent comes in all shapes, sizes, colors, and ages. Diversity must be understood and embraced if organizations are to attract the best. EQ (emotional and social intelligence) will be as relevant, if not more relevant, than IQ when considering top talent. Be prepared to work hard at attracting the best, because they will attract many others like themselves. Like a lead engine in a train, they are attached and bring with them valuable cargo outside of themselves.

In *developing* the best, the organization of the future must have a strategic human resource function. We believe that top human resources departments will have two distinct functions in the future: human resource administration, involving salary administration, labor relations, legal affairs, and compliance, and human resource strategy, involving strategic systems and approaches for attracting (recruiting), developing, and retaining human capital. If human capital is presumptively the core building block, the function that is responsible must be strategic in nature and, therefore, must be elevated to where finance, marketing, and legal affairs are today.

Finally, in *retaining* the best, organizations must be perceived as credible. And because credibility is a *perceived* phenomenon, organizations must periodically survey their talent base to determine the appropriate course of action necessary for maintaining and building credibility. Establishing a feedback loop will be critical for seizing opportunity and avoiding costly oversights. Human capital is built through organizational credibility. Demonstrating impeccable *character* in adhering to core values, exercising *competence* by continuous improvement and innovation in products and services, and always demonstrating *care* for the people who make it all happen will be the marks of the organization of the future.

21 EDWARD D. MILLER

Shock Waves from the Communications Revolution

*Edward D. Miller is an associate of the Poynter Institute for
Media Studies. He joined the institute in 1989 as a leader in
management and graphics programs as well as an originator of
new projects. He lectures around the world on innovations in
management and design. He is the author of* The Charlotte
Project: Helping Citizens Take Back Democracy, *the story
of the institute's work with the* Charlotte Observer *in 1992
to reform election coverage. He was the editor of* Eyes on the
News, *Poynter's book on the impact of color on newspaper readership, and was coeditor of* Civic Journalism: Six Case Studies.

Most of us are too young to remember wing walkers, those barn-
stormers who thrilled crowds after World War I with aerial acro-
batics, including "death-defying walks" down the wing of a biplane by the
pilot's partner, often his wife. Wing walkers had two rules. The first was
"Never let go of what you're holding on to until you have a hold on something else."

Today's executives are wing-walking between the comfortable habits
of the past and the anxieties of the future. They're trying to hold on to
what they know and believe in, despite the evidence that they have to
move down the wing to something quite new. Which brings us to rule
number two: "To get down the wing, you eventually have to let go."

Businesses of all kinds are being forced to take tentative steps down the wing. It's not an easy stunt. Traditional customers, no longer content with the one-size-fits-all approach to marketing, demand that their products and services—from jeans to information—be tailored to individual tastes. What's more, they expect to be involved in product design decisions that were formerly reserved for manufacturers. Emerging technologies of communication are fueling these expectations with the illusion of instant access to abundant information anywhere in the electronic global village. The fact is that for most businesses, cyberspace is cyberchaos, where old rules and customs have been replaced by the anarchy of uncertainty. Wing walkers who are too timid to let go try to adapt the new tools to do old things, while more adventuresome competitors, many without established enterprises worth holding onto anyway, are rapidly moving down the wing, using new tools to do new things.

Why is adjustment so difficult? Successful enterprises always find it hard to give up the routines that produced profits in the past for the mysteries of new tools and new markets. Organizations, especially large ones, tend to cling to what has worked. Even visionary leaders find courage elusive when the path they're on is still profitable. But this is hardly news; you can read all about it in any daily newspaper. What you can also clip from the newspaper's own organizational story are valuable lessons on moving down the wing amid the turbulence. Readers are changing, and newspapers are perplexed about how to keep them as customers. The tools of communication are undergoing the most profound changes since Gutenberg. Competitive threats are everywhere. Leaders fret about their own ability to keep pace. None of this is unique to newspapers, of course; most businesses today face similar turbulence. But the problems and potential solutions in the newspaper industry may be instructive.

Unlike other businesses, newspapers don't spend a lot of time cozying up to customers, and it shows. One pundit observed, "I'm all for a free press; it's the damn newspapers I can't stand!" Millions of Americans share his low regard; what's worse, millions more don't care. And many of those who do care about news have discovered attractive alternatives in the new technologies of communication. As a result, a growing number of potential customers no longer find newspapers essential.

The press has always had a paradoxical relationship with its customers. A newspaper thrives as a business by being interdependent with a community's citizens and organizations, but it succeeds as good journalism by retaining an independent voice. The equation is not always in balance. Judging by readers' current low regard for our craft, editorial independence may have come at the price of another valuable asset—a sense of belonging to a place and a people. Whatever the cause, managing the paradox of interdependence and independence is becoming more important, and more difficult.

At a recent seminar at the Poynter Institute, where we help journalists reflect aloud on these issues, one senior executive, arguing that journalists must reconnect with the "needs of readers," fumbled his words and declared that we need to fulfill the *"reads of needers."* When we stopped chuckling, we realized that he was right after all; our communities are filled with "needers" who depend on newspapers to sort through the day's events and make sense of it all by adding meaning to the turmoil. "Needers" also seek connection with each other. The Latin root of the English verb *communicate* is *communicare*. It does not mean "to communicate"; it means "to share." "Where were you when John Kennedy was assassinated?" or "Where were you when the *Challenger* exploded?" are questions of *communicare*. Newspapers have been successful precisely because they have offered readers a sense of sharing the day's events with others.

But, increasingly, citizens expect to have their own voice in those experiences, and communication technologies—from talk radio to the Internet—provide the forums. As citizens find their public voice, they are becoming more than passive spectators, thus reversing, at least for newspapers, the direction of an old push-pull equation. What had been a top-down "push" of information from news producers to consumers is becoming a demand-driven "pull" as individuals take the initiative in determining what is news and how and where they want to consume it. Henry Ford might have offered our grandfathers "any color as long as it's black," but today's pitch is "Have it your way," a difficult assignment for any business, especially for mass media.

In short, consumers are beginning to have a hand in decisions that were customarily made exclusively by producers. In the media this means gaining independence from the prevailing tastes and decisions of the editors who have managed the news through control of the distribution systems. The traditional producer-consumer transaction is being displaced by a more complicated relationship in which journalism's customers can now shape product design. Editors used to define what is news; now readers are getting into the act. These same readers can actually become entrepreneurial competitors as they deliver information and their unique brand of "news" on their own Internet home pages.

Don Peppers and Martha Rogers, in their book *The One to One Future: Building Relationships One Customer at a Time,* suggest that business is no longer just about the sale of goods to the largest number of people. It's about "creating, selling, and maintaining relationships" with individual customers, in short, "share of customer" along with market share. If that's true, many industry strategies will have to change from delivering a small line of products to a mass market to developing customized services designed to meet individualized needs. For journalism, this is a radically different concept, which explains why so many of those who make newspapers are resisting it.

Change, however, brings anxiety, and newspaper executives trying to maintain a grip on their locally exclusive franchises have a lot to be anxious about, including the following trends:

- A prime revenue base is eroding. Classified advertisements, a financial cornerstone of any newspaper, are easy targets for electronic competitors. So are sports results, stock tables, and much of the information and entertainment in a newspaper that isn't breaking news, which was taken over by television a generation ago.

- The competition is changing. To the list of traditional competitors—other newspapers, broadcasters, magazines, and free newspapers—we now add our own customers. Anyone with a computer and a modem can be an entrepreneurial publisher or journalist on the Internet. The capital costs that have kept journalism's entrance fees high and membership low have been reduced to the price of some modest equipment and local phone calls. Newspapers are just one of the many industries threatened by the phenomenon of customers who are becoming competitors.

- Technology is also altering consumer attitudes and expectations about many products and services. Print media alone will not satisfy a nation addicting itself to cellular phones, fax modems, portable computers, chat rooms, "mass customization," and the manic pursuit of faster, cheaper, better. Within newspapers, all these pressures are eroding our confidence in journalism's basic mission and traditional methods.

To cope with these threats, business leaders would do well to reread Peter Drucker, who a long time ago proposed three navigating questions: What is your business? Who is your customer? What does your customer value? For newspapers, the answer to the first question used to be easy. Our business was to sustain an independent editorial voice in a community through the manufacture and sale of newspapers. That description is still valid, but incomplete.

Our customers used to be our neighbors. Now the population is fragmenting into new communities based less on geography than on tribal affiliations defined by age, race, lifestyle, gender, occupation, hobbies, and even sexual orientation. As electronic media embrace worldwide audiences, geography itself has become less important, undercutting the traditional definition of community as a unique place.

What do customers value? News and information, certainly. But journalism has always provided something more. By putting a day's content into context, good newspapers have offered a value-added service that distinguished them from mere data bases. One of those added values has been civic cohesiveness, a sense that individuals are participating in a community. That feeling of belonging may be at risk, however, as a disturbing number of citizens choose to ignore their civic chores by volunteering less, voting less, caring less. For newspapers that have long been dependent on active citizens for their readership, any decline in public life threatens to undermine a fundamental role of newspapers in a democracy. It also jeopardizes the industry's financial stability; as citizenship erodes, so does newspaper readership.

Like other industries facing similar threats, newspapers see salvation in emerging technologies. For the media, the case is impressive. New tools will enable journalists to reach the new communities through the electronically delivered, individually customized newspaper. Interactivity will become an expectation instead of an option as customers interact with producers, including journalists, to shape the product to individual specifications. For newspaper companies, delivering electrons instead of ink-covered newsprint will save time, trees, and money. It's a seductive view of the future.

Before we stop the presses, however, we need to think a bit about tools, recalling that newspapers have seldom invented their own. Instead, we have put to profitable use the inventions of outsiders with few if any ties to journalism. What's more, we have tended to use these new tools to do old things more efficiently. Basic processes of news gathering, design, production, and distribution have remained relatively static for decades; only the tools have changed. But inventions always open up the possibility of doing *new* things with new tools, triggering spirited competition between established businesses that are wedded to customary practices and opportunistic outsiders who are quick to capitalize on emerging technologies. History shows that clever outsiders may actually have the advantage.

There is an irony in all this: the rapid transition of cyberspace into cyberchaos, as technology makes available more data than people can find, much less use. But that opens the door for journalists to step back into a traditional role as "navigator" or "agent" for the reader. This should be familiar terrain. For years, people have turned to newspapers to help make sense of their world. They might do so again, transforming a threat into an opportunity for newspapers that are agile enough to create new relationships with readers, an old idea made possible with new tools. Using a wide array of technologies, including printed, home-delivered products, news organizations need to learn how to help individuals satisfy their search for information, meaning, and community, and to do so at a profit.

What's stopping us? Success, for one thing. To put it simply, any industry that for decades has been comfortably profitable and content with the nineteenth-century hierarchical model governing assembly-line production processes will find it hard to accept and initiate radical change. Another obstacle is a caste system that has separated the priesthood of the journalists in the newsroom from not only their readers but also their colleagues who sell the ads, run the presses, deliver the paper, and meet face-to-face with customers. This caste system had an important benefit: it helped to protect editorial independence and integrity within a for-profit enterprise. But it came at the price of learning how to respond to market demands for change.

As a result, when emerging technologies and evolving customer expectations made change unavoidable, effective response was slowed by profit-fattened sluggishness, cultural isolation, and inexperience in using new tools to create new products. Organizational inertia is not limited to newspaper companies; many businesses have held onto old habits, confusing them with enduring values. But whereas values, especially those of a free press, may be immutable, routines can and must change. Business leaders need to concentrate less on what they know how to do and more on what they need to learn to do. Newspapers know how to manufacture and distribute newspapers. What they need to learn is how to apply the new tools to the creation of new relationships with readers.

Good news may still be found in all this. Despite the turbulence of technological change, a need for the essential skills of journalism will endure. The task for industry leaders is to transport these skills into new environments. Surely they have a market. As long as the information glut contributes to the complexity people face in their lives, a curious public will find an even greater need for tenacious and thorough investigative reporters, for researchers skilled at using the new tools of data storage and retrieval, and for writers and graphic designers able to assemble and explain the confusing patterns hidden beneath the headlines. As long as readers continue to be "needers," newspaper companies selling accuracy, integrity, and dependable service (and not just ink on newsprint) will have plenty of potential customers.

To bring valued skills to new tasks, however, today's production-driven assembly lines will have to become tomorrow's flexible gatherers and managers of information, initiating creative responses to individual needs instead of simply reacting to events for mass consumption. As "meaning merchants," newspapers will continue to put news into context and add value for local readers. As "information stores," they will provide extensive archival and research services, enabling readers to skim the surface of the day's offerings or plunge into a vast reservoir of supplementary data. Time will become less of a demon. Electronic delivery will enable editors to continually update stories weeks after their initial publication. Readers will no longer be captives of the newspaper's production and delivery cycles. The story will be ready when the reader is. Similarly, space limitations will be eased by around-the-clock access to almost limitless stores of information.

Despite its many obituaries, the newspaper is not dead. The durability of print has always been underestimated by those who are dazzled by new technologies. However, the core newspaper will change in form and function as news organizations help readers to make choices. One of those choices will still be subscribing to a home-delivered product (or one that may be printed in the home). It just won't be the only choice. Along the way, the relationship between news producers and customers will undergo fundamental changes. The top-down, supply-driven production model of the past will be replaced by the customer-driven information center of the future. Readers will be more than passive customers; they will become electronically linked partners in the news-selection process, suppliers of information, and even competitors.

To manage this future, the chasm between the craft and business of journalism will have to narrow. As in other industries, the tasks of management will shift from a command-and-control governance of production to the leadership of flexible organizations. Newspapers know how react to events; they need to learn to respond to reader-customers in new ways with new tools. Wing-walking was always a dangerous stunt, requiring balance, timing, and, above all, courage. Today's business leaders would find that wing familiar footing.

22 NATHANIEL BRANDEN

Self-Esteem in the Information Age

Nathaniel Branden has been described as "the father of the self-esteem movement." In addition to his private psychotherapy practice, he consults with business organizations on the application of self-esteem principles and technology to improving performance in the workplace. He is the author of The Psychology of Self-Esteem *(now in its thirty-second printing),* The Six Pillars of Self-Esteem, *and* Taking Responsibility: Self-Reliance and the Accountable Life, *among other books.*

We have reached a moment in history when self-esteem, which has always been a supremely important psychological need, has become an urgent economic need—the attribute imperative for adaptiveness to an increasingly complex, challenging, and competitive world.

We now live in a global economy characterized by rapid change, accelerating scientific and technological breakthroughs, and an unprecedented level of competitiveness. These developments create a demand for higher levels of education and training than were required of previous generations. Everyone acquainted with business culture knows this. What is not equally understood is that these developments also create new demands on our psychological resources. Specifically, these developments ask for a greater capacity for innovation, self-management, personal responsibility, and self-direction. This is not asked just at the top, but at every level of a business enterprise, from senior management to first-line supervisor and even to entry-level personnel.

A modern organization can no longer be run by a few people who think and many people who merely do what they are told. Today, in addition to a higher level of knowledge and skill among all those who participate, organizations also need a higher level of independence, self-reliance, self-trust, and the capacity to exercise initiative—in a word, self-esteem. This means that people with a decent level of self-esteem are now needed economically *in large numbers*. Historically, this is a new phenomenon.

Recent and emerging technological and economic realities may be driving our evolution as a species, commanding us to rise to a higher level than our ancestors. If this premise is correct, it is the most important development of the twentieth century and, in its ramifications, the least appreciated. It has profound implications for the organization of the future and the values that will have to be dominant in corporate culture, values that serve and celebrate autonomy, innovativeness, self-responsibility, and self-esteem, in contrast to such traditional values as obedience, conformity, and respect for authority.

The Roots of Self-Esteem

Let me begin with a definition I proposed in *The Six Pillars of Self-Esteem:* "Self-esteem is the experience of being competent to cope with the basic challenges of life and of being worthy of happiness." It is confidence in the efficacy of our mind, in our ability to think. By extension, it is confidence in our ability to learn, make appropriate choices and decisions, and manage change. It is also the experience that success, achievement, and fulfillment—and therefore *happiness*—are appropriate to us. The survival value of such confidence is obvious; so is the danger when it is missing.

Over three decades of study have led me to identify six practices as the most essential to building self-esteem. All are relevant to the organization of the future.

1. *The practice of living consciously.* This includes respect for facts; being present in what we are doing while we are doing it (for example, if our customer, supervisor, employee, supplier, or colleague is talking to us, being

present to the encounter); seeking and being eagerly open to any information, knowledge, or feedback that bears on our interests, values, goals, and projects; and seeking to understand not only the world external to us but also our inner world, so that we do not act out of self-blindness. When he was asked to account for the extraordinary transformation he achieved at General Electric Company, Jack Welch spoke of "self-confidence, candor, and an *unflinching willingness to face reality, even when it's painful*," which is the essence of living consciously.

2. *The practice of self-acceptance.* This is the willingness to own, experience, and take responsibility for our thoughts, feelings, and actions, without evasion, denial, or disowning and without self-repudiation, and to give ourselves permission to think our thoughts, experience our emotions, and look at our actions without necessarily liking, endorsing, or condoning them. If we are self-accepting, we do not experience ourselves as always being on trial; this leads to a lack of defensiveness and a willingness to hear critical feedback or different ideas without becoming hostile or adversarial.

3. *The practice of self-responsibility.* Self-responsibility consists of realizing that we are the authors of our choices and actions; that each one of us is responsible for our life and well-being and for the attainment of our goals; that if we need the cooperation of other people to achieve our goals, we must offer value in exchange; and that the question is not "Who's to blame?" but always "What needs to be done?"

4. *The practice of self-assertiveness.* Self-assertiveness is being authentic in our dealings with others; treating our values and convictions with decent respect in social contexts; refusing to fake the reality of who we are or what we esteem in order to avoid someone's disapproval; and being willing to stand up for ourselves and our ideas in appropriate ways in appropriate circumstances.

5. *The practice of living purposefully.* Living purposefully consists of identifying our short-term and long-term goals or purposes and the actions needed to attain them, organizing behavior in the service of these goals, monitoring actions to be sure we stay on track, and paying attention to the outcome in order to recognize if and when we need to go back to the drawing board.

6. *The practice of personal integrity.* Personal integrity is living with congruence between what we know, what we profess, and what we do; telling

the truth, honoring our commitments, and exemplifying in action the values we profess to admire; and dealing with others fairly and benevolently. When we betray our values, we betray our own minds, and self-esteem is an inevitable casualty.

A Leader's Self-Esteem

Leaders often do not recognize that who they are as people affects virtually every aspect of their organization. They do not appreciate the extent to which they are role models. Their smallest bits of behavior are noted and absorbed by those around them, though not necessarily consciously, and are reflected throughout the entire organization by those they influence. If a leader has unimpeachable integrity, a standard is set that others may feel drawn to follow. If a leader treats associates, subordinates, customers, and suppliers with respect, this tends to translate into the company culture.

The higher the self-esteem of a leader, the more likely it is that he or she can inspire the best in others. A mind that does not trust itself cannot inspire greatness in the minds of colleagues and subordinates. Neither can leaders inspire others if their primary need is to prove themselves right and others wrong. (Contrary to conventional wisdom, the problem of such insecure leaders is not that they have a big ego, but that they have a small one.) If leaders wish to create a high-self-esteem, high-performance organization, the first step is to work on themselves: on raising their own level of consciousness, self-responsibility, and other practices. They need to address the question: Do I exemplify in my behavior the traits I want to see in our people? (Or am I like the parent who says, "Do as I say, not as I do"?) This principle, of course, applies not only to CEOs but to managers on every level. This leads to the question: How does an individual work on his or her own self-esteem? I discuss this question at length in *The Six Pillars of Self-Esteem*, but here are a few suggestions.

Working on One's Own Self-Esteem

The practices that cultivate and strengthen self-esteem are also expressions of self-esteem. The relationship is reciprocal. If I operate consciously, I grow in self-esteem; if I have a decent level of self-esteem, the impulse to operate consciously feels natural. If I operate self-responsibly, I strengthen self-esteem; if I have self-esteem, I tend to operate self-responsibly. If I integrate the six practices into my daily existence, I develop high self-esteem; if I enjoy high self-esteem, I tend to manifest the six practices in my daily activities.

If we want to learn to operate more consciously, we need to ask ourselves: What would I do (or do differently) if I brought 5 percent more consciousness to my dealings with other people—for example, to implementing our mission, to rethinking strategy, or to creating more outlets for individual creativity and innovativeness in our organization? What facts do I need to examine that I have avoided examining?

If I operated 5 percent more self-acceptingly, or self-responsibly, or self-assertively, or purposefully, or with greater integrity, what would I do differently? Am I willing to experiment with those behaviors *now?* If I recognize that if I brought 5 percent more self-esteem to my dealings with people I would treat them more generously, why not do so *now?* If I know that with more self-esteem I would better protect my people, why not do so *now?* If I understand that with higher self-esteem I would face unpleasant facts more straightforwardly, why not choose to do so *now?* When we do what we know is right, we build self-esteem. And when we betray that knowledge, we subvert self-esteem.

Encouraging Self-Esteem in an Organization

Here are a few suggestions for leaders and managers who wish to encourage these practices in their people:

To Encourage Consciousness

1. Provide easy access not only to the information they need to do their job, but also to information about the wider context in which they work—the goals and progress of the organization—so that they can understand how their activities relate to the organization's overall mission and agenda.

2. Offer opportunities for continuous learning and upgrading of skills. Send out the signal in as many ways as possible that yours is a *learning organization.*

3. If someone does superior work or makes an excellent decision, invite him or her to explore how and why it happened. Do not limit yourself simply to praise. By asking appropriate questions, help raise the person's consciousness about what made the achievement possible, thereby increasing the likelihood that others like it will occur in the future. If someone does unacceptable work or makes a bad decision, practice the same principle. Do not limit yourself to corrective feedback. Invite an exploration of what made the error possible, thus raising the person's level of consciousness and minimizing the likelihood of a repetition.

4. Avoid overdirecting, overobserving, and overreporting. Excessive managing ("micromanaging") is the enemy of autonomy and creativity.

5. Plan and budget appropriately for innovation. Do not ask for people's innovative best and then announce that no money or resources are available. Creative enthusiasm (expanded consciousness) may dry up and be replaced by demoralization (shrunken consciousness).

6. Stretch your people. Assign tasks and projects that are slightly beyond their known capabilities.

7. Keep handing responsibility *down*.

To Encourage Self-Acceptance

1. When you talk with your people, be present to the experience. Make eye contact, listen actively, offer appropriate feedback, and give the speaker the experience of being heard and accepted.

2. Regardless of whom you are talking to, maintain a tone of respect. Do not permit yourself to take a condescending, superior, sarcastic, or blaming tone.

3. Keep encounters regarding work task-centered, not ego-centered. Never permit a dispute to deteriorate into a conflict of personalities. The focus needs to be on *reality*: "What is the situation?" "What does the work require?" "What needs to be done?"

4. Describe undesirable behavior without blaming. Let someone know if her or his behavior is unacceptable: point out its consequences,

communicate the kind of behavior you want instead, *and omit character assassination.*

5. Let your people see that you talk honestly about your feelings: if you are hurt or angry or offended, say so straightforwardly with dignity (and give everyone a lesson in the strength of self-acceptance).

To Encourage Self-Responsibility

1. Communicate that self-responsibility is expected and create opportunities for it. Give your people space to take the initiative, volunteer ideas, and expand their range.

2. Set clear and unequivocal performance standards. Let people understand your nonnegotiable expectations regarding the quality of work.

3. Elicit from people their understanding of what they are accountable for, to ensure that their understanding and yours are the same. Ask for a clear statement of precisely what they are committed to being responsible for.

4. Publicize and celebrate unusual instances of self-responsibility.

To Encourage Self-Assertiveness

1. Teach that errors and mistakes are opportunities for learning. "What can you learn from what happened?" is a question that builds self-esteem, encourages self-assertiveness, expands consciousness, and keeps people from repeating mistakes.

2. Let your people see that it's safe to make mistakes or to say, "I don't know, but I'll find out." To evoke fear of error or ignorance is to invite deception, inhibition, and an end to self-assertive creativity.

3. Let your people see that it's safe to disagree with you: convey respect for differences of opinion and do not punish dissent.

4. Work at changing aspects of the organization's culture that undermine self-assertiveness and self-esteem. Traditional procedures originating in an older model of management, such as requiring that all significant decisions be passed up the chain of command, may stifle not only self-esteem but also any creativity or innovation, leaving those close to the action disempowered and paralyzed.

5. Find out what the central interests of your people are and, whenever possible, match tasks and objectives with individual dispositions. Give people an opportunity to do what they enjoy most and do best; build on their strengths.

To Encourage Purposefulness

1. Ask your people what they would need in order to feel more in control of their work and, if possible, give it to them. If you want to promote autonomy, excitement, and a strong commitment to goals, empower, empower, empower.

2. Give your people the resources, information, and authority to do what you have asked them to do. Remember that responsibility cannot exist without power, and nothing can so undermine purposefulness as assigning the first without giving the second.

3. Help your people to understand how their work relates to the overall mission of the organization, so that they always operate with a grasp of the wider context. In the absence of this grasp of context, it is difficult to sustain purposefulness.

4. Encourage everyone to keep measuring results against stated goals and objectives, and disseminate this information widely.

To Encourage Integrity

1. Exemplify what you would like to see in others. Tell the truth. Keep promises. Honor commitments. Let there be perceived congruence between what you profess and what you do, not just with insiders but with everyone you deal with.

2. If you make a mistake in your dealings with someone or are unfair or short-tempered, admit it and apologize. Do not imagine (like some autocratic parent) that it would demean your dignity or position to admit taking an action you regret.

3. Invite your people to give you feedback on the kind of boss you are. Remember that you are the kind of manager your people say you are. Let your people see that you honestly want to know how you affect them, and that you are open to learning and self-correction. Set an example of nondefensiveness.

4. Convey in every way possible that your commitment is to operate the company as a thoroughly *moral* one, and look for opportunities to reward and publicize unusual instances of ethical behavior in your people.

The Bottom Line

In conclusion, I will quote my friend and colleague, Warren Bennis, who made an observation that goes to the heart of the matter: "About any behavior that is thought to be desirable by an organization, it's useful to ask: Is this behavior rewarded, punished, or ignored? The answer to this question tells you what an organization really cares about, not what it says it cares about."

23 DEEPAK SETHI

The Seven *R*'s of Self-Esteem

*Deepak (Dick) Sethi is assistant director of executive education
at AT&T, where he is responsible for the development of the
company's high-potential managers. Prior to joining AT&T,
he worked for Control Data Corporation, and he has taught at
New York University. He is a member of the advisory board of
the Institute for Management Studies and the New York Human
Resource Planners.*

Almost every organization professes to understand that we are now in the age of the knowledge worker and that people are the true competitive advantage. But if we look, not at rhetoric, but at behavior, we find that much of this talk is pretty shallow. We are very far from having adequately implemented what we pay lip service to. The typical U.S. corporation is still best described as a pyramid, although perhaps with some variations. The people at the top of the pyramid still have the power, set the vision, and issue directives that cascade down on and are carried out by the men and women below. When the command-and-control hierarchical structure is not explicit, it is implicit. Either way, it is insidious and tends to undermine or assault the self-esteem of most of the people "below." And of course it is not only self-esteem that suffers: performance, creativity, and innovation suffer as well.

There is absolutely no difference between creating an organizational culture that supports and nurtures self-esteem and creating one that supports and nurtures high performance. The common denominator lies in the issue of what an independent mind needs to function optimally. My own experience at AT&T and elsewhere has led me to the conviction that a company needs to implement, at the minimum, seven basic policies if it is to achieve a culture of high performance and high self-esteem. I call this the "seven R" model; it consists of (1) respect, (2) responsibility and resources, (3) risk taking, (4) rewards and recognition, (5) relationship, (6) role modeling, and (7) renewal. An inherent synergy exists among the seven R's, and the model is effective only if the components are actualized in tandem. These seven R's are directly linked to the six pillars of self-esteem proposed by Nathaniel Branden in his chapter in this volume.

Respect

This is the first rung on the organizational ladder of self-esteem and high performance. For people in an organization to be their best and give their best, they need to experience being treated with respect. The respect has to be real, authentic, and consistent. It has to make all individuals at all levels and from all backgrounds feel that their unique contribution is valued and indeed is crucial to the success of the organization. This respect cannot be made of platitudes. It has to be demonstrated by tangible action. One of the ways to express this is by encouraging everyone's expression of ideas, listening attentively, offering feedback, and factoring the ideas into the governance process. In most organizations today, only the people at the top, only the people with power, are truly listened to. People in the middle levels and on the front lines might in fact know much more about what needs to be done, but they rarely get a chance to share their wisdom and influence the course of the organization.

As organizations downsize, the number of managers is shrinking rapidly, and those that remain typically suffer a good deal of insecurity. They are unlikely to be self-assertive because they feel too vulnerable. Reluctant to challenge authority or to upset the status quo, they "go along to get along"—and the command-and-control model, far from fading away, takes deeper and deeper root. One of the challenges facing organizations that downsize is to support the self-esteem and inner security of those who remain on the job. Organizations neglect this challenge at their peril.

This is why the Branden strategies and the seven *R*'s are so crucially important today.

Responsibility and Resources

Most people in a company have a natural desire to contribute to its success by taking on some discrete and well-defined area of responsibility. Unfortunately, in spite of everything we know, organizations go to great lengths to thwart this healthy tendency. By failing to provide such an area of responsibility or by supplying inadequate resources, they inspire, not efficacy, but impotence. Self-esteem and creativity are the casualties.

This situation is often worsened by the style of management we call micromanagement. People do not and cannot give their best when a manager is standing at their shoulder—that is, when they do not feel trusted. Micromanagement is offensive to self-esteem and subversive of high performance. In fact, in the age of the knowledge worker, the whole idea of management needs overhauling. Mind work cannot be managed in the way that muscle work could. To the extent that management still means supervision, control, and manipulation, it frustrates and blocks what we need most in an information economy: the free exercise of independent minds. The organizations of the past knew how to manage. The organizations of the future will have to learn how to lead—and how to inspire.

Risk Taking

If we desire innovation, we have to support risk taking. If we want to support risk taking, we have to accept the inevitability of mistakes. Men and women who have high self-esteem are more likely to be intelligent risk takers than those who are less inclined to trust themselves, and the willingness to take appropriate risks itself reinforces self-esteem. The relationship is reciprocal. The organization of the future, in encouraging risk taking and accepting mistakes as normal, will at once be nurturing self-esteem and inspiring innovation.

In organizations, we often encounter nothing but double-talk around this issue. The message, if it were ever made explicit, would sound like this:

experiment, take risks, go after the new and untried—*but don't fail.* People who are terrified of the consequences of failure do not take the kind of chances that are the preconditions of high creativity.

As a matter of fact, failure can be the best of teachers. Failure can be used as a great opportunity to learn and to share learnings across the vertical, horizontal, and geographic boundaries of the organization. The organization of the future will *demand* mistakes and failures, as proof that its people are committed to risk taking and innovation.

Rewards and Recognition

The desire to be recognized for our contributions and achievements is basic to human nature. When an organization withholds such recognition, it may or may not hurt people's self-esteem (depending, perhaps, on the level of their independence), but it will almost inevitably undermine their motivation to go on giving their best.

One of the most effective ways we can inspire people is through the recognition we offer for a job well done. If we have read the psychological literature, we know this, of course, but the question is whether our organization implements this understanding in action. The organization of the future will have to, if it wants to attract and hold the best people. The knowledge worker, confident of his or her ability, will not tolerate the disrespect of nonrecognition in this fiercely competitive global economy, where talent is in high demand. He or she will expect, not just monetary rewards, but also spiritual rewards, of which acknowledgment and recognition are the most basic.

However, there is a problem. People of low self-esteem find it difficult to praise the accomplishments of others; envy and resentment often stand in the way. A manager who feels threatened by the talent of another person is unlikely to respond to that talent appropriately. On the other hand, if the manager learns to respond appropriately—because the organization demands it and because that is the company culture—not only will the talented individual feel better appreciated, but the manager also may grow in self-esteem through the exercise of rational behavior. The organization of the future will be built on the foundation of *mutual esteem,* as a precondition of liberating the best within everyone.

Relationship

Relationships can nurture self-esteem or undermine it, just as they can nurture high performance or undermine it, depending on whether they are personal, respectful, and benevolent or impersonal, authoritarian, and disempowering. In most organizations, impersonal relationships are more the norm than the exception. Typically, it is implicitly assumed that having a human relationship will detract from the exercise of authority and make managing more difficult—this in spite of everything we now know about how turned off people are by traditional management techniques and orthodoxy.

When people on all levels get to know one another in a respectful and benevolent way and get to understand one another's strengths, shortcomings, hopes, dreams, and fears, a context is established in which trust can flourish, as mutual and meaningful feedback is given and received. Again, we notice the reciprocal character of the self-esteem issues that Nathaniel Branden has observed: if we relate to one another personally and benevolently, we strengthen mutual self-esteem; if we have decent self-esteem, it feels more natural to relate in this manner. Or, stating the matter in the negative, if we have poor self-esteem, it can be frightening to relate on a human level; hiding behind authority, impersonality, control, and subservience deteriorates self-esteem still further.

When relationships are personal and authentic, we listen to one another, respect one another, and support one another. Among other benefits, we are then in a better position to understand the motivation of other people, judge how much responsibility and empowerment they can handle, learn what their needs are if they are to do their best, and help them to find the place in the organization that will be most satisfying for them and for the organization. There is total harmony between strengthening my self-esteem and yours, while honoring the needs of the enterprise that employs us.

Role Modeling

A high-performance, high-self-esteem organization is one where all members exemplify in their behavior the values the organization espouses.

People pay much more attention to what managers do than to what they say. Role modeling is the most powerful way of transmitting a set of values or desired behaviors. Unfortunately, managers are usually more comfortable making speeches, sending memos, or issuing orders than they are *living* professed values in observable action. The biggest single cause of cynicism in organizations is this discrepancy between what is professed and what is practiced. Just as hypocrisy erodes an individual's self-esteem, so it can discourage in others the integrity that self-esteem demands. And cynicism, disillusionment, and distrust do not create a foundation that supports high contribution.

Senior executives should be inspiring role models; that is the responsibility that goes with their position of power, that goes with the territory. When they waver on basic principles or betray their own integrity, the effects reverberate throughout the organization. They tend to lower everyone's standards, by sending the signal that a lack of principle is acceptable. And because the average man or woman is not a hero of independence, the danger is that he or she will succumb and follow suit, exhibiting no greater integrity than those above, and so the cancer spreads through every level. If such a pattern is to be broken, it can only happen from the top, by a new kind of role modeling that sends a more inspiring signal to everyone.

Renewal

There is much talk these days about the concept of learning organizations, but very few true learning organizations exist. Yet the organization of the future will have to be a learning one if it is to be adaptive to new economic realities and challenges. It will have to make continuous learning a way of life. Learning agendas and learning goals—together with the application of new learnings—will have to be openly discussed and shared across the vertical, horizontal, and geographic boundaries of the organization every day.

The organization of the future will need a culture where learning is constant; where coaching and feedback are pervasive, given and received from countless sources on an ongoing basis; and where *expanded consciousness* is the order of the day, simultaneously supporting growth, performance, and self-esteem. Increased consciousness yields increased contribution, which yields increased self-esteem, which yields the drive to continued growth. This is the meaning of renewal.

A Word About Human Resources

I believe that the human resource function has a critical role to play in supporting the interplay of self-esteem and high performance in the organization of the future. In recent years, the human resource function has gained in stature and significance as it has embarked on the journey from a purely transactional role to a more strategic one. However, business conditions are changing at a very rapid pace, and human resources needs to operate at the leading edge of these changes, becoming much more strategic and better linked to the business as a whole and playing a more proactive role in the transformation of the corporation. It must, for one thing, lead the way in all the matters discussed above.

However, it must start with its own transformation. Human resources needs to become a role model for behaviors that support self-esteem and high contribution, and then spearhead them across the entire organization. This can be accomplished, in part, by ensuring that self-esteem behaviors, including Nathaniel Branden's six practices, are embedded in all human resource functions, including the hiring and selection process, performance management, leadership development, succession planning, promotion, and compensation. All this in tandem, of course, with CEOs and other top executives who aggressively model high-self-esteem behaviors themselves. Human resources must play a role in this as well.

In an organization of the information age, each participant must be inspired to feel excited about coming to work and contributing to the fullest. This will not happen merely through mandates, or through programs, words, slogans, banners, mission statements, or declarations of values hanging on walls. It will happen only when policies and practices are followed that engage the hearts and minds of all those who participate in the process of production. It will happen only through speaking to their self-esteem.

We stand today at a historic crossroads. We are facing a new century where the U.S. role in the global economy is in question, where U.S. organizations have lost their old identity and are struggling to create a new one, and where the American dream needs to be reconceived and re-defined. To meet the new challenges that confront us, we do not have time for evolution. What we need is a revolution in the way we think about who we are and what our relationship is to one another. I see human resources as the necessary catalyst that sparks and leads this revolution. I believe that Nathaniel Branden has shown the way. He has raised a standard that the wise and honest (and far-seeing) among us must now follow.

24 FREDERICK G. HARMON

Future Present

Frederick G. Harmon serves clients in both the private and non-profit social sectors as an independent consultant. His latest book is Playing for Keeps: How the World's Most Aggressive and Admired Companies Use Core Values to Manage, Energize, and Organize Their People and Promote, Advance, and Achieve Their Corporate Missions. *Previously, he served as a senior executive with the American Management Association, where he headed AMA's Presidents Association.*

You already work in the organization of the future. Today's stressful workplace is a symptom of something new being born within an older form. The task is not to predict the future and then work toward it. It is not even to run after an evolution that is already rapidly in motion. The real leadership challenge is to hasten that evolution by understanding its components and reinforcing its direction.

Organization is a social invention of infinite capacity, flexibility, and diversity. Educational organizations distill and convey knowledge from one generation to another. Cultural and artistic organizations preserve and enhance our legacy of aesthetic enjoyment and psychological truth. American work organizations, the focus of this chapter, serve society's need to expand the productivity of individual labor.

Evolving forms of work organizations increased the productivity of the family farm, the nineteenth-century factory, and the multinational corporation. Each new form adopted useful elements of its predecessors. Each added new structures and systems to serve its individual needs. But about twenty years ago, people began to feel less at home within their work organizations. A social instrument designed to make work more productive and satisfying had grown so rigid that it often blocked productivity while increasing frustration.

Older theories didn't help. The common concept defined work organizations as a network of structures, systems, policies, and procedures. In theory, we just needed to adjust the wiring of the network to match new realities, a solution that proved woefully incomplete. The organizational chart and the policy manual are only representations of the intricate arrangement that shapes the work organization. Behind the chart lies the true organization—the managers and workers, their physical energy and skills, their attitudes, opinions, and values. At the core of the issue lie people's ability to change, their capacity to resist change, and their willingness to adapt.

As competitive pressures mounted, one choice was to rethink aging organizational forms to match new needs. For most, that proved too difficult. A second, more popular, choice was to "reengineer" existing forms. As it was originally conceived, reengineering offered a systemic way to adapt the organization to new needs. As it was applied, the technique quickly became synonymous with getting more work from fewer workers. Yet after millions of jobs have been lost, we are still faced with fashioning new organizational forms to match today's needs.

Stress within organizations is a sure sign of the urgency of this task. Stress builds as people keep trying to meet twenty-first-century needs within the nineteenth-century creations that are the dominant forms of organization today. The basic elements of the organization have changed. So have both the social climate in which the organization operates and the human components within the organization. All have changed far more rapidly than the structures that support them.

Three Global Guideposts

Organizations are society's creatures, living or dying depending on their capacity to evolve with society's fashions and needs. Hastening organizational evolution requires an awareness of the broad direction in which society is heading. Three global developments point to actions that any organization can take today.

The first development is the revolutionary shift toward democracy. In 1979, twelve out of nineteen Latin American countries had authoritarian governments. By the end of 1995, every country except Cuba had a democratically elected government. An even stronger wave of freedom swept through the former Soviet Union and Eastern Europe, spilling over to other continents. The peaceful end of apartheid in South Africa was only one surprising outcome of this process. Revolutionary currents never proceed smoothly. Evolution often risks a major leap forward only to be temporarily swept back; after a regrouping, the tide moves forward again. Although forms are now in a high state of flux, the direction away from authoritarianism is clearly recognizable.

With such a worldwide shift still accelerating, all organizational forms feel the pressure to become more democratic. The recent "revolutions" against the power of centralized governments, the education establishment, and religious institutions are only three examples of this change. What remains in doubt is not the direction of the change but the best strategies to manage it.

"Not the E-Word Again!"

Fads are often the froth atop deep ocean currents of change. "We already tried empowerment here but it didn't work," one executive confessed to a consultant. "Not the E word again!" one client moaned to me. "We're sick of it." Sick of it or not, empowerment of workers will change the form of every organization in the twenty-first century. Empowerment is not a fad that failed. It is a core idea of the future that forces antiquated organizational forms to adjust to both societal change and the expansion of workers' attitudes. Better-educated workers will reject nineteenth-century authoritarianism on the job as they have rejected it in so many other aspects of their lives.

Disillusion with empowerment arises from managers' failure to introduce it with care and treat it with respect. The word can't change anything, yet too many managers use it as a mantra for change rather than as a strategy. That makes empowerment a "feel-good" quick fix, the flavor of the month. No wonder people are sick of it.

Before empowerment can have any effect, it must enter the real life of the organization, where work gets done and evaluated. For a start, that means redrawing the psychological—and even the physical—organizational chart with front-line workers at the top. AT&T Universal Card Services Corporation of Jacksonville, Florida, takes that approach seriously. This credit-card company trusts its front-line associates to answer all types of customer requests, even requests for credit extensions. Customer representatives handle more than 95 percent of requests on the first call. The company's technology and its management system support this bottom-up strategy.

Paying real attention to empowerment means realigning the appraisal, compensation, and promotion systems. Levi Strauss and Company defines empowerment in the company's Aspiration Statement. This statement, in turn, is a prime factor in determining raises and promotions.

Rising Expectations

Paralleling empowerment, a second global economic and social evolution is transforming human aspiration. After slow progress over centuries, humanity everywhere is lifting its expectations. As summarized in a report of the International Commission on Peace and Food, *Uncommon Opportunities: An Agenda for Peace and Equitable Development:* "The old view of a Third World of politically and economically weak, aid-dependent countries is a vestige of the past that blinds us to immense opportunity. . . . In the coming years, the so-called Third World will be the major engine driving the growth of the world economy and, as a result, the greatest potential source of economic growth and job creation for the industrial nations."

For American work organizations, this means that low-skilled manufacturing and service jobs will continue to shift to developing countries for years to come, and not only low-skilled jobs. IBM, Texas Instruments, and Motorola today program software in India, for example. Current projections show that more than a billion people will be seeking jobs in the developing nations by early in the next century. The low-wage incentive will remain in place or even grow in countries that are rapidly improving the infrastructure required by development. The implications of this change are now commonplace in speech, if not in practice. We can maintain American wages and the American standard of living only by providing workers with higher skills. Our competitiveness depends on using the brains of workers as well as their hands. Companies must become learning as well as producing organizations. The organization of the future is putting such everyday homilies in practice today.

Although the global economy takes away yesterday's jobs, it holds the rich promise of expanding work at a higher level. One requirement, says Harvard professor Rosabeth Moss Kanter in *World Class: Thriving Locally in the Global Economy,* is to create more "world-class regions" in the United States. Such regions welcome foreign investment and consciously prepare to compete globally. She lays out a set of linked premises for creating such communities, including the following:

- The best social program is good jobs.
- The best jobs are those that provide linkages and capabilities for the global economy.
- The best source of those jobs and capabilities is a world-ready business.

Becoming a world-ready business is a key task for the organization of the future. The guaranteed job for life is already extinct. Everyone knows that we must replace it with a new social contract between employers and employees. Corporate leaders are already showing the way. Intel Corporation stresses employability in its implicit contract. Keeping employees employable suggests a greater emphasis on all aspects of organizational life that expand individual capabilities, such as skill training, cross-training, project teams, and vertical transfers.

Shrinking Time and Space

A third development shaping society and its organizations is the continual shrinking of time and space through technology. We've been living with this "technoshrink" so intensely for so long that we take it for granted. Our ancestors didn't. Thomas Jefferson, our most forward-thinking president, never saw a train. When Jefferson took office in 1801, Americans could only move goods, themselves, or information as fast as the ancient Greeks and Romans did. People expected that it would always be like that.

In Jefferson's day, it took six weeks for information to travel from the Mississippi River to Washington, D.C. By the time Abraham Lincoln served in the White House some sixty years later, similar information moved almost instantaneously by telegraph. Goods traveling by train or steamboat moved as far in an hour as they had in a day when Jefferson was president. Clearly, as historian Stephen Ambrose points out, Jefferson and Lincoln thought about time and distance in very different ways. And a century later, President John F. Kennedy made sending a person to the moon a "national objective," further shrinking our perspective on time and space.

This constriction of time and space is at the heart of the global economy. Today, people in organizations accept technoshrink as commonplace. Organizations accepted the fax machine as a new tool almost immediately. In only a few years, the portable phone became ubiquitous. Although acceptance is commonplace, so is anxiety. The computer is replacing middle management's primary role as a relayer of information. Technology takes home-market jobs and disperses them overseas. Many observers believe that at some point, good jobs and high employment will be lost forever. Yet despite short-term upheavals, the history of technological innovation points in the opposite direction.

The current anxiety over job losses is similar to that experienced in the 1890s when agricultural mechanization displaced 4.4 million farmworkers. That upheaval generated double-digit unemployment and visions of a dismal future. Yet in the century since then, U.S. employment has expanded by nearly 100 million jobs, or 400 percent.

Bigger Changes Coming

The original personal computers used software that was designed to speed up the work of isolated individuals. This development is now cresting. The PC is becoming what Andrew Kupfer, in a July 1994 article in *Fortune* magazine, called "a universal mailbox that organizes your voice mail, faxes, and E-mail, including messages enriched with video clips." Bigger changes are yet to come. The individual efficiency created by the computer in the 1980s is now spreading through networks to entire organizations. The networks ease the collaboration and pooling of knowledge to help whole organizations learn. Tied in with groupware, these networks create virtual meetings of people in different locations. They also can speed consensus building and group-centered decision making.

The broad shape of the organization of the future has already emerged. In leading-edge organizations, empowered employees will be even more globally competitive and technologically swift. How we get there is one key question. Another is who will get there first and fastest. Hastening evolution requires an ever-present alertness to the shifting centers of power within the organization. Organizations once functioned under the authority of a single individual. Over time, the board, representing the shareholders' money, became a second center. Changing profiles of organizational leaders reflect the expansion of the power centers. Over time, we moved from the production-oriented leader to the technology chief, the financial wizard, and the professional manager. Now organizations are becoming centerless as technology, competition, and empowerment create thousands of centers where only a few existed only twenty years ago.

Leaders start with the attitude that it is better to hasten evolution than to fight in the rear guard. In the end, hastening evolution is one definition of true leadership. Leaders seeking to direct their organizations toward the future can focus on three levers: attitudes, values, and policies.

A Shorthand for Thought

Attitudes are an integrated set of emotions, unconsciously accepted through the weight of previous experience or thought. Attitudes are one helpful shorthand for thought: "We can do this. We could never do that. This works for us. You can't trust them." Such attitudes drive actions every day. Challenging attitudes is one sure pathway to the organization of the future. Among the useful challenges are the following:

- Are we embracing change or resisting it?
- To what degree do we believe empowered people perform
  better? How well do our actions match our beliefs? If a gap

exists between belief and action, what attitude must we change?

- Do we see technology as liberating us or controlling us? How does our attitude on this influence our decisions?

Future-Oriented Values

Values are operational qualities used by organizations to maintain or enhance performance. Any successful organization reflects many values, such as customer service, quality, respect for others, and safety. The elevation of any value opens wide the opportunities for development of the organization. To move toward the organization of the future, future-oriented values should be adopted or upgraded. Here are three examples:

1. *Empowerment,* seriously pursued, moves any organization toward the emerging model.
2. *Speed* encourages the effective adoption of new technology and methods.
3. *Creativity* mobilizes the imagination of individuals and fosters the unconventional thinking required by an uncertain and competitive world.

Guidelines for Action

Policies are broad general guidelines for action. They should reflect current attitudes and values. Too often, they reflect yesterday's rules for success. Challenge policies regularly. How well do they reflect the pathway to the future? Among the provocative challenges are these:

- How well does our appraisal and promotion system match our values?
- Which of our policies promote empowerment and which limit it?
- How well do our policies support the capacity and potential of technology to change the way we work?

The speed of change has thrust us into an uncomfortable new dimension: future present. People working in our organizations are already consciously constructing the organization of the future. Detailed plans are still unavailable, although the preliminary sketches are quite clear. The most successful builders not only understand these sketches, they are acting on them now.

Part V

Leading People
in the Organization
of the Future

---

25 JAMES G. BROCKSMITH JR.

Passing the Baton

Preparing Tomorrow's Leaders

James G. Brocksmith Jr. is deputy chairman and chief operating officer of KPMG Peat Marwick LLP. He joined KPMG's Columbus, Ohio, office in 1965 and became a partner in 1971. Since 1990, he has served as deputy chairman, a member of the board of directors and the management committee, and chief operating officer.

Leadership 2000, a unique executive development program, was born in a five-minute conversation I had with Jon Madonna, KPMG's chairman, in December 1993. Whenever we're in the office on the same day, Jon and I make a point of setting aside a few minutes of "strategy time"—time to talk about the firm and where it is going. Our strategy time is a chance, too, to test out new ideas on each other, ideas we have dreamed up or have had suggested to us by partners, clients, or business advisers.

The concept of a highly focused, long-term investment in developing the firm's future senior leaders came from a discussion about passing the baton. We were talking about some of the things we had learned the hard

Note: I am indebted to the planning committee that made the Leadership 2000 vision a reality. Steve Anderson, retired partner and management committee member, who has acted as program director, and Steve Sass, director in charge of KPMG's Center for Leadership Development, deserve special thanks. I also want to thank Kitty Winkler, the program's management consultant, who assisted me in researching and documenting this chapter.

way after we were already in our current positions of chairman and deputy chairman, and we were wishing that we had somehow been given better preparation for the array of new challenges that seem to be accelerating every year. Based on our own experience, we knew that a world of difference exists between being sheltered by the infrastructure when we are a few steps removed from the top and leadership at the top, where one utterance can change the firm's image and reputation, for better or for worse.

I thought about our conversation afterward. What if we had to pass the baton to someone today? Would that person be any better prepared than we were? As I mentally reviewed the talented partners who might logically replace us, I concluded that their background and preparation were much the same as ours had been. They had grown up in a franchise structure that did not require significant business leadership skills beyond the local-office level. With the changes and staggering increases in the complexity of our jobs since we had held them, I realized that we had to give our successors more preparation than we had been given. To do otherwise would be unfair to them and potentially risky for the firm. We also were concerned with retaining the firm's top talent. Earlier that same day, Jon and I had discussed a recent key loss and realized that the firm hadn't always done a good job of recognizing and continuing to challenge our people who had the highest potential. Leadership 2000 would help to address this problem, too. We concluded that one of its outcomes needed to be a demonstration of the value the firm placed on fostering the growth of our best and brightest partners.

If it had a rapid birth, Leadership 2000 had a slow and deliberate infancy. Having conceived the idea of developing future senior leaders of the firm in extraordinary ways, we took our time in developing a framework for the program, discussing the ideas several times with the firm's management committee. Ultimately, with the involvement of the management committee, we hand-picked thirty-five initial participants, and in May 1994, we began an exciting process that is unprecedented in our firm and in others we know about.

The framework was simple. We committed the time and money to develop this group of the firm's highest-potential partners over the course of the next two to three years. Our vision was that their development would permeate all aspects of their lives during that time period: their on-the-job experiences, their formal education, and their growth and development during personal time. We saw ongoing planning and coaching as critical to the process, and we were committed to spending as much of our own time as possible in participating in the grooming of these senior leaders.

We enlisted in the program development a retiring senior partner, Steve Anderson. Along with a background in executive development and a high level of respect throughout the firm, Steve had established a reputation for being one of the firm's best coaches and had informally mentored a number of successful partners' careers. Teamed with Steve Anderson was Steve Sass, director in charge of the firm's Center for Leadership Development. Steve Sass brought to the team a long track record of educational expertise and executive development in a leading technology company before he joined KPMG. These two men also had at their disposal staff experts and consultants to assist with benchmarking and program design. We did early benchmarking with five leading companies that were known for innovative executive development programs. Although none exactly matched what we had planned for Leadership 2000, they gave us good ideas that we factored into our thinking.

With our development team in place and with our concepts and objectives in mind, we laid out an implementation plan for each of the key elements in our framework. The essence of our plan was simple, consisting of four key elements:

- Involving participants in determining the senior leadership attributes most relevant to them and to the firm

- Facilitating participants' development in the senior leadership attributes, primarily through challenging on-the-job activities

- Exposing participants to world-class thinkers

- Passing on to the group all we could of what we know and have learned in our own experiences as the firm's leaders

In the remainder of this chapter, I'll describe how we implemented these four elements and how each has contributed to the program's success.

A small, but essential, part of Leadership 2000 has been a series of three-day plenary sessions. In the first of these three-day programs, the participants developed their model of senior leadership attributes. Each of the subsequent programs focused on one or more of these attributes. The sessions gave us the opportunity to expose the group to world-class thinkers, many of whom have contributed chapters to this series. The three-day programs effectively gave impetus and excitement to the development activities each participant pursued in the six months that followed each plenary session. In highly interactive seminarlike sessions, the thought leaders challenged participants to explore the new meanings of senior leadership in the new world of business that is being shaped today. Making learning more practical than theoretical, the sessions often included role play, simulation, and workshops with feedback.

For example, in a program focused on communication, a leading business school professor had participants present controversial subject matter to a hostile audience. Fellow participants simulated the audience and put immense pressure on their peers' ability to uphold fundamental values in the face of severe criticism. In another role play, members of the group played CEOs who were reacting to a crisis involving their companies. With minimal time to prepare, the "CEOs" were faced with lights, cameras, and news-hungry members of the press played by their Leadership 2000 colleagues. A speaker on coaching used a golfing analogy to draw parallels and reinforce principles of world-class human resources leadership. Some participants were so drawn to the ideas in this session that they continued the relationship with the speaker after the session ended. Effectively, he became their personal coach on coaching.

The following list of senior leadership attributes gives an idea of the range of topics that participants developed in the first Leadership 2000 plenary session. They defined these nine attributes as essential to KPMG's senior leaders:

1. *Values:* Establish and champion values.

2. *Vision:* Have the capacity to discover vision.

3. *Perspective:* Personify the global leader.

4. *Communication:* Provide high-impact messaging.

5. *Strategy:* Think and act strategically.

6. *Decisions:* Make informed decisions.

7. *Knowledge:* Expand the knowledge base.

8. *People:* Be a resource architect.

9. *Self:* Know who you are.

Beyond naming the nine attributes, the participants also spelled out in detail the characteristics a senior leader would have to cultivate to be successful in each of the attribute areas. This was done under the guidance of another world-class thought leader. He helped participants to differentiate what the attributes meant at the senior level from what the group members had experienced up to this point in their careers. So a seemingly simple list took on new meaning as the group perceived the increased complexity of these subjects at the top of the organization.

Pursuing experiences in order to grow in the attribute areas where participants individually have the greatest need is one of the central ideas of Leadership 2000. The team's experience in executive development has taught them that real learning takes place on the job, not in the classroom, and that classroom time is wasted if it doesn't get real on-the-job reinforcement. Therefore, we designed the program so that once participants developed a list of desirable attributes, each participant went on to develop a formal plan to address his or her own attributes that were in need of development. The plans encompassed individual initiatives, educational experiences, and, most important, job-related activities to strengthen leadership skills.

When the participants had made their tentative plans, Steve Anderson met with them individually to review the plans. He didn't just act as a "checker"; he played a proactive role, challenging the participants on the attributes they had selected and how the activities they had planned would hone their skills in these attributes. Once he was convinced that the plan was on the right track, he proceeded to help them to expand the "stretch" activities they had laid out for themselves and to clear the way to make the plan a reality. We wanted to be sure that these activities, the real key to accelerated development, were significantly more challenging than anything the individuals would have been exposed to without the backing of Leadership 2000.

For example, one member of the group spent a week in a client's office interviewing managers and executives, attending senior management meetings, and shadowing the chief executive. This kind of investment in non-revenue-producing activity has been rare in the firm. However, by growing this partner's industry expertise and understanding of client issues, a significant long-term benefit has been realized—for the client, the firm, and the Leadership 2000 participant. Another participant undertook the major challenge of transforming her career from the audit side of the firm to our full-service consulting business. Although others in the firm have made that transition, few have made it at her high level. Thrust immediately into a leadership position, she was able to quickly gain the technical and leadership skills she needed for success in a totally new environment.

We had known in advance that one of the critical issues in the program design was making time for development, and it was in this area that we made one of the breakthrough discoveries that have resulted from Leadership 2000. The participants who were most successful in their development were those who saw ways to make the development part of their job. For instance, one participant set a goal to gain client credibility by becoming much more visible in his client's industry. To achieve this goal, he took a number of steps to hone his industry skills, including acting as the organizer of an industry conference. Ultimately, he was quoted as an industry-knowledgeable source in a number of industry periodicals as well as the Wall Street Journal, and he gained new respect from his client. So a set of personal growth activities was also a set of smart business growth activities.

The last of the essential elements in Leadership 2000 is the role Jon and I have played. When we conceived the program idea, we knew it would require some investment of our time and energy that might have been directed elsewhere, but we were convinced that it would be time well spent on a subject that was critical to the firm's future. Having made this commitment, we attended each of the three-day plenary sessions. With few exceptions, we stayed for the full three days, which gave us an opportunity to get to know the participants well. We also dedicated a few hours of each session to candid sharing of the decisions we faced, significant issues for the firm, and even the mistakes we had made. Beyond these events, we frequently interacted with participants during their on-the-job time. We were able to do this because we had named a number of them to lead firmwide strategic projects such as chairing annual partners' meetings for the various lines of business. Those activities have been part of their accelerated development and have let us play a personal role in their leadership growth.

Participants have repeatedly told us that the time we have spent, in the program sessions and one-on-one with them, is something they especially value. It has been a growth experience for us too; we have gained new insights and ideas from our dialogue with these bright, exciting people. Their fresh perspective on firmwide projects has given us the benefit of creative thinking from new sources.

At the time I am writing this, we are planning the final session in the series, capping two and a half years of intensive development. As we near the closing session, we are taking a retrospective look at what Leadership 2000 has accomplished. By design, our measurements for the program are informal. Its success or failure should be evident soon enough, because the participants were deemed to be only five years or so away from top jobs when we brought them into the program. We have some early indicators, though:

- About half the group has been given increased job responsibility during the two years since the program began.

- A number of the participants have led task-force efforts that are transforming the firm under the initiative we call Future Directions.

- Every participant I have talked to feels more confident and better prepared for senior leadership than would have been possible without Leadership 2000's focused growth.

A number of other indicators also exist. The firm's management committee, Jon, and I have seen enough to convince us that this investment in the firm's future is one of the best we could ever make. Our conviction is such that we have just named an additional thirty-six partners to the Leadership 2000 programs, as the Class of '96. Following in the footsteps of the Class of '94, the members of the new group will tailor-make their own set of development experiences, and Jon and I will continue to play a visible role in their coaching and growth.

When the Leadership 2000 Class of '94 meets in Washington, D.C., this spring for its "graduation" plenary, they will be sharing some sessions and experiences with the incoming Class of '96. This will continue another of the program's traditions, that of teamwork and sharing. The Class of '96 will have the opportunity to build on the best of what the Class of '94 has learned, while at the same time carving out a new set of experiences for themselves. We will also continue to refresh the commitment to development and camaraderie that has grown among members of the Class of '94. We are already planning an annual alumni get-together to keep the positive energy going.

These days, the mantle of firm leadership is a little lighter on the shoulders of our management team because of Leadership 2000. When the time comes to turn over the leadership of the firm, we feel we will have played an important role in passing the baton to a more capable set of hands.

26 MARSHALL GOLDSMITH

Retaining Your Top Performers

*Marshall Goldsmith is a founding director of Keilty, Goldsmith
and Company (KGC) (a key provider of customized leadership
development), a cofounder of the Learning Network, and a member of the Drucker Foundation board of governors. His work has
received national recognition from the Institute for Management
Studies, the American Management Association, the American
Society for Training and Development, and the Human Resource
Planning Society. He has been ranked as one of the "Top 10" consultants in the field of executive development by the* Wall Street
Journal.

Leaders in organizations around the world are debating the changing
nature of work. Discussion has centered on the perceived decline in
job security (the lifelong career at a benevolent company is a fading memory) and the erosion of corporate loyalty. In countries from Sweden to Germany, the United States, and Japan, employees are beginning to wonder,
"If the company is willing to dump me at *its* convenience, why shouldn't
I be willing to dump the company at *my* convenience?"

We tend to focus, understandably, on the profound impact that these
and other workplace changes are having on the lives of individuals. But
too often leaders overlook the equally profound impact these changes are

having on their organizations. The fact is that the "new work contract"—where employees take responsibility for their own careers and corporations provide them with career-enhancing but impermanent opportunities—can be as difficult for organizations to manage as it is for individuals. We, as leaders, still understand little of the mechanics of retaining essential high performers in turbulent times.

Our task is complicated by five additional, less widely acknowledged trends:

1. *The reduced status of working for a major corporation.* John Kotter, in his book *New Rules,* notes that from 1974 through 1994, Harvard Business School graduates who worked for smaller corporations tended to make more money and have higher job satisfaction than their counterparts in large corporations. A growing number of the top young leaders and technical specialists around the world now avoid working for major corporations. Instead, they are increasingly attracted to the risks and rewards of small start-up companies. Harvard business professor Regina Herzlinger notes that over half her graduate school students now want to be entrepreneurs.

2. *The frequent lack of connection between pay and contribution.* When I asked more than two thousand managers from a wide variety of major corporations, "What is the typical difference in contribution between a top performer and a below-average performer at the same pay-grade level?" the average answer was "Over 100 percent." When they were asked, "What is the typical pay difference?" the average answer was "Between 5 and 10 percent." In fact, many managers cited cases of younger employees who were contributing more to the company but made less money than older employees.

3. *The decline in opportunities for promotion.* Restructuring has led to fewer layers of management at many corporations. Although this change may have led to increased efficiency, it has often also led to fewer opportunities for promotion. In most companies, pay scales are still tied directly to rank, not performance. In the past, many organizations have rationalized the lack of differentiation within pay grades by pointing out that top performers tend to be promoted rapidly. Without the opportunity for rapid advancement, however, top performers can become more inclined to seek other opportunities.

4. *The increase in workload and the decline in support staff.* Most employees in major corporations believe that they are working harder today than they were ten years ago. Support staff and many of the "amenities" of working for a large organization have started to disappear. Whereas employees at small, entrepreneurial organizations have always worked hard, the relative difference in workload and support between major corporations and smaller corporations is perceived to be declining.

5. *The rise in the influence of the knowledge worker.* Peter Drucker has noted the dramatically increased importance of the knowledge worker in modern organizations. Yet we are often not sure what this means to the way we lead. Microsoft Corporation's chairman, Bill Gates, recently remarked that Microsoft would do "whatever it takes" to attract and retain the brightest software developers in the world. Innovative high-technology corporations such as Sun Microsystems are currently paying employees large bonuses to recruit top talent. In tomorrow's world, the "intellectual capital" brought in by high-knowledge employees will be a major, if not the primary, competitive advantage for many corporations. As the perceived value of key knowledge workers increases, the competition to hire these workers will intensify.

A Strategy for Retaining High-Impact Performers

Leaders can no longer afford to let the vagaries of the job market determine who leaves and who stays with the organization. We must learn to manage our human assets with the same rigor we devote to our financial assets. These seven steps can help you to accomplish that task:

1. *Clearly identify which employees you want to keep.* In recent years, many organizations have focused on determining which employees they should get rid of rather than on which ones they should keep. Many downsizing packages have been offered that gave all employees with similar experience levels the same incentive to leave. Unfortunately for the organization, the employees who decided to leave were often the high-impact performers who could find other work quickly.

2. *Let them know that you want to keep them.* Amazing as it may seem, many high-impact performers who are asked why they've left an organization

report, "No one ever asked me to stay!" Many organizations have deliberately not told high-impact performers that they were special in any way, for fear of alienating the "average" performers. In the future, it will become increasingly easy to retain "average" performers and increasingly difficult to retain high-impact performers.

3. *Provide recognition.* Although compensation is an important factor for retaining high-impact performers, several studies indicate that it is currently not the most important factor. Typically, the major reasons great people leave major organizations are lack of recognition, lack of involvement, and poor management. The CEO of one of the world's leading telecommunications companies has recently embarked on an innovative new approach. Division-level executives provide a quarterly report on high-impact performers who should be recognized. The CEO *personally* calls, thanks them for their contributions, and asks for their input on what the corporation can do to increase effectiveness. The CEO believes that this process not only helps to retain key talent but also yields great feedback and generates ideas for continuous improvement.

4. *Provide opportunities for development and involvement.* One of the world's largest consulting and accounting firms has recently embarked on an innovative program to identify and cultivate high-potential leaders. As part of the process, young leaders engage in an "action learning" project in which they work on real-life problems facing the firm. This gives young leaders a fantastic developmental opportunity and gives the firm valuable input on solving real problems. It also enhances the young leaders' commitment to stay with the firm. The firm's leaders say that such a process would not have been tried just a few years ago, for fear of alienating other partners, but that today the firm has no choice but to identify and retain high-impact partners.

5. *Challenge the compensation plan.* Organizations that are unwilling to make performance, rather than mere seniority, the key driver of pay will face an increasing challenge in keeping top talent, especially young talent. One Fortune 500 industrial company recently refused to implement a variable, performance-based compensation plan because half the employees felt uncomfortable with the concept. The corporation neglected to measure *which* half felt uncomfortable with more differentiated pay, but my guess is that it was the lower-performing employees. High-impact per-

formers of the future will be able to demand and receive substantially more pay than their lower-performing peers. A "socialistic" compensation plan combined with a lowered potential for promotion will lead to an "average" workforce.

6. *Relax the culture.* In addition to reducing bureaucracy, high-performing, high-tech companies like Netscape, Sun Microsystems, and AT&T Wireless (formerly McCaw Cellular) are known for providing freedom in dress codes, scheduled hours, and lifestyle choices. Although employees may work very hard, they appreciate the lack of rules, regulations, and strictures that can inhibit their freedom without increasing their productivity.

7. *Provide intrapreneurial opportunities.* Gifford Pinchot, inventor of the term *intrapreneur,* has shown how major corporations can provide positive opportunities for reasonably autonomous enterprises to operate within the larger corporate structure. By allowing high-potential leaders to "run a business" inside a larger business, a corporation can gain commitment and ownership of results while simultaneously developing people. People who see opportunities for ownership and personal development are much more likely to stay with the organization.

In the past, when a high-impact performer in a major corporation was offered a position at another company, the employee was likely to say no. Most managerial and professional jobs offered good pay, job security, the possibility of promotion, and status. Today the high-impact employee is much more likely to say yes. To retain such talent in the future, organizations will need to clearly identify, develop, involve, and recognize key people. Traditional compensation plans will need to be challenged, needless bureaucracy eliminated, and intrapreneurial opportunities provided.

Organizations that are unable to modify their human resource systems to match tomorrow's realities will lose the competitive edge. Those that are able to create a dynamic, new human resource model will retain the high-knowledge talent needed to succeed in tomorrow's globally competitive environment.

27

PAUL HERSEY
DEWEY E. JOHNSON

Situational Leadership in the Multicultural Organization

*Paul Hersey is founder and chairman of the board of the Center
for Leadership Studies, Inc. He is recognized as one of the world's
outstanding authorities on training and development in leadership,
management, and selling. He has authored or coauthored numerous books, including* Management of Organizational Behavior:
Utilizing Human Resources; Organizational Change Through
Effective Leadership; The Family Game: A Situational Approach to Effective Parenting; *and* The Situational Leader
and Situational Selling: An Approach to Increasing Sales
Effectiveness. *Dewey E. Johnson is professor of management in
the Sid Craig School of Business at California State University,
Fresno. Elected to more than a dozen offices in national and
regional professional associations, he is the cofounder and former
chairman of the Management Education and Development
Division of the Academy of Management, past national president
and fellow of the Small Business Institute Director's Association,
and recipient of the 1995 Provost's Outstanding Professor Award
for Service from his university. He has published many articles
in the areas of leadership, small business, and performance
management.*

Note: Situational Leadership™ is a registered trademark of the Center for Leadership Studies, Inc., Escondido, California.

More than twenty years ago, writing in the *Journal of Contemporary Business*, Ralph Stogdill, one of our most distinguished colleagues and mentors, summarized his view of leadership: "The most effective leaders appear to exhibit a degree of versatility and flexibility that enables them to adapt their behavior to changing and contradictory demands." If anything, the organization of the future will be part of an even more rapidly changing and contradictory world than it was during Stogdill's time. Therefore, how can effective leaders adapt their behavior and exhibit the flexibility that will be needed to meet the challenges of future organizations?

Warren Bennis, another of our thoughtful colleagues, has defined leading as creating and implementing a vision. We are going to build on this idea, but first let us explore more of the terrain. The future organizational environment is going to be one of increasing complexity. We can see the indicators now. Organizations are becoming multicultural and global, as opposed to national, in scope. Leaders in global organizations must function effectively with expanding diversity in cultures, values, beliefs, and expectations. But while organizations are becoming more global, people are demanding (often with increased fervor) to be treated as distinctive individuals or groups. This means that a one-size-fits-all leadership approach just will not work. The organization of the future will include members from many different cultures, and the leader of the future must be able to effectively influence people wherever they are, regardless of their culture.

Leaders in multicultural organizations are frequently, and often validly, criticized for using a style that is "too American" or "too European" to fit the needs of their environment. We will discuss an approach that adapts leadership style so that the choice of style is clearly driven by the needs of the situation, not the background of the leader. We will briefly review the Situational Leadership concept and discuss how this approach can help leaders in multicultural organizations.

Situational Leadership

Situational Leadership was developed by Paul Hersey and Kenneth H. Blanchard at the Center for Leadership Studies in the late 1960s; they originally advanced it as the "Life Cycle Theory of Leadership" in the

Training and Development Journal in May 1969. Situational Leadership is based on the interplay of three major factors: (1) the amount of guidance and direction a leader gives, (2) the amount of socioemotional support a leader provides, and (3) the readiness level of the person who is being led (the follower) for performing a specific task. The three factors are present in any leadership situation and can be easily understood by members of any culture. According to Situational Leadership, there is no one "best way" to influence people. Therefore, the model is especially useful in multicultural organizations, where flexibility is a requirement.

Task and Relationship Behavior

In the Situational Leadership model, leadership style can be classified by considering two broad categories of behavior:

1. *Task behavior* is defined as the extent to which the leader engages in spelling out the duties and responsibilities of an individual or group. These behaviors of the leader include determining what to do, how to do it, when to do it, where to do it, and who is to do it.

2. *Relationship behavior* is defined as the extent to which the leader engages in two-way or multiway communication. These behaviors include listening, facilitating, and supporting.

Task behavior and relationship behavior can be viewed as separate and distinct dimensions. They can be placed on separate axes of a two-dimensional graph, and the four quadrants can be used to identify four basic leadership styles. Figure 27.1 illustrates these styles. Task behavior is plotted from low to high on the horizontal axis; relationship behavior is plotted from low to high on the vertical axis. This makes it possible to describe leader behavior in four styles. These four quadrants can be used as the basis for assessing leader behavior. Although no one style is effective in all situations, each style can be effective in the appropriate situation.

Readiness of the Follower

As noted earlier, there is no one best style of leadership; the best style depends on the situation within which the attempt to influence takes

Figure 27.1. Situational Leadership.

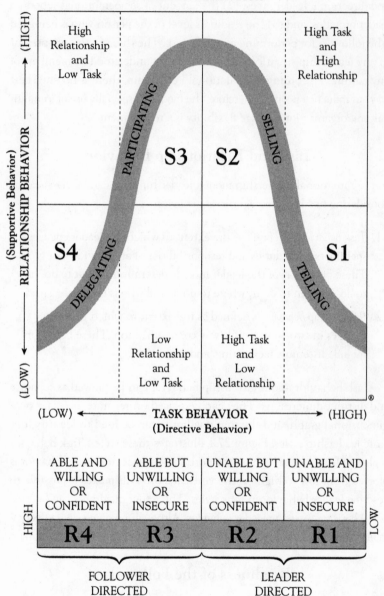

place. The more that leaders can adapt their behaviors to the situation, the more effective their attempts to influence become. The leadership situation can be influenced by many factors; however, we view the relationship between leaders and followers as the crucial variable. If the followers decide not to follow, it doesn't matter what the leader thinks or what the job demands may be. *There is no leadership unless someone is following.*

Readiness in Situational Leadership is defined as the extent to which a follower is presently demonstrating her or his ability and willingness to accomplish a specific task. People tend to be at different levels of readiness depending on the task they are being asked to complete. Readiness is not a personal or cultural characteristic; it is not an evaluation of a person's traits, values, age, and so on. Readiness is a person's preparedness to perform a particular task. This concept of readiness has to do with specific situations, not with any total sense of a person's readiness as a human being. All people tend to be more or less ready in relation to a specific task, function, or objective.

The two major components of readiness are ability and willingness. *Ability* is a function of the knowledge, experience, and skill or performance that an individual or group brings to a particular task or activity. *Knowledge* is knowledge of the task, *experience* is experience with or related to the task, and *skill* or *performance* is a demonstrated skill and/or performance in successfully completing similar tasks.

Willingness is a function of the confidence, commitment, and motivation that an individual or group has to accomplish a specific task. *Confidence* is the person or group's feeling that "I can do it," *commitment* is the person or group's feeling that "I will do it," and *motivation* is the person or group's feeling that "I want to do it."

Willingness is only one word that describes the issue. Sometimes, it isn't so much that people are really unwilling; it's just that they've never done a specific task before. Perhaps they don't have any experience with it, so they are insecure, apprehensive, or afraid. Generally, if they have never done something, the problem is insecurity. The term *unwilling* might be most appropriate when, for one reason or another, the individuals have slipped, or lost some of their commitment and motivation. It might imply that they are regressing. For many, willingness also includes a sense of purpose, meaning, involvement, and growth.

Even though the concepts of ability and willingness are different, it is important to remember that they make up an interacting influence system in which a significant change in one part will affect the whole. The extent to which followers bring willingness into a specific situation affects the use of their present ability. It also affects the extent to which they will grow and develop competence and ability. Similarly, the amount of knowledge, experience, and skill brought to a specific task will often affect competence, commitment, and motivation.

Readiness levels are the different combinations of ability and willingness that people bring to each task (see Figure 27.1). The continuum of follower readiness can be divided into four levels. Each represents a different combination of follower ability and willingness or confidence.

Readiness Level One (R1)

Unable and unwilling: The follower is unable and lacks commitment and motivation

or

Unable and insecure: The follower is unable and lacks confidence.

Readiness Level Two (R2)

Unable but willing: The follower lacks ability but is motivated and is making an effort

or

Unable but confident: The follower lacks ability but is confident as long as the leader is there to provide guidance.

Readiness Level Three (R3)

Able but unwilling: The follower has the ability to perform the task but is not willing to use that ability

or

Able but insecure: The follower has the ability to perform the task but is insecure or apprehensive about doing it alone.

Readiness Level Four (R4)

Able and willing: The follower has the ability to perform and is committed

or

Able and confident: The follower has the ability to perform and is confident about doing it.

The curved line through the four leadership styles shown in the figure represents the high-probability combination of task and relationship behaviors. These combinations correspond to the readiness levels directly below them. To use the model, identify a point on the readiness continuum that represents follower readiness to perform a specific task. Then construct a perpendicular line from that point to a point where it intersects with the curved line representing leader behavior. This point indicates the most appropriate amount of task behavior and relationship behavior for that specific situation.

In selecting the high-probability combination of task behavior and relationship behavior, it isn't necessary to be exact. As one moves away from the optimal combination, the probability of success gradually falls off, slowly at first and then more rapidly the farther away one moves. Because of this, it is not necessary to score a direct hit; a close approximation keeps the probability of success high.

Application of Situational Leadership

Use of the Situational Leadership model consists of five well-defined and interrelated steps. To determine what leadership style or pattern of behaviors the leader should use in a given situation, several key decisions must be made:

1. *What objective do we want to accomplish?* First, the leader must determine the task-specific outcome the follower is to accomplish. Without creating clarity about the desired outcome, the leader has no basis for determining follower readiness or the specific behavioral style to use for that level of readiness.

2. *What is the follower's readiness in this situation?* Once the objective has been created, the leader must diagnose the follower's readiness to accomplish this objective. If the follower is at a high level of readiness, only a low amount of leadership intervention will be required. If, on the other hand, the follower is at a low level of readiness, a more structured leadership intervention may be required.

3. *What leadership action should be taken?* The next step is deciding on an appropriate leadership style. Suppose that the leader has determined that the follower's readiness level is high in terms of accomplishing the given objective; that is, the follower is able (has high amounts of knowledge, skills, experience, and resources) and willing (has high amounts of confidence, commitment, and motivation). The appropriate leadership style would be *delegating,* because the follower has high amounts of both ability and willingness. If the follower's ability and willingness were lower, a more directive style would be appropriate.

Steps one through three reduce the constraints of culture. For example, when an objective is set within the organization's culture, the readiness of the follower to achieve an objective is based on an assessment of the follower at that time and place within the culture. Therefore, the model obviates many of the potential problems arising from importing a "foreign" leadership model and attempting to apply it to a specific culture.

4. *What was the result of the leadership intervention?* This step requires assessment to determine if the results match the expectations. People learn in small increments. Development consists of positively reinforcing successive approximations as the person approaches the desired level of performance. Therefore, after a leadership intervention, the leader must assess the results by rechecking the objectives, rediagnosing readiness, and ascertaining if a further change in style is indicated.

5. *What follow-up, if any, is required?* If a gap exists between present performance and desired performance, then follow-up is required and the cycle begins again.

Situational Leadership works best when both leaders and followers understand the model. This is especially true in a multicultural environment. By understanding the model, followers can easily realize that changes in style are not driven by cultural bias but are primarily influenced by the follower's readiness level for the task under consideration.

Applying the Model in a Multicultural Organization

Each of the key steps discussed above is task-specific and unbounded by culture. This has been demonstrated by the model's use for more than three decades in over 128 countries. The usefulness of the model crosses cultural boundaries. However, some special sensitivities need to be considered in applying the model in a multicultural environment.

Although each of the four leadership styles can be practiced in any culture, the manner in which the message is delivered may vary greatly from culture to culture. For example, whereas leaders in both Germany and Japan sometimes need to provide structure and direction, the *way* that the structure is provided may differ in the two countries. The same may be true for cultural differences inside a country. Investment bankers in New York City may provide support in a different manner from leaders in a co-op in California. Leaders need to be sensitive to cultural differences in determining the way to deliver their leadership style.

In summary, the Situational Leadership approach causes leaders to focus on the specific task under consideration and the individual's readiness for the task. This discipline helps the leader to view each situation from an objective perspective and attempts to eliminate potential cultural bias. An understanding of the model can help both leaders and followers to build bridges across cultures to get the job done. As a result, organizations of the future can function better in a multicultural, global environment and meet the challenges of a complex, rapidly changing world.

28 PIERRE J. EVERAERT

Emotions, Tempo, and Timing in Managing People

Pierre J. Everaert joined Philips Electronics NV, Eindhoven,
Netherlands, in 1993 as a member of the group management
committee and is now executive vice president of the board
of management. He spent fifteen years in six countries with
Goodyear International Corporation of Akron, Ohio, ending as
president of Goodyear's German operations. He then became vice
chairman of General Biscuits SA in Paris and later president and
CEO of General Biscuits U.S.A. In 1985, he joined Koninklijke
Ahold, Zaandam, Netherlands, as a member of the managing
board and became president and CEO of Ahold USA, Inc.
He became president of the parent company in 1989.

Organizations grow to become rigid structures that are difficult to change. The future is change by definition! So let us tackle the subject from the time when it really happens—in the future—and from the place where it really happens—in the marketplace. Who makes it happen? People as customers in the marketplace, people as employees, people who are full of emotions. People are the intellectual capital of an organization and they create change. I will focus on two specific aspects of the change process: *tempo and timing* and *emotions in managing*. Although they are very often overlooked or even completely ignored, they are crucial qualifiers in the formula for success.

The concepts of *organization* and *future* have been covered extensively in a recent flood of publications, authored by academics as well as by experienced corporate operators. Consultants have analyzed, dismantled and reassembled, reengineered, and rebuilt organizations in many ways. Their work covers not only the more classic setups in Western business arenas, but, of late, the challenges of entrepreneurial models in emerging markets and new territories. Authors seem to agree on at least two concepts:

1. To stay alive in a changing environment an *organization* must change.
2. The *future* is a defined period of time in which the changes must occur.

So what's new? I propose the concept of *tempo and timing* as a qualifier in mapping the future and *emotions* as a qualifier in managing the intellectual capital of the organization: the people.

Tempo in business is not at all different from tempo in music; *lento* and *moderato* call for a smooth rendition of the written music, whereas *presto* and *vivace* call for lively play and fast execution. In business, *lento* is the speed of the decision-making process of yesteryear and *vivace* is the time required in our tomorrows for action and reaction. *Timing* is defined as "the" moment in time when the change process is set in motion. *Emotions* are defined as feelings used in a business context. They add the human touch to the written or spoken words and modify the style of an organization.

My conclusion is that the successful organization of the future is one in which people effectuate changes required by the market instead of talking about it, and in which they implement decisions as fast as they are needed instead of piling up proposals. It is also one that allows competent managers to take charge, irrespective of their gender, age, or position in the hierarchy. It is not one in which people cover up and misrepresent emotions, thereby failing to provide the bridge between the sterility of number crunching (the current generation) and fun in working (the new generation).

The Future: Tempo and Timing

As I read reports on corporate strategy or manuals on strategic intent produced by the gurus of the past decade, I miss the concepts of timing (the time of implementation) and tempo (the speed of execution). In most organizational strategies, they may be inadvertently hidden or casually lost somewhere in the text but, in any event, they are very much understated. Tempo can make or break the musical performance of an orchestra; it can even alter the way the orchestra renders the music written by the composer. It has the same impact on the performance of an organization as it deploys the plans prepared by management. In the world of music, it affects the reputation of the orchestra—its popularity—which means its success at the box office. In business it affects the organization's success in becoming top-of-the-class or retaining that position in its industry.

The organizations of the new age, as they map their future, will include tempo and timing guidelines in the rollout of their strategy. The future of an organization, in the context of strategic planning, can be a month, a quarter, a year—but it is certainly not infinity. It is a variable that at some point in the planning stage must become a well-specified period of time typical for the organization or the industry in which it operates. However, since the mid-eighties, the financial community has looked at corporate performance on a quarterly basis. Rightly or wrongly, this has changed the timing, adapting it to the speed of the novelty industries. Computers have a novelty span of six months at the most. Software changes by the day. Investors following their advisers have reset their timing. Investment decisions, buying or selling, are more for short-term income than for long-term gain. These are the tempo drivers of the new times.

Time to market and time to money have been drastically cut. Timing is in fact a double-edged sword: timing asks, "When shall we do it?" and tempo asks, "How fast shall we do it?" In other words, when a plan for upgrading, reworking, or change is ready, it must be rolled out; it cannot be upheld by hesitation or old-fashioned bureaucracy. Ask yourself whether your plan includes both the time of implementation and the tempo of execution.

In business as in music, tempo is the choice of the composer. In fact, it is the way the composer sees it being executed: the music or the plan, rendered at the highest level of performance. Putting it on paper does not mean that it will automatically happen. Success will be the sum of three things:

The degree of acceptance by the people involved or affected

The depth of communication within the organization

The ability of the sitting management or their successors to effectuate changes

Again, what's new? The new kid on the block is *discipline in execution*.
Whether it is imposed from outside or self-imposed, it requires the organization to accept and work with tempo and timing as part of the corporate strategy. The "too much, too soon" and "too little, too late" analysis
in the postmortem of a business plan should be turned around and translated into a set of objectives for the future: "How much, how soon?" In a
competitive environment, with highly skilled players and advanced management tools, discipline at the corporate or individual level will mean the
difference between a series of successes or a one-time unforgiving failure.

Time of Implementation

Time of implementation is included in every business manual on our
shelves. So why bring it up again? Because most of these books were written *before* the Internet era and *before* high-speed notebooks came to the
market at affordable prices. The example of all examples is Bill Gates,
who started his rollout at dawn in New Zealand and finished at midnight
in Los Angeles. In the rollout plan for Windows 95, the timing was
August 24, 1995, midnight, New Zealand time; the tempo was one day
(of forty-four hours).

The state-of-the-art performance of the tools at our disposal commands
ongoing change. Personal computers on every desk and network data bases
and software to manipulate complex models have cut our time for thinking
from "See me in a month" to "See me tomorrow." Creating new ways of
doing business is now part of short-term rather than long-term planning.
Companies play simulated competitive games. The reliability of the numbers generated in these simulations is high, because competitive benchmarking is done continuously. Managers can see the requirements linked to
their proposed decisions: people to be hired or trained, products to be
upgraded, and investments needed—they see it all almost in real time.

Once a model has been approved and what is to be done is known to the decision-making body, it is only a matter of asking, "When will we start?" and "How will we orchestrate it?"

Just Do It!

The classic reason for postponing implementation is *hesitation*. Managers doubt the feasibility of their own plans, they have trouble accepting changes that are proposed by peers or associates, and they question models coming from different industries, even if they are valid and demonstrate a high degree of reliability. How many reports from experts or consultants recommending change end up in desk drawers?

Timing and tempo issues are alive in different ways in different layers of an organization. The best example is the use of PERT charts (timing charts), which adorn the bulletin boards on almost every factory floor. At the blue-collar level, timing and tempo decisions are followed to the letter. The collective performance of an assembly line or production unit is measured, benchmarked, and shown in very visible graphics at the workplace. These charts are known to have positive effects on productivity, team building, and competitive spirit. They improve quality.

As another example, timing and tempo are used by the new sales and marketing departments to plan the effects on sales and profits of an early Easter or a February 29 or a severe winter storm in New York. These are single-day events with multiple-day ripples in the investors' pond. They had little effect on the marketplace in the past, but in today's quarterly performance mode, they make a difference. Any of these three events can influence the sales and profits of the first quarter.

As an individual climbs up the organizational ladder, the notion of timing weakens and tempo is lost. Only if the boss is a real entrepreneur are timing and tempo kept alive and kicking. Hence, success will be rewarded and failure will have its consequences. In the new-age organization, lower management will not have to be told to work with timing and tempo. They will insist on doing it as part of their rollout strategy. They will assume their responsibility of ensuring on-time delivery and then claim the rewards.

For example, if corporate results are loaded on the Internet at 4:00 P.M. on January 2, at that very moment the new-generation kids will say, "Boss,

we did it! We did it better than our competitors! We've made a difference. Thank you for our bonus." This is timing. This is tempo. And this
is emotion.

Communication

The companies that are the first to publish their results, quarterly or annually, capture more of the attention of the financial community. The availability of data on-line will speed up the "what-ifs" of the investment world,
giving the early-bird company a definite advantage. If an organization has
mastered the technique of very short supply cycles, there is no reason why
it cannot provide the same speedy service in providing financial information to shareholders and associates. More important yet, the early availability of results should not be limited to improving investor relations but
should affect operations as well. It should force divisional managers to call
up their spreadsheets and revise their estimates. It is an opportunity to
reconfirm or modify the budgets and adapt the timing and tempo to the
latest sales and production data. This is a healthy form of market-driven
planning.

The Organization: Emotions in
Managing Organizations and People

Freely translated from the books on our shelves, the organization (for profit
or not-for-profit) is defined as a group of individuals (who are remunerated), working in structures (simple or complex) for a common cause
(manufacturing and selling products or providing services), who, under
the proper leadership (the boss), generate a return (payback) to the provider of funds. So what's new? I propose to bring back emotions in managing organizations and people.

Emotions

Emotions are disappearing from our Western corporate culture and are
fading away in most of our organizations. Emotional attachment to products and services is dwindling. Pride in workmanship has taken second place to numerical performance. Excellence in execution is rarely
rewarded.

The Western Way. It is very noticeable in today's financial reports that emotions are overlooked or ignored: the pictures of products are replaced by bar charts or pie charts showing percentages of growth and ratios of all sorts. Only a few years ago, most annual reports gave a vision of the future, a sneak preview of upcoming corporate developments, just enough to create interest and curiosity but not enough to give away the competitive edge. At that time the annual report was a richly illustrated compendium of new products, new sales territories, quality awareness, environmental policy, and employee incentive programs. Today it has been drastically curtailed. We currently live with the one paragraph titled "Expectations" or "Outlook," referring to the short-term outlook. This paragraph is carefully worded by the finance department, reworked by the public relations department, verified by the legal department, and signed by the CEO prior to review and final approval by the board of directors.

Have our leaders become number crunchers who have graduated in the science of noncommittal quarterly public statements and the art of profit sharing for all involved? Annual or quarterly reports are precious communication tools because large audiences as well as groups of professionals look for them at specific times of the year. These publications should be used to generate emotions: feelings of pride, expressions of happiness, and rewards, just to name a few. They must obviously present the correct picture of the state of affairs in the company at that particular time; however, they should go beyond columns and rows of mind-numbing numbers, charts, and ratios.

It takes courage to go beyond the numbers, confronting people and accepting confrontation by others. Let the person *inside* the executive do some of the communicating. Let that person be known as a leader but also as someone who relates to his or her people and the world outside the business. It doesn't hurt the CEO of a food company to be known as a good cook.

The Other Way. Our colleagues of the Pacific Rim practice the art of presenting the company, as we used to do in the past through people and products. The leader is the paterfamilias or materfamilias, the senior member of the corporate family, who is proud of his or her people and products. Reports on the organization show people accepting awards they have won for design or quality achievements. People are shown at work, in training, or at play—the human capital of the organization in all its glory. Of course, their cultures are different. Yes, their markets are booming. Aren't they part of the same global marketplace that we are?

People Management

People management requires more than just upgrading job descriptions, salary scales, and benefit plans. It includes the subtle techniques of observing employees' behavior and recognizing values related to their personalities. In the area of human resources, we have witnessed a steady stream of new management techniques from authors and seminar strategists alike, heralding an abundance of "new" people-oriented programs. We have all seen and heard them: "Managers for the Future," "Managing in Asia," and so on. And we sometimes chuckle. Of course, we learn about the six-day work week in China; the one-week-per-year, company-paid vacation in Japan; the need to provide bicycle racks for employees and to pay wages in cash in Beijing.

However, these statistical lessons are not enough. We must learn to appreciate the *cultural differences* that characterize the people from those other worlds. We must respect their traditions and learn to properly interpret their attitudes. In the next decade, human resource managers will manage attendance, productivity, training, career planning, and remuneration using the most sophisticated computer software ever, resulting in even more numbers, more statistics, and more complex pie charts, all of which create an even greater need to humanize our business lives with emotion. This new style of working will extend beyond the spoken or written word. It will include the interpretation of body language and the use of performance indicators to reward associates based on qualitative as well as quantitative parameters.

It is safe to say that presently, in Europe, growth for most industries is negligible and productivity is below the level of their Asian competitors. The cost of social programs, shorter work weeks, and early retirement have eroded profitability. European managers who will be part of tomorrow's success look for people who care about the *pérénité* (French for "survival") or continuity of their organizations, achieved by promoting pride of products and services, spearheading innovation, and implementing quality management. Some of these "old-fashioned" qualities that were lost in social battles and abandoned completely during the fat years have suddenly made a comeback. The new competition, which comes from the super-low-cost manufacturing countries of the ex–Communist bloc, provided the impetus for Western European organizations to redirect their corporate thinking to dealing with competitive pressure. The call is being answered.

A New Direction for the Organization. As markets mature in other parts of the world and new competitors make an unexpected appearance, corporations must redirect their strategic thinking. Here are some steps to help in that process:

1. *Know your current position.* Before defining any new direction and planning or replanning the future, you need an honest assessment of where you are today. Without that, filling pages on where you are going tomorrow is like jumping in the water from a ten-foot diving board without knowing which way it is pointing, how high it is, or even if the pool has water in it.

2. *Benchmark your achievements against those of the industry.* Benchmarking must be realistic. Too many organizations still compare themselves to themselves. *Our* performance this year is 8 percent over our *performance* last year. Give the maximum bonus to everybody! But what about our industry? If average sales increased by 15 percent, is the maximum bonus for our company still realistic?

3. *Benchmark your long-term plan (LTP).* The third step is to benchmark your approved LTP. Compare your goals for your organization to where you believe others in your industry will be three or four years down the road. Ask these questions:

- If we are successful and achieve all of our LTP goals, where will we stand compared to our competitors?
- Will they have taken a still bigger leap forward?
- Will they have raised the standards of the industry to higher levels?

4. *Will your industry or trade survive in the future?* The number of companies that have disappeared because of a failure to renew their product

assortments or change over to a new industry in time to survive justifies this question.

In general, the educated choices organizations must make for the future are "more of the same" or "more of something different." If we choose "something different," we must define it in terms of the upcoming user demands. Look at marketing from the standpoint of what consumers want and when and where they want it rather than from the traditional angle of "Here is what we have to offer and you will buy it." The consumer and the employee of tomorrow will operate in the "we" mode on Internet forum discussions. They will enjoy the nonstop music of MTV at ear-shattering volumes and surfing through cyberspace in living color on their computers. The new mode is for consumers to say, "Tell me what you have to offer and I'll decide where and when to buy and how to pay for it." Ask yourself these questions:

- Can your organization produce the impulses that make these surfers buy your products or services?

- Do you communicate at high volume, with loud bass, and using psychedelic colors?

- Is your organization ready for payments via telephone or cable TV? Can customers access and communicate with your data base?

- Does your organization have a site on the Internet?

- Are your product catalog and your annual report part of your Internet site? Are your data supplied in read-only form or are they formatted for spreadsheet work?

These and many more of tomorrow's consumer demands fall far outside the operational boundaries of today's senior executives. Their education, their experience, and their emotional attachments are not a part of cyberspace. Will they be flexible enough to understand the future? Have we all accepted the fact that half of the world is *younger*, either exposed to computers or already computer-literate? Do we know and appreciate the psychedelic colors and images racing through cyberspace? Have we recognized that our junior managers are operating in the virtual mode with no speed limits, modifying timing and tempo with different algorithms? It is *their* world. We (you) may just have been outdistanced.

Why not use our people management talents and allow our young executives, men and women, to lead the way. Let them prepare the plans. Let them set the parameters. Ask them to supply the input to map the future. Using their vision, new hardware, and state-of-the-art software, the leaders of today can then design an organization that can manage two generations of employees who are performing together: the seasoned executives and the data-base kids.

Change. To win the new race, we definitely need a new racing car and a new driver. A totally different person sitting in a computerized cockpit. A racing car that corners by remote computer controls. Computers setting and resetting the suspension, time and time again, in each corner until the race is won. Continuously managed change. The "not invented here" attitude, particularly at the executive level, is a well-known phenomenon that is far from disappearing. How often do older executives hide behind the statement that they are "proceeding with great care"? Are they afraid to change? This is no longer acceptable. Emotion in business, as recommended here, would require these executives to voice their objections and speak their mind. If not understanding a new technology is the problem, they should say so. Another favorite defense, "prudence in tumultuous times," further illustrates the generation gap. What may look like a hurricane to the older executive may be the ideal surfing wind for the younger manager.

Leaders of the new organizations must upgrade their own knowledge, acquire the new skills, and surround themselves with new blood. Conversion is possible. Middle-aged managers do realize that they must reschool to master new vehicles. The time of extensive training and retooling is here now. Academic institutions are ready for the task. Mixing Eastern and Western technology and cultures is no longer a problem. It is all part of managing people in a mixture of cultural environments. But it does mean changing from the comfortable position of the single markets in which we have grown up.

Organizational Structure and Governance. Emotions, timing, and tempo, fully integrated in the change process, will result in creating delay-ered organizational structures with great flexibility capable of rapid action and reaction. Organizations will be structured differently according to the markets they serve: consumer markets, business to business, entertainment, and service. They will provide stakeholders with ample data using information networks in real time. Shareholders will have a stronger representation on the boards of larger organizations. Management will be remunerated based on performance.

Lifestyle Issues. The future belongs to the (very) young who swim at age three and who at four or five learn to read and write on the computer instead of on paper or blackboards. Their teenaged brothers and sisters download their homework from the Internet. These young adults order products and pay their bills electronically while their parents struggle with the remote control of their VCR and still read newspapers and magazines. There is the gap. Three totally different generations living, learning, and working together at different speeds and different tempos. Consumers will be information-hungry, quality-conscious, and in search of bargains. Their knowledge of products and services will result from browsing electronic networks. They will select products and services from a broad global offering in the market. The data, pictures of the products, and videos illustrating their recommended use will be available instantly on the information superhighway.

Conclusion

The winning organization is one that manages people of different backgrounds, genders, and social positions, customers and employees alike, using global and multicultural management techniques in a harmonious mix of qualitative and quantitative tools. Style will be subjected to continuous changes in both substance and form. What a challenge for those of us who have the desire and the talent to design these flexible organizations. What a thrill for the courageous few who will be the first to bring them to life. What a privilege to work with well-informed, decisive people.

29 JOHN ALEXANDER
MEENA S. WILSON

Leading Across Cultures

Five Vital Capabilities

*John Alexander is vice president for communications at the
Center for Creative Leadership. Before joining the center, he
worked for more than two decades as a newspaper editor and
columnist. He is a frequent speaker at conferences and workshops
focused on leadership and serves on several nonprofit boards. He
is coauthor of* Ribbon of Sand: The Amazing Convergence of
the Ocean and the Outer Banks. *Meena S. Wilson is a research
associate at the Center for Creative Leadership. She is the lead
author of* Managing Across Cultures: A Learning Framework.
*Her research focuses on global leadership and intercultural value
differences. A native of India and former resident of Alaska,
Wilson's previous work experience includes designing programs
that foster personal development. She serves on the American
Society for Training and Development Research Committee.*

That much of the world is migrating toward an increasingly global
society is indisputable. Especially in the economic arena, major barriers have come tumbling down. New regional trading partnerships, such as
the North American Free Trade Agreement (NAFTA) and Asia Pacific

Note: We would like to thank the following colleagues at the Center for Creative Leadership for their assistance in preparing this chapter: Jerry Brightman, Maxine Dalton, Bill
Drath, Michael Hoppe, Jean Leslie, Joan Tavares, and Ellen Van Velsor.

Economic Cooperation (APEC), have emerged. Propelled by new information and communication technologies, multinational corporations have moved aggressively to offer their products and services worldwide. But if the trend toward globalization is a reality, it is not a panacea. Although the scramble for new corporate markets can boost standards of living in host countries, it can sometimes be the cause of, as well as the cure for, vexing problems such as environmental degradation, illegal immigration, and economic dislocation. Millions of global citizens still cannot partake of the fruits of the economic and information revolutions. And even in the industrialized world, anxieties caused by corporate downsizings, prolonged economic recessions, clogged governments, and—especially in the United States—a diminishing sense of family and community values have fueled new debate.

Exercising leadership in this demanding environment calls for new capacities in many leaders and new thinking about their organizations. Our focus in this chapter is on those leaders, and on how they and their organizations can perform more effectively in transnational settings. We know that managing across cultural, geographic, and national boundaries is hard work. Recent studies have shown that anywhere from 20 to 50 percent of U.S. managers fail in overseas assignments. The cost of that failure is high, an estimated $250,000 in each instance, according to one study, and that does not measure the impact of failed assignments on the families and careers of those people or the cost of training and relocating their replacements. Many attempts to establish operations in other countries fail or do not achieve the desired results.

It is not as though we lack clues about the characteristics of these boundary-spanning leaders. They go to work in countries around the world each day. They move back and forth across borders and cultural boundaries with ease. They create alliances and make friends. They get results. As one Chinese-born lawyer practicing in the United States recently told us, she can identify almost immediately the individuals who will succeed in the international business negotiations they conduct, and she can also predict those who will fail, because they cannot bridge the cultural differences between themselves and the people with whom they are negotiating. Why do some leaders succeed where others fail? Specifically, what blend of capacities and knowledge does it take to lead effectively across boundaries; how can those capacities be identified, learned, and transferred to others; and how might they contribute to originating newly configured organizations and alliances that will be capable of responding to a fast-changing external environment?

First, a cautionary note: the concept of leadership itself is fraught with cultural meaning. Though leaders have been extolled and examined for centuries, the study of leadership as a separate enterprise is relatively new. Perhaps for reasons of culture and history, the fascination with leadership has been peculiarly American—the idea of emergent or trained leaders, rather than monarchs, pharaohs, or nobility, has accompanied the rise of modern democracy. Some cultures have no corresponding word for *leader* or *leadership*. In others, the word *leader* bears a very negative connotation, because it conjures up the dictators who brought misery and suffering to millions during much of this century. An awareness of the different meanings attached to this concept is important in discussing leadership across cultures.

At the Center for Creative Leadership, both our research and our experience in working with thousands of executives from diverse organizations over the past twenty years have identified a number of generic capacities or competencies associated with effective leadership. One of the most enduring of these, not surprisingly, is a high degree of technical skill, a knowledge of how to run the business. But just as enduring are the capacities that spring from self-understanding and the ability to work with others. These less quantifiable capacities, which emerge over and over again, are the ones we choose to explore, because they hold important clues to leading across cultures. They include the following four core attributes:

1. *Heightened self-awareness*. A comprehensive understanding of one's strengths and weaknesses, how they are perceived by others, and how they affect others is essential. The effect is one of holding up a series of mirrors to see ourselves as others see us. This self-knowledge can enable the leader to change behaviors that impede effectiveness, reinforce behaviors that improve it, and devise a plan for personal growth and development that can be carried out over a period of months or years. Only when senior leaders first understand and go through their own personal transitions can they effectively lead their organizations through change.

2. *The habit of inviting feedback.* It is through the encouragement of candid but constructive feedback from others—boss, peers, and direct reports—that leaders develop the self-awareness that can become the basis for personal change and action. This feedback is usually, though not always, acquired through the use of multirater feedback instruments that are filled out by the individual and others and that have been carefully validated for accuracy and consistency with respect to their intended use.

The ability to give and receive feedback is a difficult skill to acquire and use successfully, but it is a powerful tool for helping individuals develop to their full potential as leaders, because it helps them to identify strengths and weaknesses of which they may not be aware. These strengths and weaknesses can have a correspondingly positive and negative impact on the productivity of the organizations being led. Feedback can also be used as an active, hands-on tool to improve group behavior and teamwork; it does not have to be confined to one-on-one relationships. Leaders who are artful in these wider uses of feedback can help individuals and groups to better understand their own hidden assets and thereby to render what is invisible visible and what may not seem attainable quite tangible. Such leaders straddle that elusive gap between what is and what could be. This is a rare quality, but one that may well define the successful leader—and organization—of the future.

3. *A thirst for learning.* Receptiveness to new knowledge, and the willingness to change one's perspectives and behaviors based on it, can be critical. Our research has found that on-the-job experience is the best teacher. The challenge is to learn how to learn from that experience consistently, and to adjust one's behaviors accordingly.

A passion for learning is also linked to creativity, and to the ability to frame new perspectives—to think about things in new ways. A rich learning environment creates a safe space in which people can be playful, can try out new ideas and behaviors, and can peer through new lenses—or through old ones in a different way. These dramatically altered perspectives help the leader to create meaning out of highly chaotic or ambiguous situations. Leadership as the making of meaning is a powerful concept, especially when that meaning is shared and understood by a wider community.

4. *Work-life integration.* Leading and living are intimately connected, because effective leaders must have a strong sense of themselves as whole

individuals, not simply as people who are defined by their career or job status. There is no neat divide between home and work today. The demands of family and community must be balanced—or, perhaps more accurately, integrated—with the demands of work. This does not translate into shorter hours on the job, which would be an unrealistic goal for most leaders. It does mean that to be authentic, the leader must try to be comfortable in all of these contexts and to align them, because they all draw from the same deep reservoir of personal values.

The leader has to find an oasis to which he or she can repair to be replenished, personally and spiritually. The oasis may be different for different people, but it exists, and it is the source of the leader's personal strength and stability in times of ambiguity and change. This alignment of personal and work life also generates feelings of authenticity and trust that many people seek in their leaders; it can create enthusiasm and a shared sense of purpose in the organizations or communities to which they belong.

These are core concepts of leadership development and training in many Center for Creative Leadership programs. They are learned and applied each year in hundreds of organizations, primarily in the United States. But how universal are they? How well do they apply in cultures where concepts of self-awareness, feedback, learning, and work-life integration may have very different meanings and applications? For example, our colleagues in France had to coin the phrase "le feedback" because the use of multirater feedback for personal development in European organizations is still in its infancy.

To what extent are these concepts more narrowly rooted in the American tradition of optimism and individualism, the notion that people can improve themselves and their lives through hard work and that steady progress along this path will yield a more productive and happier person? To what degree does the concept of a self-aware, self-developing leader make sense in a culture where the norms of the group are used to subdue individualism or in a culture where styles of learning support the authority of the teacher more than the experiences of the learner or where beliefs about the meaning and purpose of work itself may be different?

Consider, for example, the case of the U.S. human resource manager of a global pharmaceutical company who was assigned to the Far East. He discovered, to his surprise, that his biggest challenge was to persuade his company's managers from China, Malaysia, Taiwan, and Korea to accept promotions. They did not wish to compete with their peers for career rewards or personal gain, nor did they wish to break their ties to their communities in order to assume cross-national responsibilities.

We believe that these core leadership attributes do have meaning and application in other cultures. But, as in all things cultural, they require translation and reframing. Self-awareness, for example, is honored in many different societies, but the motivation for it may vary widely. Self-awareness in a Western culture may serve as a springboard for individual development, whereas in an Eastern culture it may be more an end in itself or a route to a higher spiritual plane. Feedback as a tool for self-awareness or behavioral change is not unknown; in some cultures, it simply may be confined to family or school settings, rather than the workplace. Learning is also respected in most societies, but often for different reasons and in divergent ways. Strategies for learning differ. For example, some societies encourage learning through mentors or gurus and emphasize the personal relationship between the teacher and learner; others stress learning through textbooks.

Further, the concept of balance between work and family can vary, depending on the centrality of work to individual identity. In the United States, where jobs and career occupy a central role, laid-off workers consistently report a feeling of having been fundamentally violated, of having lost a vital part of themselves. In some cultures, however, people do not define themselves by their work or job status, or they blend work into the larger rhythms of life such as family relations, child rearing, and religious observances. War-torn societies provide few incentives to work hard because no meaningful connection exists between hard work and individual or social progress.

The global leader should be able to understand, accommodate, and synthesize these perspectives, no easy task when cultural barriers work against synthesis. In effect, the leader must be not only a learner but also someone who can learn how others from different cultures learn. Therefore, we propose to add a fifth ingredient of effective leadership:

5. *Respect for differences in others.* In order to be effective in the emerging global environment, the global leader must be aware of, and sensitive

to, dramatically different people and situations. By this we mean more than sensitivity to differences of language, customs, and culture, which is certainly important in itself. We mean an ability to find complementarity and synthesis of radically different points of view, and to give voice to the other person's perspectives and values. This skill, in many ways, is universally applicable. It is needed in cross-cultural situations but also in any situation in which divergent points of view are typically expressed or acted out, in business, politics and government, or community settings. It also integrates the other leadership skills we have outlined: self-awareness, feedback, learning, and balance. All of these skills, working harmoniously together, help the leader to take action in situations where different perspectives need to be mediated or merged. In taking action, the leader gives voice to various perspectives and honors them, fostering an inclusiveness that transcends parochialism yet does not stifle differences.

Examples of this phenomenon abound. Action-oriented U.S. managers on international assignments often find themselves blocked until they begin to exhibit a receptivity to their host culture. As one such manager told us, "Unbelievable value comes from nonbusiness discussions. There are points of view out there that are valid that don't match up with the way you see the world. Your sensitivity increases and then team membership becomes possible." Or, as another manager said, "You have to put your own culture aside and be willing to prepare yourself to accept what you are going to be confronted with."

It took a young Peace Corps volunteer, a teacher in central Panama, four months to begin to understand why he had made no progress in the classroom or in building relationships with local people. "Somewhere in the back of my mind I realized that a different set of rules existed here, but I couldn't figure out what they were," he later wrote. Only when he realized that teachers in Panama gain respect when they act as authority figures did the wall of separation begin to come down. The more he played the role of expert, rather than that of friend or counselor, the more he gained his students' respect and ultimately their trust and friendship. After a full year at the school, he wrote, "I was not Panamanian but had become assimilated into the culture to the point where I could function successfully. My differentness became an asset as long as I stayed within certain culturally defined parameters."

That is the most difficult lesson of all for the boundary-spanning manager or leader. Such leaders need three things. They must first have a firm understanding of their own culture and how it is likely to be viewed by others. They must then have a strong sense of their place within their culture of origin and know whether their personal values represent or run counter to their home culture. Finally, they must be able to see the world from the perspective of the different culture in which they are operating without losing their own cultural moorings. This sense of being anchored while moving is akin to the technique of the ballet dancer who keeps his or her eyes concentrated on one spot while whirling in place. Such skill can be breathtaking.

We see the capacities of the global leader and the leader of the future as one and the same. Even if the leader does not operate directly in an international setting, she or he must be able to reconcile differences and assume a global perspective that transcends parochial boundaries. If the workplace of the future is certain to have one characteristic, in addition to constant change, it is its widely divergent points of view. John W. Gardner recently wrote in *National Renewal*, a joint publication of Independent Sector and the National Civic League, "As one surveys the world scene today, one is driven to believe that wholeness incorporating diversity is the transcendent goal of our time, the task for our generation at home and worldwide."

And what of the organization of the future? Need we add that the truly productive organization of the future will create a climate in which the leadership capacities we have outlined are consistently nourished? These organizations will undoubtedly take many different shapes—flat, virtual, team-based, centralized, dispersed, large, small—but the exact form does not matter. What matters is not only that self-awareness, feedback, learning, work-life integration, and respect for differences are encouraged but also that opportunities to develop these capacities through such channels as training programs, mentoring, and developmental job assignments become an integral part of the organizational culture. From these organizations will spring the new generation of global leaders.

30 DIANA CHAPMAN WALSH

Cultivating Inner Resources for Leadership

Diana Chapman Walsh is president of Wellesley College. A leading expert in public health policy and the prevention of illness, she most recently was Florence Sprague Norman and Laura Smart Norman Professor at the Harvard School of Public Health, where she chaired the Department of Health and Social Behavior. Prior to joining Harvard, she was at Boston University as a University Professor and as a professor of social and behavioral sciences in the School of Public Health. She has written, edited, and coedited twelve books, including a study of the practice of medicine within corporations, Corporate Physicians: Between Medicine and Management.

I want to tackle what I'll call the "inner work of leadership," an aspect of being a leader that is essential for success, but one about which far less is written than is available on strategic and tactical considerations in the leader's external world of power and relationships. I'd like to reflect on things a leader can (and, I would venture, should) be doing or trying to do, even while she or he is managing the relentless demands of running an organization or other enterprise, in order to continue growing and developing a sense of self that is deeper and more fully rounded, more firmly grounded, more at peace, and increasingly trusting of her or his own intuition, imagination, and inner resourcefulness. The great Irish poet, William Butler Yeats, said that life "is a mystery to be lived, not a problem to be solved." This chapter focuses on the challenge of living the interior mysteries of leadership, while still managing to get on with exterior life.

My inspiration on these questions comes partly from an essay titled *Leading from Within,* by Parker J. Palmer, a well-known speaker and consultant in higher education. He begins with the 1990 address by Vaclav Havel, president of the newly declared Czech Republic, to the U.S. Congress and pivots off two of Havel's key points: that "consciousness precedes being" and that "the salvation of the world lies in the human heart." From these two points, Palmer infers that we all share responsibility "for creating the external world by projecting either a spirit of light or a spirit of shadow on that which is 'other' than us." We can approach the world with a spirit of hope or one of despair: "We have a choice, and in that choice we create the world that is."

Such choices should weigh especially heavily for leaders who, by virtue of their position, have an unusual degree of power to project shadow or light on other people, to create worlds for others that are filled with hope or with despair. All leaders, then, have a special duty to attend to what goes on inside themselves, "lest the act of leadership create more harm than good." Parker Palmer's ideas here resonate with the writings of Max DePree, one of whose precepts is that good leaders absorb pain rather than inflicting it, and with those of Warren Bennis, who has observed that truly effective leaders have set out not so much to be leaders as to fully express themselves. They are people who accept responsibility and do not blame others, people who are learners and seekers of self-knowledge.

In Palmer's essay, the "shadow side of leaders" refers to the harm they can do when they operate without awareness or consciousness of the ways in which they are projecting onto the external world the fears, insecurities, and self-delusions that they have lacked the courage or the skill to confront internally. He enumerates five ways in which leaders who aren't leading from within can project their unexamined shadows on individuals, on organizations, and on the larger society.

Leaders who are insecure about their own identity and self-worth create institutional settings that deprive other people of their identities. They tend to perceive the universe as essentially hostile and life as a competitive battleground. They believe and act as though ultimate responsibility for everything rests with them. Fearing "the natural chaos of life," they impose rigid rules and attempts at control. Finally, their fear of negative evaluation and public failure (a "denial of death") keeps projects and programs on life support systems long after they are moribund.

The release that comes from all the great spiritual traditions, Parker Palmer reminds us, is that those who find self-knowledge and inner wisdom need not be afraid. This does not mean that they cannot or will not have fears (they will), but they need not *be* their fears, need not create worlds in which those fears dominate their lives and affect the working or living conditions of many others. People who ascend to leadership positions usually function especially well in the outside world. They are skilled at reading the environment and adapting to it, and they often go through life with a deeply divided self. Leading from within means finding a unity between one's carefully crafted, successful outward self and one's cautiously hidden inner shadow self.

Now, you may wonder, what does any of this have to do with being president of Wellesley College? Little less, I believe, than everything. My challenge as the leader of a great institution of higher learning—one dedicated to providing an exceptional liberal arts education for women who will make a difference in the world—is to do everything I can to hold open a space in which a community of growth and self-discovery can flourish for everyone. The president of a college or university is constantly beset and besieged by a cacophony of competing claims for resources, attention, and validation. Unlike an organization whose function is to produce a particular product as efficiently and effectively as possible, a college is committed to teaching and learning. In education, the process is inextricably bound up with the product. Learning is nothing if not a process of discovery and unfolding.

As a result, how we do our work at a place like Wellesley College— where we put our emphasis and what values we embody and express—is fully as important as the outcomes we actually seek to produce. We teach as much by the example of what we do and how we do it as by what our professors actually profess in the classroom. We teach a silent curriculum that is not detailed in the catalog. This is a humbling realization for an organization that, like any human arrangement, has imperfections and gaps between what it says (expressed aspirations) and what it does (the lived reality). I am constantly being called to account by students, faculty, staff, alumnae, and even strangers for lacunae they see between what they think we ought to be and what they think we are. And those gaps matter if we are serious (and we are) about protecting a process that has integrity and legitimacy. Every college president faces this challenge, every single day.

The good news is that human creativity arises in just this gap between vision and reality, in the disquieting but galvanizing structural tension we experience between where we are and where we aspire to be. Holding that tension in active consciousness is the first step in the creative act. Creativity is stifled when we paper over the tension with self-delusion about where we are or, conversely, when we lower our ambitions rather than tolerating the tension. Creativity requires the confidence to grant what we may not know and the courage to look failure in the face. "It is necessary to any originality," Wallace Stevens wrote, "to have the courage to be an amateur."

If we in higher education are serious about this business of teaching and learning together, then one of the most important tests we shall always face is how we deal with our imperfections, vulnerabilities, and inevitable mistakes—whether we seize on them as learning opportunities without which we will never stretch and grow to our full capacity, whether we support one another in that sometimes painful process of self-discovery and growth, or whether we allow ourselves to be so chary of the anticipated humiliation of criticism and failure that we avoid the risks altogether and hold ourselves back from exploration, from creation, from self-invention.

The courage to learn, it seems to me, is among the most pressing challenges we all share as students, as teachers, and as workers; in our families, communities, organizations, and other social enterprises; and, most profoundly, as human beings whose nature it is to seek to know ourselves in all our messy complexity and whose life task it is to keep adapting to ever-changing circumstances. At a time of enormous confusion and conflict around the world—a time of mounting tribalism and ethnic hostilities—residential liberal arts colleges are among the few places in our society where people from diverse backgrounds are coming together and trying to find ways to live in peace and learn from each other. They are engaged in vitally important work, delicate, sometimes painful, sometimes even explosive work, but work, I think we can say without too much hyperbole, that we as a species must do, and do well, if we are to ensure our safe passage into the twenty-first century.

This delicate community-building work will not be done well in the absence of the inner work of self-discovery. People of diverse backgrounds cannot come together and suspend their suspicions and hostilities, cannot let down their guard to learn from one another, until they are secure enough in their own identities so that they do not have to risk everything to open themselves to others. On our college campuses, we can create safe places for these learning encounters to occur—cautiously, haltingly, and, we hope, with progressively more confidence and skill. That is what is unique, and uniquely important, about a residential learning community.

What makes these efforts so important for the larger society is that we hope the young people who do this hard work during their college years will go out into the world and will work to transform it in important ways, taking responsibility for the contexts in which they find themselves in workplaces, families, and communities. We hope that our graduates will not adapt to dehumanizing environments or blindly accept the kinds of destructive mores that Parker Palmer enumerates, but will continue to undertake the hard work of confronting their own interior demons and acting with courage and conviction in the exterior world.

In my travels around the country I have had many heartening and moving conversations along these lines with our young graduates. Many of them are quite eloquent about what they have carried from their Wellesley experience into the world: an unshakable confidence that what they have to say is worth saying and worth hearing, irrespective of negative signals they may be getting from the environment, and an inner conviction, cultivated at college, about their own self-worth as women. What I see in them is access to an inner teacher, an inner wisdom, an inner voice that will be an extraordinary resource for them throughout their lives.

So much of leadership in our society is radically cut off from any inner voice. So much of leadership emphasizes form over content and style over substance. It trades on simplistic, cynical notions about how to lead: through manipulation, bullying tactics, slickness, hollow rhetoric, image management, spin doctoring, sound bites. These manipulations are devices on which leaders seize out of a need to paper over their unexamined fear of exposure, isolation, or rejection. They create unhealthy organizations in which no one can be free. It is for these reasons that ideas about leading from within are, in my view, exceptionally important for the kind of future we will choose to have. How do we go about doing this inner work?

We begin, I believe, with a profound, patient, and reverential respect for our own lifelong process of unfolding. The work requires attention, commitment, and discipline, but of a gentle, loving, forgiving sort. It means living our questions (as the poet Rainer Maria Rilke advised) calmly and with deep trust in our own inner wisdom and judgment.

Let me conclude with a short list of things I try to do, habits and disciplines I try to cultivate (not always successfully) to maintain a sense of balance and wholeness in my busy life.

First, I make a conscious decision to nurture my own identity and integrity. I try to resist the projections others place on me (usually out of their own need for me to be a certain kind of leader: decisive, strong, or visionary, for example). I try to stay grounded in who I am, what I bring to my work, and what is mine to give, and to separate that from the office I occupy. I try to stay in touch with who I will be when I'm no longer the Wellesley president, to remember who I was before I embarked on this adventure.

Second, I try to carve out time to connect and reconnect with an inner truth. Gandhi advised regularly asking oneself this provocative question: "What have I done today that expresses my truth?" Notice that his question is not "How have I advanced my goals?" but "How have I connected to a deeply rooted inner truth?" I try to find time every day to spend alone with myself, often while I am out running in the morning, and to use that solitude as a time of personal renewal. I don't always succeed at fending off the worries and projects of the day, but I do try. I also write in a journal when I have time or the need to work something out.

Third, I try, as well, to make opportunities to come together in community with people who bring out my better self, friends with whom I can be calm, courageous, and authentic. Being authentic fundamentally means being one's own author. I'm blessed with a number of friends who play this role for me. I make it a point to connect, whenever possible, with old friends with whom I have a history of shared joy and shared pain and to cultivate new friends who, for whatever reasons, call forth in me this feeling of safety. I find that the observations of friends who know me well and who care about me as a person—sometimes even offhand observations in a rambling conversation—can send me down a path toward a fundamentally new insight about myself, and often it is one that has a kind of healing quality.

Fourth, I try to draw on the resources of various wisdom traditions. I confess that I am a bit eclectic and experimental where organized religion is concerned. I was raised in the tradition of the Society of Friends—the Quakers—and have enjoyed Friends' meetings at various times in my life. But I've also tried forms of mindful meditation and have found them valuable, depending on the particular pressures and needs I'm experiencing. What I find remarkable and reassuring in sampling various wisdom traditions is not only how much wisdom their stories convey, but the commonalities that emerge from them and speak to the bonds of humanity that unite us all.

Fifth, I try to deal as well as I can with feedback, which is hard. Evaluation is one of the thorniest problems in the business of teaching and learning—and of managing. Few of us give or receive feedback honestly and well, despite the many management rules and protocols on the subject. The truth is that it is always painful to come into awareness of our mistakes, limitations, and deficiencies, even if the news is delivered in the most constructive and sensitive way. There is no birth of consciousness, Jung said, without pain. Discomfort and denial are part of the challenge, then. In addition, effective feedback requires attention to a subtle but important balancing act. An intensive and relentless self-improvement project that is focused on deficits and flaws and that dwells on mistakes can mask the reality that our mistakes often result from an overreliance on our most precious assets, skills, and gifts. I try to be conscious of how my behavior affects other people and to minimize any damage, but I also try not to dwell too much on my flaws and mistakes without recognizing and protecting my compensating gifts. I don't always succeed at this, but I consider it important.

Sixth, I try to remember to allow myself to take in the affirmation—the love—that comes my way, to feel the relief and gratitude of connectedness to others. The need to be aware of this came to me first as an insight from a friend who saw something in me of which he was becoming conscious in himself. At a meeting one day, he slipped me a note that simply said, "Take it in." I wasn't sure what he meant at the time, but I am now. I try to stop and let myself feel satisfaction, gratitude, and affection before I rush off to the next encounter. I am not always successful at that either, but when I am, I certainly feel better.

Seventh, I try to be attuned to the cycles of life, to give myself permission to be somewhere in a cycle and not to fight it too hard. Mary Catherine Bateson, in her book *Composing a Life*, observes that women's lives are more cyclical than men's, even just biologically. We have cycles of growth and of consolidation, cycles of celebration, of mourning, and of loss. We can honor those parts of us that are falling away even as we grow in new directions.

Eighth, and finally, I try to be my own good teacher. Great teachers are challenging, caring, inspiring, alert to their students' intellectual travails, attuned to their inner conditions. It's interesting to wonder what it would mean to be that kind of teacher to oneself. Or one's own good parent, or one's own good supervisor, if that is what one does well. Good teachers, good parents, good supervisors listen intently for what is being spoken and what is still unspeakable, ask probing questions that open avenues to self-awareness, strike a careful balance between nurturing and challenging, and always encourage and support deep reflection on experience. I believe that we can be good teachers to ourselves, and to one another, as we work to discover new and healthier possibilities for deploying our power in ways that cast more light than shadow. We often hear what a difficult time it is now to be a successful leader—and it surely is—but it is an exciting time as well, a time of possibility and promise in an era of profound change.

31 ROBERT H. ROSEN

Learning to Lead

Robert H. Rosen is founder and president of Healthy Companies Institute, a not-for-profit organization promoting a new vision of organizational health as the key to America's social and economic success. Since 1984, he has held the position of assistant clinical professor of psychiatry and behavioral sciences at the George Washington University School of Medicine. He is a principal in the Healthy Companies Group, a national consulting group committed to building healthy, successful enterprises. Rosen is the author of The Healthy Company: Eight Strategies to Develop People, Productivity, and Profits *and* Leading People: Transforming Business from the Inside Out.

Leading profitable, responsible organizations is difficult these days. We live in a time of chaos and complexity, full of breathtaking technological advances and international competition. Our workforces grow more diverse every day and our attitudes about work are constantly changing. Customers are demanding better, cheaper, and faster service. And just when you think you've got it down, another change comes spinning around the corner. Everyone is operating in the new "knowledge economy," where

Note: Portions of this chapter appear in *Leading People: Transforming Business from the Inside Out,* by Robert H. Rosen (Viking Penguin, 1996). Reprinted with permission.

people are the intellectual assets that make things happen and the costs of mismanaging them can be disastrous. Success goes to companies whose leaders mobilize their people and unleash their competence, creativity, and commitments.

Over the past five years, American businesses have undergone massive changes—reengineering, retooling, and restructuring. Many of our companies are now strong, lean, efficient organizations. Yet under the surface of these short-term profits, companies may be emotionally volatile and vulnerable; mistrust and cynicism are at an all-time high as tensions simmer between leaders and followers.

Americans are hungry for new leaders, emotionally intelligent leaders with vision and character who can guide their downsized organizations back to health and high performance. I have spent the last fifteen years studying and advising leaders from all walks of life, and I believe that the leadership mind that brought us managed costs and reengineering is not the leadership mind that will mobilize people and build healthy, profitable businesses for the twenty-first century. Here are some of the lessons I have learned from working with leaders and their organizations as they struggle through the difficult challenges of leading people.

Understand Yourself at a Deeper Level

Learning to lead starts with getting to know yourself. You must first dig deep and get your own house in order before you can lead others. Each of us carries emotional baggage around from childhood. What mental models do you hold about yourself and others? What are your greatest fears and most vivid aspirations? In what ways do you sabotage these aspirations? What values and principles really matter to you? You will want to bring these thoughts to the surface to understand how they influence your day-to-day behavior.

We also carry a picture in our mind of what we consider to be an ideally healthy leader. Which principles are your strengths and which are your shortcomings? How are they reflected in your words and actions? You will want to strengthen your leading capabilities by understanding yourself at a deeper level and closing the gap between your ideal and your current performance.

Practice Positive One-on-One Relationships

Numbers are easy. It's relationships that are hard. Relationships are messy. People are always bumping up against one another. It is critical that you become agile in managing the space between people. The best leaders build relationships one at a time. You can start by understanding your external self, the part of you that people see on a daily basis. Ask yourself these questions:

- What is your basic demeanor and operating style?
- What do people typically like and dislike about your personality?
- How comfortable are you with interpersonal relationships?
- Are you authentic and honest with others?
- Can you make demands on people and do you keep your commitments?
- Are you caring and respectful of others?
- How comfortable are you with the dark side of relationships—the side that's full of conflict, competitiveness, anxiety, resentment, and self-interest?
- Do you react differently with different groups of people?

Examining your relationships is an excellent way to assess your ability to lead. Some of us interact positively with certain types of people. Others know the right way to act but lack the necessary interpersonal skills. Still others deal badly with crises, and we all know people who are simply blind to their own shadows. Where do you stand on this continuum? The best way to improve your relationship skills is to find people to practice with. Ask them for feedback and listen carefully to what they have to say.

Develop a Diverse Leadership Team

It is now time to build a leadership team. The most successful organizations develop a strong, diverse team at the top. This is important because no one person can master all the necessary leadership skills. The team will always be stronger if diverse talents are sitting around the table. Your job as the leader is to identify and leverage those differing talents into a whole that is greater than the sum of its parts.

The first step is to assess the team's strengths and weaknesses. The key is to capitalize on people's strengths and manage around their weaknesses. This requires you to understand your team members as well as yourself. Each person must be viewed as a complex human being with unique values, aspirations, and motivations. Each has his or her own temperament, learning style, prejudices, and resistances. Knowing people at a deeper level will help you to navigate through the inevitable complexities of team dynamics and organizational life.

Diagnose the Health of Your Organization

To build a high-performance company, you must assess the current health of your organization. Does it operate like a muscular, aerobically fit athlete or a vitamin-deficient, homebound anorexic? Are your employees, customers, and shareholders undermining each other, or do they work well together as a balanced team? The key is to examine the gaps between your vision and your current performance. The best way to do this is by assessing your company's strengths, weaknesses, threats, opportunities, and areas for improvement. Use a combination of interviews, focus groups, audits, and surveys. Analyze your work environment to see whether its values, policies, systems, and structures are aligned with your vision. Conduct a survey of your stakeholders to identify their satisfactions and concerns. Conduct an employee survey and follow it up with interviews so you can feel the very pulse of your organization.

As you assess the health of your organization, you will appreciate the multiple causes of business problems and solutions, and the fact that everything operates as one system. The health of this system has a direct effect on employee commitment and performance and, ultimately, on the company's success.

Build a Mature, Adult Workforce

Traditionally, we have underestimated the extent to which the new workplace requires a very different kind of adult employee-partner. Just as leaders must reinvent themselves, so must the people following their lead. Everyone must share the responsibilities for an organization's success.

Leaders must first paint a picture of the ideal employee. The best candidates are mature, principle-driven, adult partners who are hard-working team players and who are committed to their own development. Here is a list of responsibilities we have found to be important in employees:

- They listen well, respect the confidence of information, and communicate with honest dialogue.

- They contribute ideas, take responsibility for decisions, search for new and better ways to work, and assume leading roles.

- They understand the mind of the customer, see their role in the customer chain, and anticipate and meet customers' needs.

- They commit to lifelong learning, share knowledge, learn from mistakes, and develop multiple competencies.

- They bring their unique beliefs, talents, and experiences to the workplace, work effectively with the prevailing culture, value the differences and uniqueness of others, and censure discrimination and prejudice.

- They observe the policies and practices of the organization and share responsibility for improving work relations.

- They give full value in their work, understand and support the company's goals, and accept the organization's multiple stakeholders.

- They share commitments and burdens and recognize that individual security is directly linked to the long-term success of the organization.

- They adapt to new technologies, learn how to use new tools, and support innovation and technological changes.

- They take personal health seriously, observe safety rules, share the cost of managing health and illness, and actively seek optimum fitness for work.

- They strive to achieve high levels of quality, ethical behavior, and customer satisfaction.

- They actively seek to balance their commitment to work, family, and personal needs.

- They share public responsibilities as active citizens, environmental stewards, and volunteers for social good.

Create a Culture of Leaders

Today, the world is too complicated, change is too swift, and the issues are too technical to expect any leader or team of leaders to solve every problem. That is why the best organizations create a culture of leaders. The goal is to build a stronger capacity for leading at all levels in the organization. The first step is to develop an organizationwide process for assessing these leaders. This is done best by assessing strengths and shortcomings, then developing feedback systems so that the employees can learn how well they are performing. Feedback should come from all directions—top management, team members, and customers—and in all forms.

Next, an organizationwide leadership development program should be developed to help each leader learn and grow. Each leader should have a developmental plan based on the feedback systems and have access to a full program of education and coaching. The goal is to develop a rich pool of leaders, at all levels, who will be change agents inside the company.

Build a Healthy, High-Performance Organization

Your ultimate challenge is to build a healthy, successful enterprise, one that is values-based and vision-driven internally and customer-based and market-driven externally. You are the chief people officer in the firm, and people are the leading indicators inside your business. How they are led, and the environment you create, will predict what happens to the business over the long term.

Your goal is to strengthen your organization's capability—to increase the competence, commitment, and creativity of your people. This will require a top-down, bottom-up strategy. It will require managing costs and developing assets at the same time. And it will require transforming your culture until your leading principles are reflected and reinforced in the policies, practices, and systems of your organization. Ask these questions:

- Do leaders walk their talk?
- Do they use them to guide the way they lead and work?
- Are the leading principles used in deciding how people are recruited, valued, managed, developed, and rewarded?
- Are these principles reflected in your selection, performance management, career development, and compensation systems?

This is all part of developing an integrated approach to leading people.

Be Wise About Leading Change

Leading people is always about leading change. Every person, at every company, from the shop floor to the executive suite, is always in white-water conditions and there is turbulence ahead. Many of our change and reengineering efforts have failed. When this happens, we typically blame outsiders for causing the change or we accuse the insiders of resisting the change. But success or failure generally has to do with how leaders manage change. Many of us are unwilling or unable to deal with the complexity of change. Some people feel angry, fearful, or resentful when they confront it; others deny these feelings altogether. But change is constantly around us, and we must all learn how to survive and thrive in it.

We all resist change. It is a human phenomenon caused by our search for control and predictability in our lives. We put up protective barriers and turn down the noise in order to survive. People need time to work through the change process. Some people resist change more than others, and many of us experience multiple, overlapping changes at the same time. None of us move through change at the same pace or in the same way, nor are we motivated by the same things. All of this suggests that the leader needs to pay special attention to why and how people deal with change.

During organizational transformations, leaders cannot reengineer people's commitment. They must build it one person and one relationship at a time. And if the goal is to help people feel engaged and committed to the organization's future, then these people will need to feel respected, understood, listened to, and valued along the way. Otherwise, they will likely sabotage the change effort.

Learn to Follow Your Own Leaders

We are all leaders and followers. As we become better leaders, we also learn to become better followers. In time, we begin to expect more from our own leaders. What is it like for you to work with your current leaders? Are you inspired and challenged in their presence? Or do they criticize you and deplete your energy? As you examine your leaders more closely and look around at other leaders, you may gain an added appreciation of what you have. If that's the case, give your boss some feedback. He or she is probably starving for recognition and will enjoy your honesty.

If you are not so fortunate and happen to work for a dysfunctional leader, you might consider doing something about it. It is important to evaluate your boss's ability to hear candid feedback, particularly if he or she lacks people skills; then make a decision about whether it's safe to give feedback openly. In many cases, our fears about retaliation are greater than the reality of what would actually happen. But this is not always the case, so be careful. Some people find it easier to approach a thin-skinned leader with a group of colleagues, whereas others decide to work more independently. Or you may simply decide that you are unwilling to work in this type of environment anymore.

Learn How to Measure Your Success

What we measure is what we treasure. Today, managerial accounting omits from its accounts, and accountability, large portions of behaviors and outcomes that we associate with leading people. Labor is still viewed as a cost of production, so we end up measuring the consequences of mismanaging our people on the balance sheet. These costs are important. Here are some examples:

- Underinformed employees
- Lack of urgency and initiative

- Limited new ideas and innovations
- Underdeveloped products and markets
- Excessive absenteeism and accidents
- Costly disputes and grievances
- A negative public image
- Lack of employee commitment and goodwill
- Tampering and sabotage
- Conformity and overcompliance
- Stress-related workers' compensation claims
- Underperforming technologies
- Angry, alienated customers
- Excessive health and disability costs
- Decaying communities and environments

People are both appreciating assets to be developed and depreciating costs to be managed. And as knowledge, relationships, and the ability to learn and adapt become paramount factors of productivity and the creation of wealth, new ways of measuring and accounting for intangible "soft" assets are needed. Consider these questions as you measure your organization's success.

- Do you have a clear sense of your business?
- Are you attracting, satisfying, and retaining the right customers?
- Do employees have the right skills, knowledge, and abilities?
- Is the work culture conducive to learning and innovation?
- Do you have a positive reputation in the community?
- Are you adapting and thriving amid change?
- Have you designed the appropriate organizational structure?
- Do you maintain an enthusiastic and committed workforce?
- Is there a shared mindset inside the company?

- Are your work processes efficient and effective?
- Are all your stakeholders delighted?

A new way of leading is emerging—one that is slowly, quietly, and decisively transforming our organizations. Never before have our challenges been so great and the need for responsible leaders so profound. Successful enterprises know how to excel and compete. They make the most of their resources—their financial, marketing, and technological capabilities—but it's their people who make the deciding difference; they are the engine for growth and productivity. Mature, wise leaders make it happen.

Part VI

New Definitions of Organizational Health

32 LEWIS E. PLATT

Employee Work-Life Balance

The Competitive Advantage

*Lewis E. (Lew) Platt is chairman of the board, president, and
chief executive officer of Hewlett-Packard Company, headquartered
in Palo Alto, California. He joined HP in 1966 and has held a
variety of senior management posts. In 1992, he was elected
president and CEO and a member of the board of directors and was
elected to succeed David Packard as chairman the following year.
In 1995, Platt was appointed to the Advisory Committee on Trade
Policy Negotiations by President Bill Clinton and is chair of its
World Trade Organization Task Force; in 1995, he also was elected
cochair of Joint Venture: Silicon Valley (California) Network.*

Shelley Comes, a Hewlett-Packard veteran of fifteen years, knows about
family turmoil. When her father died, her sixty-eight-year-old mother
was left alone on her farm. Shelley was worried sick. The farm was at the
end of a winding mountain road, and the nearest neighbor had no phone.
Shelley's job was in Mountain View, California, in the same state as her
mother's farm but 260 miles away. It was too far. She was torn between
family and work responsibilities. She needed and wanted to keep her job
as a senior training consultant. She also wanted to be close to and care for
her mother. Shelley began searching for ways to cope. She had heard that
various work alternatives were sometimes available to Hewlett-Packard
employees.

Within months, she was telecommuting from the farm for three weeks of every month. With her family secure, Shelley's mental and physical health improved. Her job productivity increased, leading to a promotion. And the story doesn't end there. Last year, Shelley's husband died at the age of forty-four. She told me that she might have just given up had she not been able to continue her work during the many phases and layers of grief that she, her daughter, and her mother endured. Telecommuting helped solve the work-family dilemma for Shelley, and HP kept a valued employee. It was a feel-good, win-win situation. Shelley tells her story often, adding gracious comments about her commitment and loyalty to our company, its culture, and its people. This bodes well for HP.

Organizations of the future will have to address these real people concerns if they plan to be industry leaders and build committed, talented workforces. People need and deserve support from their employers. We all face life changes and need help from time to time. I certainly have. When my daughters were eight and ten years old, my wife died. I was an HP group manager at the time. Tough job assignments were familiar, one might even say comfortable, compared to my new situation: taking sole responsibility for the care of my daughters. It was a tough time. Though I had financial resources and family members to help me, I still had trouble meeting the rigorous demands of my job, especially its travel schedule.

I was lucky that I was at HP. My management team chipped in and lightened my load. We have no thick rule books in our company, but it's culturally unacceptable not to help people who are facing life-altering situations.

Work-Life Balance

Now, as CEO, I believe that it is an important part of my job to nurture this valued culture and encourage an atmosphere that leads to an even more positive work-life balance for employees. It's something I find personally rewarding and, I believe, the right thing to do. Also, I believe that this balance is imperative to business success. Good people are a competitive advantage. We can't keep them or recruit them if we don't recognize the value of this important balance.

In Silicon Valley, where I work, jobs become more demanding every day. Technology is accelerating at a dizzying pace. Product life cycles are shorter. Consumer power and expectations are escalating and competition is relentless. We're continually expanding activities though partners and forging alliances, always looking for a variety of survival strategies. It's a constant push, pull, and shove. Put these things together and you'll see why a tremendous amount of stress builds up in our jobs. These realities are what make it so tough to balance work and life, particularly when they are set against the backdrop of rapidly changing demographics in the workforce.

The Changing Demographics

A lot of changes have taken place in our workforce. According to the U.S. Bureau of Labor Statistics, in 1995 women comprised 46 percent of the workforce, up from 33 percent in 1960, and 46 percent of these women came from families where both spouses worked, up from 34 percent in 1960. These working women have the toughest balancing act. At HP, professional men and women both spend about the same amount of time at work in a week, roughly fifty hours. But women spend an average of thirty-three hours a week on household chores or child care, compared to about nineteen hours for men. So on average, men have about two hours a day more leisure than women do. This puts a lot of extra pressure on the women in our workforce.

Another interesting insight is found in the very divergent family patterns of our managerial employees (see Figure 32.1). Only 29 percent of the men have a working spouse, compared to fully 86 percent of the women. That means that 69 percent of the men in our workforce, over two-thirds of us, simply have never experienced the challenge of trying to complete the business plan, then pick up the dry cleaning on the way home, buy the groceries, and prepare dinner.

Although work-life balance is particularly relevant to women, men in the workforce are increasingly concerned as well. Trends are changing. Many of the younger men I talk to in my company are less willing to sacrifice family get-togethers, children's birthdays, and school plays to the

Figure 32.1. Managerial Employees at Hewlett-Packard Company.

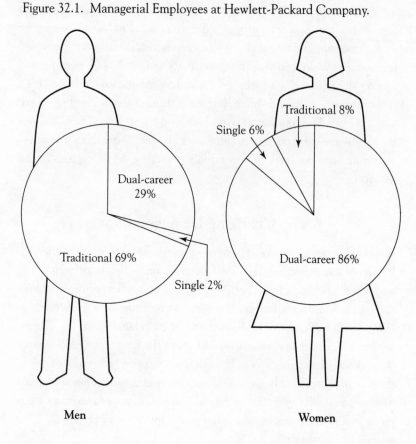

corporate job. In our present-day workforce, between 23 and 50 percent of our parents have child care responsibilities: 50 percent of the parents of children under the age of eighteen and 25 percent with children under the age of thirteen.

Another growing issue is elder care. This is the situation I find myself in, and I expect that many of you do also. Those of us in the Baby Boomer generation are now seeing our parents, fortunately, living to much older ages. Twenty-five percent of HP employees now have the responsibility of caring for their parents. Of these, one-fourth have their parents now living with them.

Changing Expectations

Not only are demographics changing, but so, too, are attitudes and expectations. Seventy-two percent of the members of today's general workforce say that they need a job that doesn't interfere with their personal or family life. This is up from 62 percent just three years ago, and I predict that the percentage will go higher. People entering the workforce today tell us that they are looking for a particular work environment, and to them it's much more important than salary. They are looking for a balanced lifestyle. Sixty percent rate the effect of their lifestyle, or being able to find a balance in their lives, as among the top five considerations when they sign up for a job. Where are salary and benefits? They are at numbers 13 and 16 on the survey. So those of us who thought that paying a big salary would make up for everything else in life probably had better start thinking again. Changing employee values and needs are beginning to get our attention, as they should.

We on the business and management side have very good data that lead us to believe that it's in the best interest of the business to provide employees with the tools needed to achieve the right balance. I've become a strong believer in the past few years. Work-life balance improves employee retention and yields much greater employee initiative and commitment. We know that it helps to reduce stress and burnout, and we are learning that it increases employee productivity. And although much of our focus normally is on changes in the business environment, I think it's imperative that we also recognize the changing nature of our workforce.

But even though we can provide the tools for people to balance their lives, it's not up to management to do the actual balancing. Employees must take the initiative to do that. We can't make the job easier, but we can add significant flexibility in the way our people work.

Policies

HP has always had a number of policies that support work-life balance. We've had flexible work hours since 1972. Recent studies have noted that flexible work hours are seen as one of the most desirable benefits. Educational reimbursement also is very high on the list, as is the time given off for certain kinds of educational programs. Employees need to keep up and learn new skills. We think that employees must retool themselves about every five years in our environment, and most of today's workforce realizes this. I believe that it's up to the company to provide help to those who are trying to keep up or move ahead.

Another policy, management by objective, also works well in helping us to achieve work-life balance. It's something that Dave Packard and Bill Hewlett put in place in the company more than fifty years ago. Simply stated, in management by objective we focus on the results, not on the methods used. As we begin to do this, we find that we can actually give people quite a bit of flexibility in the way they get from point A to point B.

So we've had these things in place for a very long time, in most cases for twenty, or thirty, or fifty years. And these relatively old programs are still serving us very well as we strive for an even better work-life balance. But we've found that we've also had to add some new policies. For example, we changed our leave-of-absence policy. In all honesty, employees could always get a leave of absence from HP, but until fairly recently it was kind of a federal case to get it done. These days, it's pretty simple. Employees can get a leave of absence for just about any reason. So if an employee has reached a point in life when he or she simply needs to "chill out" for a little while, it's easy to do. Perhaps tending a dying parent or spending more time with one's children is the reason. It doesn't matter. If an employee asks for time, we give it to him or her. We continue health care contributions, and we provide a return employment guarantee. We've also made rehiring easier for the person who goes beyond the leave of absence. Perhaps a person needs to be out of the workforce for five years. We now bridge service and basically pick up benefits. These things help the employee who, for whatever reason, simply needs to take a few months or a few years off.

We've also made a number of investments to help employees with dependent care. HP recently made a long-term commitment to the American Business Collaboration for Quality Dependent Care to increase the availability and improve the quality of child care services. HP is one of twenty-one corporations who together have pledged $100 million to develop and strengthen a broad range of dependent care programs around the United States. In addition, we sponsor an insurance program that allows employees to sign up and make contributions for long-term care, not only for themselves but for others in their family.

We have formally endorsed alternative work schedules. For example, in our financial services center in Colorado Springs, thirty-eight people out of a team total of sixty chose to work a four-day, ten-hour schedule instead of their regular eight-to-five, five-day schedule. The environment could be controlled, so we did a study. Our pilot showed these results:

1. Overtime was reduced by 50 percent.

2. Productivity—transactions per day—exceeded that of colleagues who remained with the typical five-day, eight-hour schedule.

3. Customer satisfaction and employee satisfaction increased.

These results speak for themselves.

Not only are schedules flexible, but so are locations for work. Telecommuting has become a popular option for many. As technology continues to advance, working from almost anywhere has become possible. Work has, indeed, become portable. Between 10 to 15 percent of our employees telecommute. It is very easy to work from places other than your office, and often you can work better and more efficiently. Telecommuting also reinforces the importance of management by objective, that old HP practice. The focus really does have to be on accomplishments and meeting objectives. It's no longer on "face time," and I think that's good. It suits the world in which we live.

I'm often asked about the price tag of providing the equipment for telecommuting. Our company has a very liberal policy. If we go through the economics of it and determine that telecommuting makes sense, then we give the employees the tools they need to do the job. It's part of being a modern employer. If you look at the cost of equipping an employee to work at home compared to items such as employee health insurance or a cafeteria subsidy, the technology is a drop in the bucket. Everybody gets caught up on what it might cost, but I really believe that equipping employees according to their requests will differentiate employers.

Cultural Changes

Cultural change is the most difficult change of all, especially in organizations that are led by a generation of managers who had at-home spouses and were willing to sacrifice much of their personal lives for their careers. For example, one of our senior managers had a meeting with his staff to discuss work-life balance. The meeting started at 5 P.M. and ended at 9 P.M.—and the manager didn't see the irony.

But even though change is slow, I do believe it's happening. We will continue to work through the key themes I've mentioned: the flexibility of where and when work gets done, support of our employees through help with issues concerning their dependents, and the development of a management climate that is prepared for employees who want more family time and control over their personal lives. We have spent considerable time and energy developing an appropriate work-life vision for our company. I'd like to share it with you: it is the vision of "an environment that encourages employees and managers to work together to achieve common company objectives for business success, while creating opportunities for balancing work with other life activities."

We don't pretend to have all the answers. Nor do we believe that there is a single correct one. Only the goal of creating a positive balance is clear. Some like to find it by integrating their work and private lives; others prefer a very clear demarcation between the two. The answers are as individual as the individuals seeking them. I believe that work-life balance is an issue that all companies should address. Neither the size of one's company nor the length of time it has been in business should matter. A positive work-life balance, as illustrated in Figure 32.2, will be reflected in the good health of our families and communities, and everyone should share in that.

As we all look for answers, I hope that many of you will accept and promote this agenda. The health of our organizations and our families depends on our ability to find the right solutions. I believe that a win-win solution to the seesaw of work-life balance can be attained and that achieving it is one of the greatest management challenges of the decade.

Figure 32.2. The Goal Is Work-Life Balance.

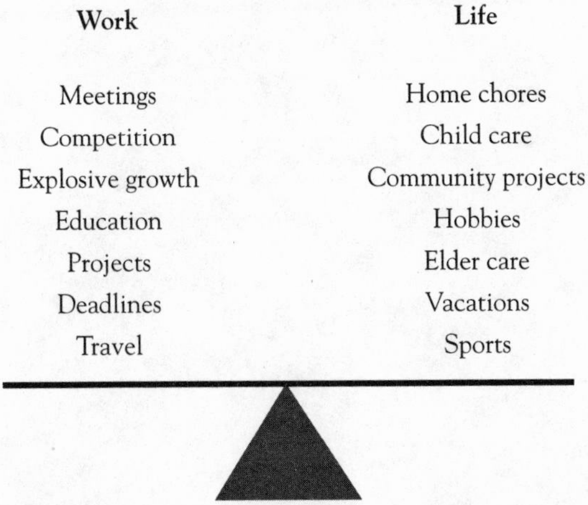

Work	Life
Meetings	Home chores
Competition	Child care
Explosive growth	Community projects
Education	Hobbies
Projects	Elder care
Deadlines	Vacations
Travel	Sports

33 RICHARD BECKHARD

The Healthy Organization

A Profile

Richard Beckhard is an organizational consultant who specializes in working with leaders in the area of organizational and institutional development and management of change and complexity. He is the author of The Fact-Finding Conference, Core Content, Organization Development, *and* Explorations on the Teaching and Learning of Managing Large System Change. *He is coauthor of* Changing the Essence: The Art of Making and Managing Fundamental Change *and* Organizational Transitions. *Beckhard was a professor of organizational behavior and management at the Sloan School of Management at the Massachusetts Institute of Technology, where he served on the faculty for twenty-one years. The Sloan School honored him by creating the Richard Beckhard Prize, awarded annually for the best article on this subject in the* Sloan Management Review.

As we approach the millennium, we are living in a world that is the most unstable, dynamic, exciting, and frustrating in modern history. Technology is exploding. We can contact anyone in the world in milliseconds. Surviving organizations, particularly in the private sector, are increasingly global entities.

Paradoxically, the need for local and community power is growing. The sectors of society are changing places. As the social sector becomes more powerful in influencing the direction of national policy, governments are devolving from national to local. Soon, the private sector will no longer be the only source of wealth. The public sector will need to reexamine its role of serving the people. The social, or volunteer, sector is exponentially increasing in importance.

Throughout history, the "world's work" has been done through institutions and organizations. As our global society tries to cope with the differences between rich and poor, North and South, developed and developing countries, and global and local issues, organizations increasingly serve as the bridges between issues and people. But just as individuals have personalities, which are a function of both heredity and environment, so organizations have personalities with the same causes.

Many individuals spend major amounts of energy in trying to understand and manage their behavior in an ever-changing environment. Increasingly, organizations and their leaders are engaged in the same inquiries. Look at the recent explosion of interest in the learning organization. Listen to executives struggling with managing dilemmas, rather than being faced with simple choices. Organizations are no longer stand-alone entities that can operate autonomously in a relatively stable environment. They are part of a system of relationships and interactions that is in a constantly dynamic state.

We can describe healthy people in a number of ways, from "not sick" to "moving toward highest potential" to "having it all together." There is no consensus, however, on how to define healthy organizations. I have spent a major part of my professional life exploring the nature of the health of organizations, and I have come to the conclusion that, although every aspect of our environment is in a turbulent and rapidly changing condition, both individual and organizational health can be measured now and in the future by the same criteria.

Profile of a Healthy Organization

- A healthy organization defines itself as a system, and the organization's work is to take in needs and raw materials and to transform them into goods and services. The organization's stakeholders include its owners and staff, its suppliers, intermediate customers, the ultimate consumers of the product or service, the media, and the communities in which the organization operates.

- It has a strong sensing system for receiving current information on all parts of the system and their interactions (systems dynamics thinking).

- It has a strong sense of purpose. It is managed against visions of its future.

- It operates in a "form follows function" mode. The work to be done determines the structures and mechanisms to do it. As a result, it uses multiple structures: the formal pyramidal structure, horizontal structures and teams, project structures, and temporary structures (as when managing a major change).

- It employs team management as the dominant mode. There is an executive team at the top; teams manage divisions and functions and also manage projects; there are interfunctional councils; and the professional development teams are composed of both specialists and users of services.

- It respects customer service—both to outside customers and to others within the organization—as a principle.

- Its management is information-driven. Large amounts of information can be received and processed in seconds. Access to information is widely shared across geographic areas, functions, and organization levels.

- It encourages and allows decisions to be made at the level closest to the customer, where all the necessary information is available.

- It keeps communication relatively open throughout the system.

- Its reward systems are designed to be congruent with the work and to support individual development. Managers and work teams are appraised against both performance and improvement goals.

- The organization operates in a learning mode. Identifying learning points is part of the process of all decision making.

- It makes explicit recognition for innovation and creativity and has a high tolerance for different styles of thinking and for ambiguity in all things.

- Its policies reflect respect for the tensions between work and family demands. Work at home is encouraged where appropriate. Job sharing is supported. Parental leave and child care are seen as responsibilities of the firm.

- It keeps an explicit social agenda. Community citizenship, protecting the environment, and supporting the arts are corporate policies, not isolated activities.

- It gives sufficient attention to efficient work, quality and safety awareness in operations, and identifying and managing change for a better future.

34 R. ROOSEVELT THOMAS JR.

Diversity and Organizations of the Future

R. Roosevelt Thomas Jr. is founder and president of the American Institute for Managing Diversity, a research and education
enterprise with the objective of fostering the effective management
of diversity. He is also chief executive officer of the consulting
firm R. Thomas and Associates. Thomas is the author of Beyond
Race and Gender: Unleashing the Power of Your Total Work
Force by Managing Diversity; Differences Do Make a Difference; and Redefining Diversity.

Organizations of the future, like those of today, will operate in an uncertain, highly competitive, and complex business environment.
Their profitability and viability will depend on the efforts of an increasingly
diverse workforce—one that is characterized by managers and employees
who differ greatly and who insist that their differences be recognized.

Some components of the workforce mixture—race and gender in particular—have long been viewed as "diversity" issues. Other, less traditional
components—age, sexual orientation, work and family issues, education,
work experiences, tenure with the organization, personality, tolerance for
risk and ambiguity, geographic origin, and religion, to name a few—also

---

Note: I would like to acknowledge and thank Marjorie Woodruff for assisting in developing
and organizing this chapter.

are viewed by some companies as part of the workforce diversity mix. In reality, however, the situation is even more complex than this. *Diversity*, stripped of its cultural and political baggage, refers to any collective mixture (people, systems, functions, lines of business, and so on) characterized by similarities *and* differences.

Suppose, for example, that you have a jar of red jelly beans and you add some green and purple ones. Many people believe that the green and purple jelly beans represent diversity and that attention should be paid to them and their differences. I believe, however, that diversity is the collective mixture of jelly beans, which are similar on one dimension—size— and different on another—color. I believe, as well, that the relative visibility and complementarity of the beans is influenced greatly by the size and shape of the jar.

Diversity, thus defined, leads to very different assumptions than do inclusion-focused definitions. An unspoken but common assumption in both affirmative action and "understanding differences" initiatives, for example, has been that white men are the norm in organizations; all others are "different." As a consequence, attention to diversity has meant attention to these "others." The basis of this assumption is clear, given the equation of diversity with inclusion and the longevity, numbers, and relative power of white men within America's corporations. But the result has been to effectively remove white men from the diversity mix. It is as if we were to photograph the jar with a lens that hides the red jelly beans from view and then attempt to analyze the placement of the green and purple beans.

The equation of diversity with inclusion has rendered other aspects of diversity's dimensions largely invisible, too. For example, it has led many to ignore the seminal work of Paul Lawrence and Jay Lorsch, in *Organization and Environment*, in addressing relationships among functional subunits and the work of Lorsch and Stephen Allen III, in *Managing Diversity and Interdependence*, with respect to multiple lines of business organized as divisions. In effect, the "inclusion" focus has inhibited our ability to see diversity along dimensions other than race and gender. Equating diversity with inclusion has hidden the distinction between a diverse population and a diverse jar (or organizational culture, structure, and systems) as well. As a result, organizations have routinely attempted to stuff a demographically diverse workforce into a one-size-fits-all jar. Few have understood the need to examine and, where necessary, to change their culture, structure, and systems to reflect the diversity mix of their employees.

Clearly, definitions matter. Just as clearly, organizations of the future can ill afford to retain narrow, outdated notions of diversity. They must, instead, adopt a definition that illuminates and clarifies the environmental and organizational complexity that the future holds. This complexity will both result from and contribute to diversity. The two phenomena go hand in hand. Together, they will dictate, for example, that organizations seek synergistic relationships among functions and lines of business; among corporate organizational units that result from acquisitions, mergers, reorganizations, and partnerships; and among nations, cultures, strategies, and people, as globalism becomes ever more important.

Managers have had many of these issues on their plate for some time. However, most have lacked a framework that would allow for enhanced awareness of and systematic thinking about diversity mixtures and their implications. Projections into the future suggest that such a framework will become imperative. Peter Vail, in *Managing as a Performing Art*, has compared the turbulence, danger, and volatility of the present business environment to permanent white water. I see this white-water environment as becoming even more volatile and dangerous, extending as far as the eye can see.

As corporations respond to the relentlessly changing environment, managers will be required to cope nonstop with two very intricate diversity mixtures: (1) mixtures associated with environmental turbulence and (2) mixtures associated with organizational transformation and change. Managing diversity of this magnitude will require that managers have both a broad-based understanding of diversity and a conceptual framework, with attendant structures and techniques that go beyond those provided by affirmative action and "understanding differences," the traditional workforce diversity initiatives. I believe that diversity management—a process for addressing all relevant diversity mixtures in ways that maximize the achievement of organizational objectives—meets these requirements.

The Diversity Management Framework

My twelve years of helping organizations address diversity have convinced me that poor or no management is the biggest barrier to doing so effectively.

Key to diversity management is effective *managing*, where to manage is to empower and enable, not to command and control. Key to the diversity management *process*, which I introduce in my book *Redefining Diversity*, is a framework that facilitates a systematic approach. This framework delineates a sequence of analytic steps, identifies a number of possible action options, and defines a contingency context for selecting an appropriate option for a given circumstance.

The Diversity Management Process: A Contingency Approach

Step one of the diversity management process is to get clear on the problem. Achieving this clarity requires articulation of the company's vision, mission, strategies, and culture and an understanding of the environment in which it does business. Clarity concerning an organization's culture can be particularly hard to achieve. Edgar Schein, noted MIT organizational psychologist, in his book *Organizational Culture and Leadership*, described culture as the "basic assumptions" that drive an institution. Like the roots of a tree, these assumptions are out of sight yet determine what can grow and evolve in an organization.

The basic taken-for-granted, unspoken, out-of-awareness assumptions govern organizational responses to diversity. If these assumptions—many of which were put in place in the midst of homogeneous historical realities—do not reflect current internal and external diversity and subsequent complexity, they can sabotage the organization's ability to address today's business realities.

Once the company's vision, mission, strategies, culture, and external environment are understood, managers can differentiate requirements from traditions, preferences, and conveniences. Such differentiation will become essential as complexity multiplies and resources dwindle.

Step two of the diversity management process is to define the situation in terms of a *diversity mixture*. A manager who is concerned with product lines, for example, may find differences and similarities in the mechanisms by which they are manufactured, the way they are distributed, their profitability ratios, their current or potential customer base, their development costs, their position in the product maturity cycle, and their governmental regulatory requirements. Awareness of all of the mixture's dimensions is essential when planning a solution.

Step three is to check for *diversity tension*—conflict, stress, or strain associated with the interactions of the elements in the mixture. Two questions matter here: Is the diversity mixture creating tension? If so, does anything need to be done about it? Not all diversity mixtures are accompanied by tension, and not all tension is bad. Diversity tension is a problem only when it interferes with achieving organizational objectives. When it does, it's time to review current and possible approaches to addressing the problem.

Step four of the diversity management process is to *review* current approaches and to *replace* those that aren't working with something else. The question for managers has been what that "something else" should be. To help with this, I have identified nine possible action options and have defined a system for selecting the appropriate option for a given set of circumstances. The use of the action options facilitates diagnosis, understanding, and action planning and provides a way to organize data and to discover and understand patterns.

Nine Action Choices

The following nine action options are available to managers as they address diversity and complexity issues:

1. *Include*. Expand the number and variability of the components of the diversity mixture.

2. *Exclude*. Minimize the number and variability of the components of the diversity mixture.

3. *Deny*. Minimize awareness of the existence of the diversity mixture by highlighting similarities or downplaying differences.

4. *Assimilate*. Minimize the diversity of the mixture by insisting that "minority" components conform to the norms of the dominant factor.

5. *Suppress*. Minimize the diversity of the mixture by allowing knowledge of differences to come into awareness, then consciously deciding to keep it from surfacing.

6. *Isolate*. Address diversity by including and setting "different" mixture components off to one side.

7. *Tolerate*. Address diversity by fostering a "room for all" attitude, albeit with limited superficial interactions among the components of the mixture.

8. *Build relationships*. Address diversity by fostering quality relationships, characterized by acceptance and understanding, among the components of the mixture.

9. *Foster mutual adaptation*. Address diversity by fostering mutual adaptation, in which all components change somewhat for the sake of achieving common objectives. (Business requirements, not preferences, traditions, or conveniences, determine which component changes and when.)

Understanding the Action Options

Five points can be made about the action options:

1. *None of the action options is inherently positive or negative*. All options are legitimate and can be used for good or ill. The early *isolation* of new lines of business, for example, may provide needed distance and time to allow full implementation with minimum complexity. *Assimilation* in the interest of conformity to an organization's genuine—and carefully delineated— requirements ensures adequate individual and organizational performance. The challenge is not with assimilation per se but with the inappropriate use of this overused option. *Denial* can be an appropriate and effective coping mechanism until a state of readiness to acknowledge and address diversity can be achieved. It is not the option per se but the context of its use that determines its benefits and limitations. Negative perceptions of the options can be traced to the fact that in the past, our experience with certain options has been limited to the area of race and gender relations.

2. *Each option can be used with any collective mixture of differences and similarities*. Although we are most familiar with the options in the context of race and gender, they are operative whenever diversity of any kind exists. The options may be particularly useful, for example, when addressing diversity mixtures that are associated with organizational change and transformation.

3. *Action options can be and often are used in combination.* People, for example, may be recruited (included) and isolated, recruited and merely tolerated, or recruited and asked to suppress and assimilate. Similarly, a company might buy (include) another company and then set it up as a subsidiary (isolation).

4. *Of the nine options, only fostering mutual adaptation unequivocally endorses diversity.* The first seven options seek to minimize or eliminate diversity and complexity. In theory, the eighth—building relationships—has the capability to enhance diversity. But in practice, it is seldom used to do so. The predominance of options that diminish levels of diversity and complexity reflects the desire of most individuals and organizations to minimize, even deny, differences when possible. Indeed, at times it is appropriate to limit diversity or to simplify complexity. At issue is the ability to embrace and manage diversity when circumstances make it essential to do so.

5. *The selection of action choices is dynamic and determined by context.* As circumstances change, so does the most effective action option. It is important to monitor the results of any option and make changes when appropriate.

Competencies of Effective Diversity and Contingency Managers

The effective manager of diversity will use the diversity management and contingency approach to identify key diversity mixtures. She or he will recognize, however, that not all diversity mixtures require attention. Many such mixtures create no problems. Some diversity mixtures that do cause problems may prove inconsequential to the organization's mission or bottom line. Here, the manager's judgment becomes essential. The effective diversity and contingency manager will place the identified diversity mixture and consequent tension into an appropriate context. This context will include the external environment as well as the organization's mission, vision, strategies, and culture. She or he will then ask two questions:

1. Given this context, what is the diversity tension's potential effect?
2. Given this effect, does this particular diversity tension warrant my attention?

A no answer to the second question allows the manager to move on. A yes answer is cause for action.

Managers who identify significant diversity tension must then ask, "What next?" Effective managers begin by reviewing past actions and asking, "Did this work?" A yes answer poses the question, "Why didn't the solution stick?" A no answer points to the need to do things differently. The action options, with their clearly defined choices, can help managers to reach a decision. The choice and implementation of one or a combination of action options, however, is just a beginning. Managers must monitor and "tweak" their selected option to ensure that it achieves its goal. Again, nimbleness and adaptability will be key to their success.

Diversity Management: A Necessity for Future Organizational Success

I believe that *all* of the water downstream is white and will remain so in the foreseeable future. Only the companies that transform themselves into nimble, adaptable organizations will thrive. The achievement of nimbleness and adaptability requires a continuous search for new success formulas. This search will be difficult at best, given the profound changes in the business world and the fact that many current organizational assumptions and practices discourage change and adaptation.

Qualities of Organizations That Will Thrive

Companies that thrive will value the following attributes:

- Commitment to a shared mission and vision, as context for the reformulation
- Effectiveness, a focus on determining the right thing to do
- Reflection and a learning capability
- Empowerment (when searching for something new, informed self-direction is needed)
- Multifunctional roles with collaboration across units
- Management of performance, not just potential

- Strategic thinking, the process of identifying approaches for gaining a sustainable competitive advantage in the future
- Cultural renewal, a sustained change in root assumptions
- Continuous searching and learning

Organizational transformation of this magnitude creates several non-traditional diversity mixtures with which to come to grips. All can be approached through the diversity management process. The way in which the process works will be illustrated below, using two of the most significant of these mixtures: environmental perceptions and organizational change.

Environmental Perceptions and the Action Options. Managers constantly receive impressions, or "snapshots," of their external environments. Collectively, these snapshots constitute a picture of the current environment and serve as a framework for determining strategy and action. A manager may, at any time, depend on her last several environmental snapshots to provide an operative portrait of external realities. In a stable environment, these snapshots are similar to each other and to past snapshots, and they can reassure the manager that she will be able to continue business as usual.

But the more unpredictable and dynamic the environment, the more diverse the current snapshots are and the more they deviate from previous sets of snapshots. This manager must ask, "Do I need to change my understanding of external reality?" and, if so, "Is a change in the way we do business required?" Her answers will be influenced greatly by how she responds to the snapshots' diversity. She may choose to *exclude*, in which case she discards the snapshots that deviate significantly from the status quo. She may *deny*, by including snapshots that are different but minimizing the differences. She may *isolate* the snapshots, setting them aside and ignoring them when making action plans. She may *assimilate* them by interpreting all current snapshots as part of the status quo, thus maintaining the illusion that the environment remains unchanged. Alternately, she may *tolerate* or *suppress* the snapshots. These options, like the previous ones, allow her to ignore the "deviate" snapshots and proceed with business as usual.

Only two choices will allow the manager to begin the necessary process of organizational transformation. The first is to *build relationships* by testing the different snapshots in order to determine how they deviate from the status quo. The second is to *foster mutual adaptation* by accepting the reality that different snapshots will require her to adjust her composite view of the environment.

Organizational Transformation and the Change Management Process.

As organizations continue their transformation process, their managers will have to adapt to constant and ubiquitous change. The ability to clarify the nature of a desired change depends on an ability to analyze and understand the diversity mixture of the status quo and its alternatives. A manager may choose to *exclude* or refuse to consider the possibility of change. A typical remark here is: "Things are okay. If it ain't broke, don't fix it." Alternately, he may choose to *include*—to consider the possibility of change and to create diversity mixtures of the status quo and alternatives. He may, however, pair the "include" option with *deny,* in which he disallows claims of differences that would make them worth considering.

The manager may also choose to *isolate*—to include alternatives but label them "special." He may, for example, put total quality in place but treat it as complementary rather than integral to the rest of the organization. As a result, the status quo remains in place. Managers who *assimilate* attempt to redefine the alternative so that it fits the status quo. They may say, "We will develop our own version of Succession Planning." The "assimilation" option allows managers to appropriate the jargon of change while maintaining the status quo. Only the *foster mutual adaptation* option seeks to develop a new status quo, one that blends the alternatives with the status quo to come up with a new desired state.

Achieving the Desired Competencies

Organizations of the future will experience ubiquitous diversity mixtures in multiple settings. Some diversity mixtures, such as those found in the business environment or among the workforce, will be inherent in the nature of our world and national culture. Others will be the result of an exponential increase in the interdependency of organizations, functional units, and lines of business. Still other diversity mixtures, such as those associated with organizational transformation and change, will result from managerial efforts to respond to previously identified mixtures. Organizational transformation and change will, in turn, result in additional and previously unaddressed mixtures.

This means that, at a minimum, organizations must reexamine their previous conceptualizations and approaches to diversity. In the past, diversity-related efforts have focused on the inclusion of previously excluded people and harmony within the resulting diversity mix. Such desired states are still valid, but they are not enough. Both the abundance and nature of the diversity mixtures will make their effective *management* critical to continued organizational viability. This, in turn, will depend on managers who possess diversity competencies—managers who understand and use the diversity management framework and can predict accurately the effect of using specific action options.

Much more than in the past, organizational diversity competence will also depend on employees—not just managers—who possess diversity management skills. The need for diversity management skills on the part of employees will place added responsibilities on already challenged managers. They must facilitate the needed employee competencies through a combination of empowerment management and specific modeling and training of diversity management skills.

Finally, achievement of essential diversity management competencies will require organizational cultures and systems that reinforce the competencies of the corporation's managers and employees. Here, the burden is on organizational leaders to clarify and communicate their organization's mission, vision, strategies, and culture, and to be willing to change those that no longer work in a turbulent, challenging external environment.

35 GREG PARSTON

Producing Social Results

Greg Parston is chief executive of the Office for Public Management, London, an employee-owned trust, which provides organizational development for public service organizations and socially responsible businesses. His work focuses on strategy formation with chief executives. He is currently an adjunct lecturer at the Kennedy School of Government, Harvard. He has worked as a manager and consultant in many countries, including senior appointments with New York State, the Province of Ontario, the U.S. National Science Foundation, and the World Bank. He has written and lectured widely and has been on the faculty of New York University.

An organization is defined by its accountabilities. During the brief history of large commercial organizations, accountability and the hard measure of the bottom line have traditionally and principally related to the interests of owners. The business world has measured the success of its organizations and their management largely on the basis of profits. Today, business analyses are filled with references to shareholder value as the main criterion for judging the success of organizational change. Accountability to shareholders and to their interests is the key driver of organizational performance, design, and behavior. Performance management, business process reengineering, and competitive advantage are all aimed at transforming today's organizations into ones that can deliver bigger dividends tomorrow.

341

Accountability to shareholder interests is not everything, however; customers have always run a close second in the accountability stakes. Frontier store signs that stated "The customer is always right" might have been little more than good marketing, but they were also a recognition that the claims of customers played an important role in the ways in which commerce organized and ran itself. More recently, with the help of gurus like Tom Peters and, more compellingly, with the success of competitors, particularly Japanese competitors, management has learned how to focus organizational efforts more clearly on customers' requirements. And with that learning, organizations have moved from Henry Ford's production lines to Disney's worlds. No longer is the customer faced with the prospect of "any color you want, so long as it's black." Indeed, Michael Eisner attributes the Walt Disney Company's success in becoming one of the world's best-performing organizations to simply giving people what they want. Accountability to customers has reshaped organizations, resulting in greater devolution and more responsibility in the hands of front-line workers who are there to ensure that customers are well served.

Shareholders and customers both demand accountability from their organizations, and executives have learned how best to fashion the design of organizational structure and process in response. Under the influence of innovative leaders like Max DePree and Ricardo Semler, many executives have learned that responding to the claims of workers can also bring rewards. By allowing organizations to give more *to* their workers, in terms of career development, flexible and supportive working conditions, recognition, and participation in work design, executives have been able to get more *from* their workers, in terms of increased productivity, nonrestrictive working practices, and even corporate loyalty. Cynical observers might say that this new attention to the workers and their conditions is used by some managers only as another way to achieve bigger profits—that is, as a way to better serve shareholders. But many of the progressive employment practices that exist in organizations like Levi Strauss and Company have happened because CEOs like Bob Haas have a genuine desire to serve and to empower others to contribute meaningfully to their organization and, ultimately, to their own lives.

Over time, we have seen the accountabilities of enterprises grow, and the structures of organizations and the processes of management have matured in response. Shareholder values still dominate the stock exchange floor, but customers and employees have become recognized as important and legitimate claimants of the values that enterprises produce. However, as we look to tomorrow, many leaders acknowledge that the demands now being placed on their organization and the things for which they are being held to account are becoming far more complicated. Something is happening to challenge the effectiveness of their management, to alter the profile of their leadership, and to change the very shape of the organization itself.

In many industries and in most developed countries, a new interest is being claimed in commercial organizations and a new accountability has been placed on their management. External stakeholders who, as customers, had placed expectations on business for such things as high quality, good service, and fair price have begun to demand more. They have begun to expect business to think beyond profit and to be held to account for performance that goes beyond shareholder value, beyond serving customers and employees. They have begun to hold business accountable for social results.

Accountability for Social Results

Unlike the charitable donations that many businesses make, accountability for social results is enduring. It is one thing for a company to give money to the arts one year and to higher education the next—and, when times are bad, to give no money to anyone. It is quite another matter when the organization's very standing with customers, shareholders, and society requires that it continually respond positively to the expectation of public good. Failure to meet this social expectation can be as dangerous as failure to meet the expectations of shareholders or customers.

One example of how apparent failure to meet one's social accountability can hurt may be seen in the case of The Body Shop. This English cosmetics company had been seen as the paragon of socially responsible business. From the start, its founder, Anita Roddick, built an expectation among customers and the public that her business was doing all it could in the spirit of enlightened capitalism to change society for the better, to protect the environment, to oppose animal testing, and to promote ethical trade. In meeting those expectations—or at least in conveying the impression that it did—The Body Shop thrived. But in 1994, when its social commitments were questioned in a series of unfriendly news reports, The Body Shop's public image *and* market worth suffered. Its products and prices had not changed. Yet the public knowledge that The Body Shop might not be contributing anything more to the social whole than its drugstore competitors raised serious concerns about whether those who supported its propounded social values as citizens might now, as customers, buy somewhere else. Its share value and its profits plummeted.

The research on socially responsible businesses shows that in the case of many organizations—The Body Shop included—corporate commitments to "public good" are initiated, not just in response to external public pressure, but often because of the personal values and philosophies of founding entrepreneurs. Ben Cohen is probably the most notable American example. His own personal values drive the broader social agenda of Ben & Jerry's Homemade ice cream business. Community development, especially in the agricultural communities that supply its raw materials, is broadcast by the company as an enduring commitment and one to which it holds itself accountable. The consequence of this is an organization with a flatter structure, wider employee participation, and greater opportunity for flexible work patterns than might otherwise be the case; this allows the social agenda to be shared by shareholders and employees alike. But at the same time, the consequences of this internally driven social commitment resonate in the marketplace. I and other customers buy Ben & Jerry's Homemade because it *is* good ice cream, but we also buy it because we want to support or even benefit from the company's community development programs. As a CEO myself, I am pleased to learn that the company runs itself well and that its employees seem happy. But, in the end, what I really want as a customer is good ice cream *and*, as a citizen, the public benefit of community development. If Ben & Jerry's had no social agenda, ice cream from another company might be just as good.

New Public Expectations

This new claim on business is partly a result of the relative growth of wealth in Western society. More and more people are finding the comfortableness of relative affluence disturbed by business practices and side effects that they cannot condone or sustain, including the environmental and social consequences of private production. Their worries about what business does besides manufacture and deliver the goods and services they enjoy are probably made more urgent by the apparent failure of governments to respond to social needs. As a result, people are looking to other institutions, including business, to ensure justice and fairness, to fight social exclusion, and to sustain environmental well-being. The result of all this social change is that people outside our commercial enterprises have begun to exert a new pressure on those inside them to be more concerned about public issues. The people outside organizations that produce goods and services for private use have begun to expect that these organizations do so in a way that recognizes public concerns, if not by producing some sort of social benefit, at least by ensuring that they do not contribute to any type of social harm, such as pollution or racism or increases in violence.

Demands for "green" products and production, concerns about asset stripping when companies move out of town, and worries about the impact of media and toy guns on youth crime are illustrations of larger social issues that commercial organizations have had to address (or have chosen to ignore) for many years. But today the concern is growing that companies have a responsibility to do more than merely deal with the darker side effects of their business. The idea that a business should be a part of the community is a growing consciousness and a growing demand. "What is your business doing for our schools? for our health care? for our elderly?" are questions that are being asked more and more frequently of leaders of organizations that in the past usually played only a minor role in community development. What is different now is that this is not just the influence of consumer associations or environmental lobbies; it is the consequence of millions of nonaffiliated individuals exerting their collective rights as citizens to a safer, healthier, and fairer society.

These growing social expectations are imposing a new accountability on business organizations and their leaders that is different from those they faced in the traditional marketplace. Business success will still continue to be gauged by how well management has fulfilled its responsibilities to shareholders. It will increasingly reflect how well the interests of customers and staff play out on the bottom line. But in more of tomorrow's organizations, success will also have to include a measure of how well the business contributes to meeting the new expectations of citizens.

Developing and Leading the Socially Responsible Organization

Regardless of whether the new social accountability arises from within the organization or from the demands of those outside, it presents a quite different challenge in organizing business, developing the organization, and exercising leadership than we have seen in the past. As demands increase, leaders across a wide array of enterprises will see being held accountable for public good as a difficult challenge, but they will also see it as an opportunity. They will understand that although their businesses face more complex and more rapidly changing expectations and demands than they did before, they also have before them a growing sector of business activity that can respond to consumer choice *and* to larger claims for social responsibility. And they will be enjoined by the expanding body of ethical investors to reconsider the meaning of their bottom-line results.

Today, with some knowledge of what this future could be, many executives are becoming frustrated by the fact that the traditional ways of organizing in order to meet the traditional measures of success, most of which are related to shareholder value, are not good enough to cope with these new complexities. Traditional approaches to management and organization are not helping them to strike an acceptable balance between shareholders and society. Those who will be tomorrow's leaders are struggling to develop coherent responses to the growing pressure for social outcomes, as is apparent in the many conventions and conferences on socially responsible businesses, most notably the Social Venture Network, founded by Ben Cohen, among others. Clearly, the new set of often-conflicting and nonsubstitutable accountabilities is one that many of today's leaders do not feel well prepared to meet. But leaders of some of today's socially responsible organizations, like Ben & Jerry's, Château de Lastours in France (which employs only people with learning disabilities), and Sweden's IKEA (where environmental protection is each employee's key objective), *are* developing new ways of organizing to meet these new social demands.

There is much to learn from them and much to be done to develop the organizations that tomorrow's social responsibilities will demand.

Tomorrow's organizations will have to develop new types of relationships with shareholders, staff, and customers. But most important, they will also require a new type of relationship with the public as a whole. These organizations will be built on far-reaching visions in which they define themselves as active participants in community life and as active contributors to social well-being. Socially responsible organizations will no longer be defined by their financial limits, their ownership, their products, or their organizational charts but rather by their roles in society. A business's place in its community will challenge the traditional boundaries within which its leaders have confined their visionary designs. Socially responsible leaders will have to design new futures that go beyond their organization's physical and legal limits. This will not only introduce a new systemwide architecture in their business thinking; it also will change the nature of the leaders' own role in their organization.

The leaders of tomorrow's socially responsible businesses will coach and educate and facilitate others in their organization to contribute to a social result that is bigger than themselves and bigger than their organization. They will place as much emphasis on building understandings about the complex set of accountabilities that the organization faces, and about the societies within which they live, as they do on improving the organization's capabilities and skills to meet these accountabilities. And they will work with people outside their organization to form new partnerships and new dialogues focused on social results.

In this role, the leaders of tomorrow's organizations will have to be social activists. In order to meet their new accountabilities, they will have crucial roles to play in establishing and clarifying the social agenda of their organization. They will have to do the tough political work with shareholders, staff, and customers to agree on the new social bottom lines of their business. And they will have to work in the wider public arena to declare their personal and organizational commitments and to make them stick. Leaders of tomorrow's organizations will not be able to remain anonymous executives; they will be known by what they stand for and by the social results they produce.

Tomorrow's organizations will produce social results, not just profits. Their leaders will not have an easy job, and their rewards will not conform to our traditional measures of success. But tomorrow's leaders will have a more important role than merely managing tomorrow's organizations. They will be helping to improve our lives.

36 JOHN R. SEFFRIN

The Voluntary Health Organization of the Future

*John R. Seffrin is the chief executive officer of the world's largest
voluntary health organization, the American Cancer Society. He
is also a trustee of the American Cancer Society Foundation and
serves as vice chairman of the board of the National Health
Council. Until 1992, he was professor of health education and
chairman of the Department of Applied Health Science at Indiana
University. During his years in academia, he distinguished himself
as a national and international leader in health education, disease
prevention, and public health.*

I magine a future in which our society was no longer committed to assigning resources to the poor and disadvantaged, thus multiplying current
problems related to health care and resulting in a split, or the creation of
two separate health care systems, one for the rich and one for the poor.
The likelihood of this bleak future is not impossible; in fact, many would
argue that we are well on our way to this end point. Rapidly advancing
technologies, changing demographics, and mounting economic and political pressures are dramatically changing this country's health care system.
Managed care, for instance, portends the likelihood that the family practice physician will be the primary cancer therapist, and that he or she will
be the main gatekeeper who determines which cancer patients are seen by
specialists, if at all. Moreover, with capitation methods becoming the

norm, monetary incentives will encourage less rather than more use of new and often expensive medical care innovations. Furthermore, as the health care system changes, voluntary health organizations have to change along with it.

Unfortunately, many leaders of voluntary organizations are too busy concentrating on the problems of today, and thus they are unable to look to tomorrow and the creation of a health care system that would promote health for *all* members of society. The American Cancer Society (ACS) recently organized the landmark Futures Symposium, bringing together leaders from inside and outside of the cancer community, to help us develop a "statement of intent" in terms of long-term outcomes to be achieved by the society. With help from the Institute for Alternative Futures, a nonprofit research and educational organization cofounded in 1977 by Clement Bezold, Alvin Toffler, and James Dator, we looked ahead to the year 2013 (the society's hundredth anniversary) and created a vision for the prevention and control of cancer by the early part of the next millennium. The preliminary elements of the proposed statement of intent included the following expectations for the year 2013:

- More cancer will be prevented, and the disease will not be the leading cause of premature death.

- Age-adjusted incidence will be reduced.

- Age-adjusted mortality will be sizably reduced.

- The public will no longer perceive cancer as a death sentence.

- After diagnosis, more people will survive longer, with excellent ability to function and enjoy life.

- All cancer patients and their families will have a better quality of life.

- Uncontrolled pain will be eliminated as an effect of cancer.

All voluntary organizations need to develop a similar vision of what they want the future to be so that strategies can be devised and commitments made toward having that future be a reality. We might do well to remind ourselves regularly of the prophetic words of Lewis Carroll in

Alice's Adventures in Wonderland, when Alice "was a little startled by see-ing the Cheshire Cat sitting on a bough of a tree a few yards off. 'Would you tell me, please, which way I ought to walk from here?' 'That depends a good deal on where you want to get to,' said the Cat. 'I don't much care where—' said Alice. 'Then it doesn't matter which way you walk,' said the Cat. '—so long as I get *somewhere*,' Alice added as an explanation. 'Oh, you're sure to do that,' said the Cat, 'if you only walk long enough.'"

The ACS has already made changes in the way it will operate in the early twenty-first century. Based on several years of strategic planning and the launching of its futuring initiative in 1994, the society is now com-mitted to ongoing processes that allow the organization's top priorities to drive our budget on an annual basis. This represents a reversal from many decades in which the various departments drove the budgeting process by competing for ever-increasing amounts, thus forestalling our ability to launch well-funded new initiatives, no matter how important such efforts might have been to the realization of the society's mission.

Through the futuring initiative and our commitment to serious strate-gic planning, we now have in place the key mechanism to allow our large and rather traditional organization to change more quickly, as it must do to be maximally successful in the ever more competitive marketplace.

Major Forces Shaping Health Care and the Future of Voluntary Health Organizations

Currently, the United States is the only advanced, industrialized nation in the world that does not guarantee basic health care for its citizens. As the health care debates continue in Washington, D.C., it is becoming increasingly clear that the American people not only are ready for, but are demanding, significant change. This change will greatly affect the roles and missions of voluntary health organizations. We need to prepare for these coming changes as well as to devise strategies that will enable our agencies to shape the future in ways that will ensure our organizational vitality and relevance and maximize the prospects of realizing our respec-tive goals.

The move toward managed care will shape the health care system in many and profound ways. Although a number of these changes may well result in greater efficiencies and less waste in health care expenditures, it is also likely that certain desirable health care services will not be broadly available to all in need without more effective advocates for patients. The area of cancer care is especially worrisome, because past experience has shown that a person with a history of cancer is more likely than most other patients to be discriminated against. In addition, although the public clearly wants better ways to prevent and cure cancer, such improvements are not likely without research and clinical trials. Funding for the needed trials will not come easily, in any case, but may be virtually impossible if our organization is not an effective advocate for the needs of all people facing cancer.

As the health care system evolves, we are seeing a shift toward viewing diseases as "syndromes of risk." Poverty would be the number-one syndrome that leads to ill health among our population. Many factors are included in this syndrome, such as poor housing conditions; poor nutrition; increased use of tobacco, alcohol, and other drugs; and higher levels of stress and crime. Health voluntaries may be called on to combat these agents of ill health. This could mean collaborations with other voluntary groups as well as the formation of partnerships with community entities such as educational, housing, and law enforcement agencies.

Breakthroughs in technology will change the way in which we communicate, treat disease, and run our organizations. Genetic therapies will affect prevention and the treatment of disease. Mapping of the human genome will enable the development of tests that will identify at-risk members of the population for many diseases. The current trend toward the "forecast, prevent, and manage paradigm" of disease emphasizes prevention as well as lifestyle changes as a way to create healthy communities. Disease will come to be seen as the result of various syndromes such as poverty and poor environment. Voluntaries will be called on to expand their role beyond the disease to address issues of environmental stress as well as to focus on the whole person at risk. That is why the ACS has changed its broad and disease-oriented mission statement to one that is both more focused and more people-oriented.

The major demographic shifts taking place as well as the aging of our overall population will require very different services from the health care system. These shifts have implications for health as well as for other areas of our society, such as education and housing. More elderly people and minority populations will be using the health care system. These minority populations will have their own cultural backgrounds and beliefs that might affect how they access the system and perceive its benefits. Many of these minority groups will be poor and have limited access to preventive health care as well as to good nutrition and safe housing. These are all contributing factors to ill health.

The pool of volunteers will change for voluntary health organizations as well. More elderly and minority people will become prospective volunteers. The shift toward ever-greater accountability in health care will affect our agencies as well. Volunteers and donors alike will want outcome measures in place so that they can see the results that their money and time have produced. Voluntary organizations need to recognize this so that they can adapt their recruiting and educational strategies to ensure that they are getting the highest-quality volunteers and are deploying them to use the best of their abilities and interests. I predict that the larger elderly population will be the major force affecting the changing volunteer base in the early twenty-first century.

The use and acceptance of complementary and alternative therapies is growing in the United States and worldwide. This might change the way in which people access the health care system and at what point in their illnesses they opt for traditional medical care. The rise in health care costs is starting to make these nontraditional therapies more attractive. Health voluntaries can choose to take an active role in making sure that the practitioners of these therapies are well trained and provide services that are useful to their patients. Voluntaries can also become proactive in the uses of these therapies by accepting responsibility to (1) do research dealing with the efficacy of complementary and alternative therapies and (2) provide objective and valid information to the public regarding safe and effective therapies, including nontraditional approaches. We must remember that as the cost of care and profit motives pervade the health care system in America, the voluntary health organization may become the one institution whose *only* interest is what is best for the patient.

Lifestyle and behavioral patterns are another major force shaping health care. Although many people are moving toward healthier lifestyles by eating better, exercising more, and making use of nontraditional stress-reducing therapies such as yoga and meditation, signs of an increase in non-health-promoting behaviors are very disturbing. Despite the overwhelming evidence that smoking is linked to cancer, heart disease, and many other health ailments, statistics show that about a quarter of the adults in the United States continue to smoke, and that young people are taking up smoking in greater numbers.

Why is this? Understanding human behavior and learning how to modify it to promote healthier lifestyles will be one of the greatest challenges facing health voluntaries in the twenty-first century. Again, some areas of psychosocial and behavioral research are best done by social sector organizations rather than by the for-profit sector or the government. In the future, voluntary health organizations and all other social sector organizations that purport to improve the quality of life must, out of necessity, make a commitment to understand human behavior better and to evaluate the effectiveness and *appropriateness* of all interventions aimed at changing that behavior.

Many non-lifestyle-related factors affect health worldwide and need to be addressed. We are just beginning to understand the extent of the ill effects of increased exposure to petrochemicals, artificial radiation, and the thinning of the ozone layer on our health. What will be the role of health voluntaries in dealing with these issues? Should we be called on to become advocates for health by lobbying against the forces that are creating these health threats? It is the responsibility of every voluntary health organization to decide what position it is going to take to combat these forces. As was previously mentioned, attacking these syndromes of risk will require new collaborations and pooling of resources between voluntaries and across communities. Providing safe housing, adequate nutrition, and good education, to name just a few factors, will be a large and daunting task. The future of voluntary health groups will be to use what resources are at their disposal to help the people they serve. After all, in the last analysis, the very existence of our organizations is predicated on the notion that some important human and community needs are not being adequately addressed by either the private, for-profit sector or the public (governmental) sector. Therefore, our reason to exist is to fill those voids and to promote the overall welfare of our democratic society at the community level.

The American Cancer Society
in the Early Twenty-First Century

What does all of this mean for voluntary health agencies? I believe that the best way to illustrate this would be to provide a profile of how I see the American Cancer Society in the early twenty-first century. One possible scenario is as follows.

The ACS is increasingly incorporating accountability and outcome measures into its ongoing operations. Cancer control interventions and other programs are evaluated on their effectiveness. The use of electronic town meetings on the Internet and other forms of cyberspace communication are being considered to poll members on their opinion of the efficacies of interventions, health promotion programs, and other support functions of the ACS. Feedback on these issues is used to revise programs that are not working well, eliminating those that prove to be ineffective and creating new ones to meet existing needs.

Acknowledgment of lifestyle factors as a major contributor to ill health has led the ACS to change its research focus to an increased concentration on the behavioral sciences. Attention is paid to determining what it is that causes people to behave in certain ways and to devising strategies, such as health promotion campaigns and behavior modification programs, to combat these behaviors and promote healthier lifestyle choices. Prevention of cancer as well as control of the disease have become the society's primary goals. The strong ACS research base is supported by donations as well as by community partnerships to ensure adequate funds that enable all ACS programs to succeed.

The aging population of the United States has caused the society to redirect its voluntary recruitment strategies. Younger senior citizens (fifty-five to sixty-five years old) are recruited and trained to help older seniors (over seventy years old). Increased minority populations have led to different demographics for volunteers. Bilingual trainers and recruiters are required by ACS. The way in which the society recruits its volunteers has changed also. The ACS is committed to using the latest technological advances in all areas of its operations, not just in screening and referral. Volunteers are recruited on-line and many of the ACS-sponsored patient support groups are conducted on the Internet. As the Internet moves toward more video capabilities, the on-line support groups will soon be able to interact "face-to-face" in cyberspace. This requires the society's staff and volunteers to be trained in the use of these new technologies as well as to keep abreast of other technologies as they emerge in the future.

The increased use of proven supportive therapies is accepted by ACS as a way to enhance pain management efforts. The ACS supports the use of several related techniques such as massage, biofeedback, and meditation, and it serves as a resource to the public on complementary therapies. Although ACS acknowledges that at present there are no cures among these nontraditional therapies, they can be useful in reducing stress and alleviating pain in some cancer patients. Moreover, when they are used as an adjunct to state-of-the-art conventional therapy, pain can be reduced dramatically—and even eliminated—as a part of terminal cancer, thus enhancing the prospect of dying with dignity.

Through increased behavioral research efforts, ACS was able to find hard evidence showing that syndromes such as poverty lead to increased tobacco and substance abuse, poorer nutrition, and increased exposure to environmental toxins (as a result of unsafe living and working conditions). All of these things are known to be contributing factors to the development of cancer. ACS responded to this information by launching an aggressive campaign against poverty. They began collaborations with other health voluntaries (mostly dealing with the issues of alcohol and substance abuse and environmental concerns) and with community organizations in poor and urban areas. As ACS has created community partnerships with educational, small business, and housing organizations, it has become more and more deeply rooted in the creation of healthy cities. The promotion of healthy lifestyles is very closely tied in with the "healthy cities" movement. When communities are environmentally safer and have better housing for lower-income people, safer public areas, and improved community support networks, it is easier for people to lead healthier, better lives.

Issues for Leadership in Creating the Voluntary Health Organization of the Future

In order for any voluntary health organization to be an effective change agent in its community as well as nationally (and, as is increasingly the case, worldwide), it will need to instill and nurture certain beliefs and feel-ings among its members. People need to feel that the organization they contribute to and/or volunteer for shares their values, is run by people who understand their needs, does not tolerate excessive overhead, and does not have conflicts of interest involving other constituencies. The voluntaries of today and tomorrow will need to meet ever more stringent standards of accountability. People want to see *results* for their investments of time and money.

Voluntaries must be committed to incorporating the ideas of *account-ability* and *outcome measures* into their organizational philosophy, struc-ture, and operations. In the future, these bottom-line accountabilities will be assessed and, ultimately, judged more on the progress toward and impact on the mission of the organization. This is opposed to other impor-tant but lesser standards related to the cost of raising money and the per-centage of gross receipts dedicated to certain program activities. In other words, the public *trust* is on us to use our resources in ways that are pru-dent, are defensible, and, most important, will get us where we want to be. Whether or not we are making reasonable progress with our chosen legal and ethical methods will, in fact, determine whether we deserve fur-ther public support.

In conclusion, I believe that the voluntary health organization of the future will differ vastly from any of today's contemporary organizations. This future organization will have the following characteristics:

1. It will be much more dynamic and will be able to change more quickly in order to compete in an even more competitive marketplace. The most successful organizations will be marked by decade-to-decade progress, rather than decade-to-decade tradition.

2. It will be both high-tech and high-touch. Technology will be used to make communicating, training, and networking both more efficient and more effective. Diffusion time for new policies and program strategies will be measured in days and weeks rather than in years, as is often the case today. However, the successful organization will also provide the necessary resources for face-to-face meetings of its members and constituents. The emphasis will be on high-quality interaction among staff, volunteers, and constituents.

3. It will become increasingly people-oriented and mission-driven, rather than organizationally driven. Although it will always be important to keep focused on positively changing the course of a disease, that desired outcome will come about much more quickly and effectively if the organization understands the preeminent importance of people—both its members and its customers.

4. It will be more businesslike in its strategic planning and ongoing operations. It is certainly true that our cause-related organizations are much more than just businesses, but they are also businesses that have top and bottom lines.

5. It will understand that measurable factors such as public name recognition, volunteers recruited and retained, and people touched will become top-line measures of success. Likewise, such factors as dollars raised, actual numbers of people served, and numbers of lives saved will be bottom-line measures of success. Our future leaders will be judged by the stewards and stakeholders on these highly relevant outcomes that relate to mission—our very reason for existing in the first place.

Leaders of voluntary health organizations need to understand that volunteerism does not occur in a vacuum. Many factors affect the recruitment of new volunteers as well as the ability to keep the ones we have. Technological advancements such as the Internet will change the way in which volunteers are recruited and trained. Nonprofit organizations must learn to manage in the turbulence of today while planning for a tenuous tomorrow; as leaders, we must learn to communicate what we do and how we do it while mobilizing our organization around a clear and compelling vision.

37

A. W. DAHLBERG
DAVID W. CONNELL
JENNIFER LANDRUM

Building a Healthy Company–
For the Long Term

Recently named "America's most admired electric utility" by
Fortune *magazine, the Southern Company is the largest electric-*
ity producer in the United States and is rapidly becoming a player
in the global electricity market. Southern's chairman and CEO,
A. W. "Bill" Dahlberg, was recently honored as "Georgia's
most respected CEO." David W. Connell is founder and dean of
the Southern Company College, which is responsible for develop-
ing among the workforce the competencies required for future suc-
cess and for supporting company leadership in strategic cultural
interventions. Jennifer Landrum is a performance consultant,
bringing a background of change management and leadership
development from her past work with Andersen Consulting.

Sometimes it seems that we, in the Southern Company, are dealing with every conceivable type of change that an organization can experience. We are moving from a more regulated, monopolistic environment toward an environment that is more open and competitive. We are changing from a smaller, regional organization to a much larger, global organization, and finally, we are leaving behind a relatively stable world and entering a new world that has both greater risks and more incredible opportunities.

One of our great challenges is continually to develop our long-term health and vitality as an organization while we are at the same time thriving in the midst of massive change.

Health is something that we all strive for personally and professionally. But what does it mean when we apply this concept to an organization? We will try to answer this question from the unique perspective of our rapidly changing company.

As the last major industry in the United States to go through deregulation, we are fortunate to have had the opportunity to learn from the gas, banking, telecommunications, and airline industries. On the one hand, we have had the opportunity to enjoy a long history of stability. On the other hand, we believe that we will now face deeper, swifter changes than our counterparts in other previously regulated industries. Our perspective has been developed from a variety of sources, including what we have learned from our company, our industry, and other industries.

Key changes in the utility industry—especially deregulation and the move toward greater competition—have resulted in many companies' breaking their implied contract with employees. Loyalty to the company has declined, and short-term financial indicators have been used as the sole measure of success. Deregulation of other industries has often led to a decrease in customer satisfaction and an erosion in the partnership between companies and their communities. We believe that dealing with these issues proactively is crucial to the success of any healthy company, including our own. We therefore take a three-pronged approach to defining a healthy company. In our minds, a company that will be healthy for the long term will be respected financially by investors, internally by talented people, and externally by customers and communities.

Balance of Focus

To meet our definition, a healthy company must determine how to give appropriate attention to both performance measures—customer satisfaction, earnings and costs, and market share—and employee satisfaction. James C. Collins and Jerry I. Porras speak in *Built to Last* of the "genius of the and." This idea becomes critical in managing the tension and trade-offs that result from determining the appropriate balance of focus. Without such a balance, significant organizational problems will arise. Performance will decline, customer satisfaction will decline, employee retention will decline, and the company could ultimately be forced into short-term survival mode. An emerging responsibility of leadership will therefore be to minimize the tension and to manage the balance of focus, ensuring in times of increasing competition that the pendulum does not become permanently lodged on the side of financial performance. The business case for balance of focus is abundantly clear to the Southern Company. Our internal data have shown a strong correlation between employee satisfaction and business unit performance.

So how does the Southern Company's leadership apply the concept of balanced focus? It is evident in the company's clearly articulated "BAG" (bold aggressive goal) to be America's best-diversified utility and in the "BIGs" (big intermediate goals) that focus on costs, overheads, cash flow, power marketing, earnings, customer satisfaction, and being a "great place to work." It is evident in our leadership's accountability and rewards systems. The balance of focus is also evident in the allocation of schedule time of top leadership. In 1991, the Southern Company Leadership Council, made up of senior offices representing the Southern Company's eleven subsidiaries and key members of the corporate staff, created the College Board of Advisors to ensure that the company is building the competencies and culture required for success in the future. Under the direction of this board, the college, responsible for training and development in all eleven subsidiaries, designed a top-down curriculum that provides leaders with the technical and people skills and competencies necessary for success in our changing environment. All members of the top management team were the first participants in the weeklong Leading Empowered Leaders program, designed to provide the leadership or "people" component of this curriculum. During this experience, the team defined tools and systems that will support the balance of focus between financial performance and employee needs. These actions and others make it clear that "we are in for the long haul."

Determining What You Do

A key component of a healthy organization is the ability to determine *what* the organization does on an ongoing basis. In other words, organizations that will be healthy for the long term must continually reexamine strategies and reassess the markets in which they want to compete. Healthy companies will become far more clear about the true core competencies of the business and will outsource everything else. Strategic planning will become a continuous process, engaged in daily by all levels of the organization, instead of an annual event conducted by a mere few. Planning will be driven simultaneously by the global marketplace and by the market around the corner. Of course, these processes will again heighten the responsibilities of leadership. Business unit managers will actually run their units as individual businesses, building skill sets in the form of a flexible workforce and creating a fluid organizational structure. As the marketplace changes, so too will company strategies. An amoebalike workforce and structure are critical to weathering the transitions that will be required to thrive in the rapidly changing future.

The Southern Company's strategy for the future will be driven by the changing electric marketplace, which is swiftly moving from regulation to competition. No one can know for sure what type of competition we will face. We must prepare for the most competitive environment imaginable.

Although we may not know the details of how the competitive circumstances will play out, we are certain that things will be different, and we can plan for that. We can create a fluid, capable workforce that is organized in a flexible structure so that regardless of what marketplace changes occur, we will be ready and able to meet and exceed the evolving requirements.

Determining How You Do What You Do

Perhaps even more than knowing what they do, healthy companies must become skilled at determining *how* they will do what they do. They must have a very clear organizational vision and values that will resist erosion in a sea of change in the marketplace and in the organization. The vision and values must be shared by all in the organization to create a common basis for action.

In our company, employees can all rally around our vision to be America's best-diversified utility. We have also set out our values statement, "The Southern Style," which defines the behaviors that we strive to live by. To ensure that our values do not become organizational platitudes, all members of the leadership team strive to model these values, measure each other against them, and publicly discuss the day-to-day actions that best demonstrate these values. Courses delivered through the Southern Company College provide opportunities for all levels of employees to discuss how each value applies to their daily work routine. Commitment to this vision and shared values will not be erased by changes in the marketplace or business objectives.

Another key "how" component is the way in which a company is organized to do the work. Healthy companies will become far less obsessed with organizational structure and far more focused on key processes. Work will be done through seamless partnerships with suppliers and customers. The success of each entity will be interdependent, leaving no room for turf fights. Healthy companies must have the ability to make networks work and must have people who can manage multiple relationships because a single entity may turn out to be a company's customer, supplier, and perhaps even competitor, all at the same time. Communication about business realities must be relentless throughout the organization, utilizing all possible media. In our own company, we have learned that the absence of communication breeds mistrust. We are committed to eliminating the barriers to the open flow of candid communication in all directions.

Speed will become the watchword, requiring that an organization aggressively commit to organizational learning as a way to integrate lessons learned from recent experience and apply them to current actions. For example, in our company, one reason we are interested in international diversification is that we believe that it will enable us to learn lessons that will be of great value in the future. When we make international investments, we are not just trying to get bigger—we are trying to get better!

Determining Who You Need

Once a company is very clear on what it will do and how, *who* it needs will become far more apparent. The core competencies of the business will determine the skills and aptitudes around which a company selects and develops talent. Healthy companies will hire for skill sets, not for jobs. They will import new talent as required and will "rehire" existing talent, doing whatever it takes to hire the best *as defined for that organization*. The most desired employees in both the internal and the external workforce will have the capacity and the desire to learn and think critically. And the learning process only begins with their hiring. Employees of healthy organizations will commit to daily learning as key to their personal and corporate success.

We have learned through our experience that the skill sets that made us successful in the past will not take us where we need to go in the future. This does not require that we change our entire workforce but rather that we clearly define the competencies required for future success and then develop those competencies within our organization, complementing our current workforce with new talent as necessary. Our individual development philosophy emphasizes understanding the business, producing results, and assuming joint responsibility. The employee commits to seek out opportunities to develop in ways that add value, and the company commits to provide tools and resources to support the individual's endeavors. We believe that the time and money spent appropriately on developing people are an investment in the future of the business.

Keeping Who You Need

As increased competition forces the breakdown of the implied employment contract, how can companies *keep* the people they need? We have seen that moving from monopoly to a competitive environment shatters employees' sense of job security. We understand that people will never give 100 percent to their job if they live in fear of losing it. Healthy companies must replace that shattered sense of security with something that redefines the company's commitment to employees and employees' commitment to the company. Otherwise, fear and its long-term consequence, paralysis, will fill that void. Seeing that lifelong employment is no longer possible in corporate America, our company is in the process of developing a new compact with its people. This compact commits the company to provide encouragement for people to grow and develop so that they can maintain their marketability within or outside the company. Coupled with the development philosophy and the systems to support the compact, we strive to ensure that our employees are positioned to understand the future of our business and to craft their individual roles in that future.

At a fundamental level, to keep the people they need, healthy companies will have to create the kind of company that talented people will want to stay with. Our company is dedicated to being a "great place to work."

Fundamental to this concept is letting people know what is expected of them and providing feedback on how well they are performing against those expectations. In healthy companies, feedback from all directions (up, down, and sideways) will become the norm. If people are not clear about what is expected of them or are not satisfied that they know their level of performance, they have a right and are expected to pursue this understanding vigorously. Expectations include the "whats" of a job (the hard performance criteria), the "hows" of the job (the behavioral dimensions, including the values), and the required skills and knowledge.

Also central to our view of a great place to work is the goal for our company always to be a winning team. We believe that we are not in the game merely to play but to win. We will continue to set high goals for ourselves and the team. We will each take individual responsibility for the success of our team. We will act with speed, decisiveness, and individual initiative to solve problems through our team. And we will do this with our belief that the people closest to the customer and the work being performed are best qualified to make decisions related to that customer and that work. A healthy company will provide people with as much freedom to act as is feasible. We believe that a key part of enjoying work beyond delivering better results is the *freedom* to apply capabilities to opportunities. Our leadership is committed to increase authority and accountability among our people, to improve the flow of information needed to make good decisions, to augment people's decision-making capabilities, and to recognize and reward people for their accomplishments.

Another crucial element of a satisfying and enjoyable work environment is the quality of leadership. The Southern Company is focused on ensuring that our leaders are not only technically and managerially capable but also ethical—always telling the truth even when it means saying "I don't know," keeping their promises, and dealing fairly with everyone. As eluded to earlier, healthy companies must provide ethical leadership that supports and serves as an organizational architect, continually linking appropriate groups of people to get the work done. Healthy companies must have leadership bench strength so that if a key contributor does leave, the organization will continue to thrive.

In these times of increasing responsibility and uncertainty for all members of an organization, healthy companies must focus on work and personal-life balance. As demanding as our jobs are becoming in our company's evolving competitive environment, we must be proactive about achieving this balance. As demands in our jobs go up, healthy companies must be committed to providing resources that allow us as individuals to make personal decisions to achieve some acceptable level of balance. Good health and quality time with our families and for ourselves, balanced with the work environment we have described, represent the bedrock of a "great place to work."

Again, to ensure that these concepts do not become platitudes but rather actions ingrained in our daily work, we hold each employee of our organization accountable for making sure this happens. We have learned through company and personal experience that what gets measured, focused on, and attached to a consequence system will improve. We are therefore using our own cultural index, known as the Vision Progress Survey, to measure the qualities of a "great place to work," benchmarking against the best, establishing programs and processes for improvement, and making leaders accountable for actions.

Although defining what it takes to be a healthy company for the long term is a monumental task, we have attempted to do so in this chapter—and attempt to do so daily for the long-term viability of our company. We will continue to learn and will be constantly seeking to share our lessons and to apply them to our practices. As a company that is getting up from a really comfortable, lived-in easy chair from a decade ago never to sit down again, we think that the leadership, workforce, and programs we have in place at the Southern Company will keep us standing, even soaring, for the long term.

38 CHRIS ARGYRIS

The Next Challenge

Chris Argyris is James Bryant Conant Professor of Education and Organizational Behavior at Harvard University. He was formerly a faculty member at Yale University, serving as Beach Professor of Administrative Sciences and as chair of the Administrative Sciences department. His books include Personality and Organization; Integrating the Individual and the Organization; Interpersonal Competence and Organizational Effectiveness; Organization and Innovation; Intervention Theory and Method; Inner Contradictions of Rigorous Research; Theory in Practice; Organizational Learning; Knowledge for Action; Strategy, Change, and Defensive Routines; Overcoming Organizational Defenses; *and* On Organizational Learning. *He is currently working on a project that will relate the perspective presented in* Knowledge for Action *to the ideas of other researchers and practitioners.*

Currently, a great emphasis is placed on organizational learning. Yet organizational defensive routines, one of the most powerful factors that inhibits learning, are becoming stronger every day. Why?

Organizational Defensive Routines

Organizational defensive routines are any actions, policies, and practices that are used to prevent the participants in organizations (as well as

367

members of groups, departments, and other areas) from experiencing embarrassment or threat, at the same time preventing them from discovering and correcting the causes of the embarrassment or threat. Politicking, game playing, layering, and creating unnecessary structures are but a few examples that come to mind. Organizational defensive routines encourage individuals to bypass the causes of the embarrassment or threat and to cover up the bypass. They also encourage making this action undiscussable and the undiscussability undiscussable. The consequences of using organizational defensive routines include creating errors that are not detected and corrected, blaming others for errors, and limiting learning. These consequences feed back to reinforce the defensive routines and make it more difficult to correct them. Not surprisingly, the participants soon begin to express helplessness about reducing the defensive routines. This helplessness feeds on itself, persists, and eventually is taken for granted.

Item: The February 1995 issue of *The Executive* reprinted a twenty-year-old article by Steven Kerr that contained many examples of organizational defensive routines. The editors contacted their executive advisory group, who represented fifty of the best-known and most managerially advanced organizations, and asked if the advisory group members thought that these defenses still existed. They said that they did and, indeed, were flourishing. In the same issue, Jeffrey Pfeffer identified thirteen practices that could involve people in ways that would help to make their corporations more competitive. He wrote as if organizational defenses did not exist or, if they did, they would not erode the effective implementation of his ideas.

Item: When Thomas Watson Jr. was CEO of IBM, he was very concerned about organizational defenses. In many meetings with his top group, he led earnest inquiries into the possibility that someday IBM could become too bureaucratized, too rigid, too inflexible, and unable to change as fast as might be necessary. I attended at least a dozen such meetings. Watson's immediate reports told him not to worry. IBM was a world-class organization with world-class employees. Privately, the same executives reported that they did not want to upset Watson because he often worried too much about the human factors.

Item: A CEO and his immediate reports participated in a learning session where the faculty members focused on the importance of leading versus managing. The session was rated very highly by the executives. The next day, the same reports attempted to tackle key management problems of the future. The moment the issues became "hot," the discussion became distant and focused on the routine features of the problem. The very executives who, the day before, voted for the importance of leading over managing produced a discussion that was consistent with managing and not leading.

How is it that organizational defensive routines are so powerful, yet no one teaches them in executive programs, no formal policies and practices reward them, and the informal activities that do so are seen by managements as counterproductive? I usually hear two answers to this question. First, organizational defensive routines are somehow genetic in organizations. Second, individuals, especially managers, cause them with their unilateral leadership styles. After a few minutes, a third explanation is usually produced, namely, that organizations and individuals jointly cause them.

I agree that the third explanation is what we tend to see when we observe organizations. But I believe that this explanation is incomplete, if not wrong. Individuals are the first cause of organizational defensive routines. They create the organizational cultures whose feedback causes individuals to continue their defensive actions.

Item: The directors and owners who founded Monitor Company, one of America's leading and most innovative consulting firms, did so with the idea of creating a firm that had few, if any, organizational defenses. Yet within several months, defenses surfaced, even in their own deliberations. They attempted to solve the problem through admonitions and even set financial fines for perpetrators. None of these measures worked.

We have here an example of a brand-new firm with defenses that the directors and owners did not want. How can the organization be blamed? It had just begun. Why did the people at the top, with financial and organizational power, create the very conditions that they decried, and why did they appear to be helpless to do much about it? Incidentally, they did take corrective action and, as the *Financial Times* reported in June 1993, they did a superlative job.

Our research indicates that directors, and almost all human beings, regardless of their age, sex, race, education, or wealth, are programmed early in life with theories in action to deal with embarrassment or threat. Individuals espouse a wide variety of theories of action. To our surprise, we found almost no variance in the theories that they actually used. But we did find a systematic discrepancy between the theories of action they espoused and the ones they actually used. Furthermore, the individuals were unaware of the discrepancy while they were acting. Finally, we were surprised to find that when the theory in use was used effectively, it led them to be unaware of the program in their heads that made them unaware.

To explain these findings, we have developed a theory. The premise of this theory is that human beings and organizations are designing systems. The way to understand them is to focus on these designs. The way to get at the designs is to observe their actions. The majority of methods presently in vogue to understand individuals and organizations are based on a different premise. For example, take the issue of leadership. Numerous tests exist to understand leadership behaviors and leaders' attitudes, beliefs, and values. All of these instruments relate to espoused theories, not theories in use.

Item: Two hundred senior executives, during a period of two years, participated in workshops created by their human resources division in order to enhance their executive leadership. As part of the learning, each executive completed four different leadership and personality tests and discussed the results in depth. The executives evaluated these sessions very positively. Several months later, the top-line officials still felt that one of the most exasperating problems had not been corrected, namely, the presence of organizational defense routines. I was invited to create a series of workshops for the top fifty executives. In preparation for the workshops, the executives completed a case describing a problem and the way that they actually dealt with it or would strive to deal with it. They included the conversation that they used or would use and the thoughts and feelings that they censored or would censor in order to be effective.

As predicted by the tests the fifty executives took, they varied in their leadership styles, personalities, decision-making predilections, and other factors. But in their cases, they all used the same unilaterally controlling, bypassing, covering-up theory in use. At the theory-in-use level we saw no differences. The differences the tests produced represented differences that did not affect the ways the executives designed and implemented their actions. In every case we found that the executives created self-fueling, antilearning processes. No wonder the organizational defensive routines were as robust as ever.

Another approach to leadership that is more experiential focuses on the behavior of individuals. The fundamental assumption is that a group of participants who are interested in learning to lead more effectively can provide each other with feedback to correct their errors and therefore can become more effective. For example, a leader (L) learns that many of his subordinates view him as autocratic and unilateral; if they give him this feedback constructively, he can change to be more effective. The most favorable scenario is that L wishes to change and become less controlling, and therefore he listens more and holds his views until others have spoken. The causal reasoning behind the change is that if L is too controlling, he should act in a less controlling manner. But this causal reasoning excludes L's reasons for being overcontrolling in the first place. It may be that he sees his subordinates as weak, wooly-headed thinkers. Thus he may change his behavior but not his causal reasoning about why his "original" behavior was valid.

The superficiality of the changes can be seen in at least two ways. First, L is often awkward in being genuinely participative. His awkwardness makes sense because he does not trust his subordinates' reasoning and competencies. Moreover, he struggles hard to cover up the bypass of his true views. This leads to the second problem. The subordinates rarely focus on their reasoning regarding effective leadership; therefore, they do not have to learn about the mediocrity of their reasoning processes. If L were to attempt to test his opinions about their mediocre thinking, they would respond that he was being autocratic. With those views in mind, it makes rational sense (to them) to see L as defensive and to ignore their own defensiveness.

Both of these approaches, in my opinion, will always be seriously limited because they cannot get at the unilaterally controlling theories in use and the causal reasoning that are the fundamental basis of the organizational defensive routines without focusing on his causal reasoning and theory in use. The best L can do is the opposite of his present theory in use. He does this by suppressing his overt adherence to his theory in use. If he has talked too much, he now talks less. If he has been aggressive, he can be more passive. These behaviors do not represent a new theory in use. They represent the opposite features of the old one. Hence, they are often short-lived, especially when the individual experiences embarrassment or threat.

Defensive Reasoning About the Human Resources Function

If our theory is correct, all of these defensive actions are designed. Thus the behavior is skillful even though its consequences are counterproductive. Underlying these "skillfully incompetent" actions is defensive reasoning. Defensive reasoning constructs actions in ways that allow the actor to remain in unilateral control. Actors craft their conclusions about what is going on and how they should behave in ways that do not put their designs to a genuine test. The test that is most often used is one that supports the reasoning that was used in the first place.

I would like to illustrate defensive reasoning and its antilearning consequences by using a case written by a very bright, highly successful consultant who has recently accepted the task of being head of the human resources function in her firm. Her case represents the age-old problem of individual versus organizational requirements. She describes her attempts to deal with a partner who was representative of other partners who wanted her to return to consulting. I have purposely chosen a case written by a woman because I also want to illustrate one of our most important findings about gender. It is fashionable for women (though not this one) to espouse the theory that they are more sensitive, more interpersonally alert, and less unilaterally competitive than men. All these findings wash out when we study their theory in use. In a cumulative sample of over 7,500 individuals to date, we have found that women use the same unilaterally controlling, win-lose theories to design and implement their actions as men do. Men and women use the same defensive reasoning processes when they are dealing with issues that can be, or are, embarrassing and threatening.

Susan (names have been altered) began her case by framing the issue. The frame included the following assertions. First, human resources activities are as important as consulting activities. Second, all human beings "have unique gifts and talents." And third, "They are the happiest and most productive when they are able to use them in a way that fulfills their purpose in life."

The way these claims are crafted, it is difficult to subject them to a tough test. Susan may respond that she has tested her claims by observing colleagues and herself. Such a test, based only on her private logic and experience, is soft. A harder test would be to seek out individuals who, for example, are productive and dissatisfied or unproductive and satisfied. I suggest that such cases would not be hard to find. If this is true, then her claims that the human resources function is based on these views is full of gaps. Susan does not appear to recognize the gaps. Perhaps the partner with whom she was having the dialogue did recognize them. If so, he may have seen Susan as being shortsighted and as overemphasizing the importance of the human resources function. Interestingly, Susan, in her private conversation, evaluated the partner as shortsighted and as overemphasizing billings and money.

If Susan had framed her discussion to learn about the limits of her views before she focused on the partner's limitations, it could have led to a more productive dialogue. It could also have led to a richer and more valid view of the human resources function. Susan wrote in her case that she was stunned to hear that the partner wanted her to return to consulting. She dealt with the surprise by carrying out two conversations, one private and one public. The private conversation included the statements: "Oh my God, I can't believe that I'm hearing this," "[This is evidence] that the partner has no idea of how important the human resources activities are to the firm," and "The partner does not have a clue about what it takes to do this job well."

Susan also carried on a public conversation. She stated: "Well, June [the individual who was to replace Susan] is very capable. She's a real jack-of-all-trades. But I think being a consultant is an important qualification. The CEO believes this." Because of Susan's causal reasoning, she decided to hide the negative evaluations and attributions and act as if she was not doing so. She said something positive about June and used the CEO's comments as the basis for questioning the partner's suggestion.

The result was an encounter dominated by bypass and cover-up, leading to attributions about the other person being closed to learning and helping to frame human resources as the soft function and consulting as the hard one. Toward the end of the conversation, Susan said to herself, "It's okay. Don't let it get to you. It's just the partner being [himself]." Don't take offense, she said to herself. She concluded that she was underappreciated by the partner. The partner could conceivably have had similar private thoughts about Susan.

The case illustrates how individuals using defensive reasoning create consequences that are counterproductive to their own intentions. They utilize a unilaterally controlling strategy coupled with private conversations that censor important information; therefore, they develop self-fueling processes that limit learning. Because organizations are populated primarily with human beings who have the same theory in use, the result is that organizational defensive routines arise to protect the individuals and to reinforce the counterproductive behavior.

I suggest that the challenge for the twenty-first century is to reduce these kinds of self-fueling, antilearning actions. It is the function of leadership to begin and reward this important quest.

The Last Word

The Last Word

CHARLES HANDY

Unimagined Futures

*Charles Handy is a writer and broadcaster living in London. He
has been an oil executive, a business economist, and, for many
years, a professor at the London Business School. His writings
on organizations and the future of work are well known, the latest
being* Beyond Certainty. *His book* The Age of Paradox *is
a sequel to* The Age of Unreason, *which was named by both*
Fortune *and* Business Week *as one of the ten best business
books of 1994.*

One thing is sure. The organizations of the next century are going to
be very different from the ones which we knew in this one. Much
of the past analysis and writing on the subject will be, frankly, wrong or
at best irrelevant. That leaves us with a huge challenge. We have to
rethink what an organization is, conceptually, and why it exists, for what
and for whom. This is a task for a philosopher more than a researcher, for
philosophers pose questions which have yet to be asked and suggest
answers which are often too new to be studied in action. I write, therefore, as a self-styled social philosopher intrigued by the future, its possibilities, and its problems.

Virtuality and the New Science

Margaret Wheatley, in *Leadership and the New Science*, has written of the danger of believing in Newtonian organizations in a quantum age. Newton wasn't wrong. He just wasn't right enough to cope with the dilemmas of science now. Similarly, the old way of looking at organizations wasn't wrong; it just does not capture the real essence of what it means to organize today. Organizations aren't the visible, tangible, obvious places which they used to be. No longer, for instance, do you have to have everyone in the same place at the same time in order to get things done. Place and time are now independent of one another. Global organizations will pass a project to a chain of groups around the world to keep pace with the time zones. More mundanely, people can work together connected only by phone, fax, or E-mail. If information is the raw material of the work, then there need be no common space at all. Already the office blocks of our cities are being turned into apartments as their previous inhabitants find it too expensive to keep an asset available for 168 hours a week and yet have most of their people doing their work elsewhere—on the train, in the plane, with the client, in their homes, or on assignment.

More important, organizations no longer feel that they have to own all the people needed to get the work done, let alone have them where they can see them. Partnerships, outsourcing, flexible labor, and interim managers are a way of keeping risks within bounds and of exporting the slack needed to cope with the peaks or the emergencies. A favored formula today is $1/2 \times 2 \times 3$, which means that half as many people will be employed in the future as are now employed, paid on average twice as well (and working twice as hard), but producing three times as much. Some organizations are, in reality, little more than "boxes of contracts," contracts with suppliers, agents, and specialists of one sort or another, with no visible presence at all. The new library created in Dubrovnik, Croatia, to replace the one destroyed in the fighting a few years ago, is tiny, but it is computer-linked to all the libraries in the world. It has few books or journals of its own and needs no large acres of shelves to satisfy its readers, who, in fact, do not need to go near the place at all if they have the necessary technology in their own homes. It is not so very different, in fact, from the Open University in Great Britain, which is, for its students, only a conceptual space, not a physical one.

Such organizations are increasingly "virtual"; you can describe what they do but cannot see them. What, then, is this thing called an organization? The word seems to be more of a verb these days than a noun, a means of organizing instead of a thing or a body. And how do we manage something we cannot see or people whom we never meet? For many a manager, these new organizations are something to be kept as far away as possible for as long as possible. Most of us prefer to walk backward into the future, a posture which may be uncomfortable but which at least allows us to keep on looking at familiar things as long as we can.

Unfortunately for our comfort, neither quantum theory nor the new order can be ignored. We have to try to understand it so that we can live with it and use it, as we do with science. In the new science, matter is not something which is fixed; it is a mix of particles and waves, a mix which can never be completely captured because the two can never be measured at the same time. In the same way, the new organizations are more properly viewed, I suggest, as patterns of relationships, an ever-changing mix of particles (or people), and waves (or transactions). Physicists speak of particles as "bundles of potentiality." I see that as quite a good description of the people we want in the new organizations, no longer role occupants in prescribed boxes but would-be butterflies, as in chaos theory, capable of starting perturbations which ripple out to cause a thunderstorm across the world.

Prediction and uniformity are no longer, now, possible in any detail. Just as Werner Karl Heisenberg pointed out that the very act of observation changes the thing observed, so, too, the way we see someone affects the way they behave, and our own actions often help to create the environment we think we are responding to. Power, in the new organizations, comes from relationships, not from structures. Those who have established reputations acquire authority which was not handed down from above; those who are open to others create positive energy around themselves, energy which did not exist before. Love, or, to give it a more corporately respectable title, "unconditional positive regard," may not make the world go around, but it can certainly release unsuspected potential. This makes for an untidy world but one with its positive side. Unlike physical systems and older models of organizations, the new organizations do not obey the Second Law of Thermodynamics, with its relentless downward drag, but have the capacity to find new sources of energy and so to renew themselves. They contain within themselves the real clue to a so-called learning organization.

To heighten the unpredictability, isolated events can cause unanticipated major changes, as they do in science; for example, a customer inquiry, a mistake, or an unexpected experimental result can lead to a whole new product range. There is order, of a sort, in the world, or daily life would be impossible, and there has to be order in its organizations, but order no longer implies control. The new organizations are, in fact, always tending to be slightly out of control, their structures flexing, their people innovating. Nonlinear systems, a concept which includes people, tend to feed back on themselves, creating unforeseen results, rather like what often happens in marriage. In these new organizations, therefore, some older ideas, such as management hierarchies, spans of control, grading systems, job descriptions, or career planning can seem as time-bound and out of place as trying to send a telegram in the world of E-mail, nostalgic but unreal. Instead, a new language is emerging, a language which would seem strange and weird to the old order, a language of metaphor and simile, low in definition but rich in suggestion.

The New Language

What is this language? Once again, we might be tempted to borrow our metaphors from science. Field theory is one appealing idea. Electrical fields, for instance, are real; their effects can be seen, measured, and, within limits, predicted, but the field itself is invisible, intangible, and unmeasurable. These fields create energy, activating inert points and holding the whole together. I believe that the metaphor can usefully be carried over to the organization, if we think of the fields being such things as culture, values, ethics, beliefs, or vision.

These words are now commonplace in organizations as they fumble for ways to hold the thing together, to give it a common thrust when a tight plan is no longer feasible, a central ethic takes the place of control, and norms of behavior exist instead of rules. One such field is that of trust.

Francis Fukuyama, in *Trust: The Social Virtues and the Creation of Prosperity*, argues that societies of high trust do better economically. I would extend his idea to organizations. Organizations which rely on trust as their principal means of control are more effective, more creative, more fun, and cheaper to operate. They are, however, very different from the organizations we know today, most of which are based on hierarchical control systems, with an unspoken undercurrent of fear. Nor are these organizations easy places to run. Trust imposes its own constraints and has its own rules. I have written elsewhere about these rules, rules which make it clear that running trust-based organizations requires their leaders to adopt radically different attitudes and assumptions.

Trust is one example of the way a field can be used as a way to obtain some leverage on the new disaggregated organization. Field theory works best, however, if it is combined with another metaphor from the new science, that of the "strange attractor," which, in chaos theory, becomes the organizing focus of the emerging patterns, the way out of chaos, the thing which gives meaning to movement. Chaotic and energetic but uncontrolled organizations can exhibit movement without meaning unless they have found their strange attractor, which gives them point and purpose. Some have called this the "soul" of the organization, another soft but pregnant word which fits the new language of organizations. It is, I now believe, the principal task of leadership to find the strange attractor which will give meaning to movement, and around which a field of trust can be built which will allow the organization to devote most of its energies to its product instead of to its own entrails. Underlying it all, however, will be the emergence of a new organizational contract.

The New Contract

Under the old order, instrumentalism ruled OK. The organization was the instrument of its owners, particularly if it was a business, and the workers were the instruments of the organization. The managers were there to see that the organization delivered what the owners wanted and that the workers did what the organization needed. The contract was clear: the organization was not only an instrument but a piece of property to be disposed of if the owners tired of it.

But if the organization is a changing mix of people and relationships, not a building with plant and machinery, it makes less sense to talk of the people who put up the money "owning" it, for how can one morally or practically own other people or their relationships? If the organization is largely virtual, a box of contracts, then there is, in any case, nothing tangible at all to own. If the organization has a building, it is probably on a short lease, and any computers are likely to be leased as well. To add complication to complication, the workers are now the principal assets of the organization; if they walk out they take their skills and know-how with them. Assets are more than instruments. They are things to be cherished, guarded, and invested in as well as used.

Self-directing assets are a new phenomenon in organizational behavior. Karl Marx would be amused. He longed for the day when the workers would own the means of production. Now they do. He meant, of course, that the workers would, through revolution, become the financial owners. Instead, they are literal owners, because the means of production in most organizations these days resides in the heads and hands of the workers themselves; if they leave, almost nothing is left.

We need a new contract, a new way of spelling out the responsibilities of financiers, workers, and managers and of their relationship to each other. In the process we will probably rediscover that a "company," if the organization is a business, is, in law, much more than a mere instrument of the owners. In English law the company is equivalent to a person. It can be sued as a person, charged as a person with criminal offenses, held responsible for good behavior, and required to conform to regulations. A company has always been more than a piece of property, although common usage has tended to forget that; it has allowed instrumentalism to pervade our way of thinking, turning people into things or, at best, into human resources.

A new contract will probably forgo the language of property and property rights in favor of talking about membership, associates, and investors. Members belong to a company, as they would to any association or club. No one owns a voluntary association; no one needs to, but members have a feeling of psychological ownership which becomes crucial when they are themselves the principal assets. Members have rights, which eventually need to be defined by law, but investors also should have rights, although ones which are not as all-embracing as they are at present, as should associates such as suppliers or agents. No one, for instance, should have the right to dispose of the company over the heads of the members any more than a club could be sold along with its members.

A membership contract along these lines would redefine the role of management. The managers now become the agents of the members rather than their bosses. They manage because, in a sense, the workers want them to manage. They draw their authority from the people over whom it is to be exercised. That is already the way it is in many organizations which are struggling to find a way to harness the talents and skills of the people who are now their principal assets rather than their instruments. It makes the job of the manager more difficult but much more legitimate.

It is more legitimate, for instance, for the managers to question what should be the driving purpose of the organization, the strange attractor which will give it meaning. No longer will it be possible to evade the question by maintaining that the sole purpose of the business is to enrich its owners, for there will be no owners, only investors. Clearly the business, any business, needs to reward its investors and to provide for its future, but that has always begged the question: What future? For what and for whom does the organization exist? Under the new contract, there will be no evading that crucial question. No standard answers will be possible, just as in future no standard organizations will exist. It will be for each organization to determine its own destiny, its own strange attractor.

I have no doubt that the new organizations will be less easy places than they have been. They will certainly be less predictable, less measurable, less amenable to the traditional disciplines. But we cannot reject the future just because it is uncomfortable. What we have to do is find a way to understand it so that we can make the new organizations work for us. The first step to that understanding is a new conceptual vocabulary and a new way of defining these strange creations.

Index

The Drucker Foundation Future Series

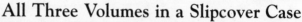

All Three Volumes in a Slipcover Case
Boxed Set   ISBN 0-7879-4696-6 $75.00
The paperback set will be available in Spring 2000 for $49.00

Business Week Best-Seller!
The Leader of the Future
New Visions, Strategies, and Practices for the Next Era
Frances Hesselbein, Marshall Goldsmith,
Richard Beckhard, Editors

World-class contributors offer insights into the future
quality of our lives, businesses, organizations, society, and
the leadership required to move us into the exciting
unknown.

Hardcover   ISBN 0-7879-0180-6 $25.00
Paperback   ISBN 0-7879-0935-1 $16.50

Now in Paperback!
The Organization of the Future
Frances Hesselbein, Marshall Goldsmith, Richard Beckhard, Editors

"Required reading. If you don't use this book to help guide your organization
through the changes, you may well be left behind."
—Nonprofit World

Hardcover   ISBN 0-7879-0303-5 $25.00
Paperback   ISBN 0-7879-5203-6 $18.00

Now in Paperback!
The Community of the Future
Frances Hesselbein, Marshall Goldsmith, Richard Beckhard,
Richard F. Schubert, Editors

"This book of essays is full of rampant idealism. Its authors share a desire to
better the world through their ideas and actions."
—Christian Science Monitor

Hardcover   ISBN 0-7879-1006-6 $25.00
Paperback   ISBN 0-7879-5204-4 $18.00

FAX	**CALL**	**MAIL**	**WEB**
Toll Free	Toll Free	Jossey-Bass Publishers	Secure ordering at:
24 hours a day:	6am to 5pm	350 Sansome St.	www.josseybass.com
800-605-2665	PST:	San Francisco, CA	
	800-956-7739	94104	

Leader to Leader

A quarterly publication of the Drucker Foundation and Jossey-Bass Publishers

Frances Hesselbein, Editor-in-Chief

Leader to Leader is a unique management publication, a quarterly report on management, leadership, and strategy written by today's top leaders *themselves*. Four times a year, *Leader to Leader* keeps you ahead of the curve by bringing you the latest offerings from a peerless selection of world-class executives, best-selling management authors, leading consultants, and respected social thinkers, making *Leader to Leader* unlike any other magazine or professional publication today.

Think of it as a short, intensive seminar with today's top thinkers and doers— people like Peter F. Drucker, Rosabeth Moss Kanter, Max De Pree, Charles Handy, Esther Dyson, Stephen Covey, Meg Wheatley, Peter Senge, and others.

Subscriptions to **Leader to Leader** are $149.00.
501(c)(3) nonprofit organizations can subscribe for $99.00 (must supply tax-exempt ID number when subscribing). Prices subject to change without notice.

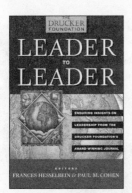

Leader to Leader

Enduring Insights on Leadership from the Drucker Foundation's Award-Winning Journal

Frances Hesselbein, Paul M. Cohen, Editors

The world's thought leaders come together in *Leader to Leader*, an inspiring examination of mission, leadership, values, innovation, building collaborations, shaping effective institutions, and creating community. Management pioneer Peter F. Drucker; Southwest Airlines CEO Herb Kelleher; best-selling authors Warren Bennis, Stephen R. Covey, and Charles Handy; Pulitzer Prize winner Doris Kearns Goodwin; Harvard professors Rosabeth Moss Kanter and Regina Herzlinger; and learning organization expert Peter Senge are among those who share their knowledge and experience in this essential resource. Their essays will spark ideas, open doors, and inspire all those who face the challenge of leading in an ever-changing environment.

For a reader's guide, see www.leaderbooks.org

Hardcover 402 pages ISBN 0-7879-4726-1 Item #G379 $27.00

FAX
Toll Free
24 hours a day:
800-605-2665

CALL
Toll Free
6am to 5pm
PST:
888-378-2537

MAIL
Jossey-Bass Publishers
350 Sansome St.
San Francisco, CA
94104

WEB
Secure ordering, tables of contents, editors' notes, sample articles at
www.josseybass.com or
www.leaderbooks.org

Lessons in Leadership

Peter F. Drucker

Over the span of his sixty-year career, Peter F. Drucker
has worked with many exemplary leaders in the nonprofit sector, government, and business. In the course
of his work, he has observed these leaders closely and
learned from them the attributes of effective leadership. In this video, Drucker presents inspirational por-
traits of five outstanding leaders, showing how each
brought different strengths to the task, and shares the
lessons we can learn from their approaches to leadership.
Drucker's insights (plus the accompanying *Facilitator's Guide*
and *Workbook*) will help participants identify which
methods work best for them and how to recognize their
own particular strengths in leadership.

1 20-minute video + 1 *Facilitator's Guide* + 1 *Workbook*
ISBN 0-7879-4497-1 $89.95

Excellence in Nonprofit Leadership

Peter F. Drucker, Max De Pree, Frances Hesselbein

This video package is a powerful three-in-one development
program for building more effective nonprofit organizations
and boards. *Excellence in Nonprofit Leadership* presents three
modules that can be used independently or sequentially to
help nonprofit boards and staff strengthen leadership
throughout the organization. The video contains three
twenty-minute programs: (I) *Lessons in
Leadership* with Peter Drucker (as described
above); (II) *Identifying the Needs of Followers*,
with Max De Pree and Michele Hunt; and
(III) *Leading Through Mission*, with Frances
Hesselbein. The video comes with one
Facilitator's Guide, which contains complete
instructions for leading all three programs,
and one free *Workbook*, which is designed to
help participants deepen and enrich the learning experience.

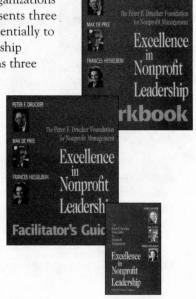

1 60-minute video + 1 *Facilitator's Guide* + 1
Workbook
ISBN 0-7879-4496-3 $129.95

FAX	CALL	MAIL	WEB
Toll Free	Toll Free	Jossey-Bass Publishers	Secure ordering at:
24 hours a day:	6am to 5pm	350 Sansome St.	www.josseybass.com
800-605-2665	PST:	San Francisco, CA	
	800-956-7739	94104	

The Drucker Foundation Self-Assessment Tool

Since its original publication in 1993, the best-selling *Drucker Foundation Self-Assessment Tool* has helped and inspired countless nonprofit boards, executives, and teams to rediscover the direction and potential of their organizations. This completely revised edition of the *Self-Assessment Tool* now offers even more powerful guidance to help organizations uncover the truth about their performance, focus their direction, and take control of their future.

The *Self-Assessment Tool* combines long-range planning and strategic marketing with a passion for dispersed leadership. It allows an organization to plan for results, to learn from its customers, and to release the energy of its people to further its mission. The *Process Guide* by Gary J. Stern provides step-by-step guidelines and self-assessment resources, while the *Participant Workbook* by Peter F. Drucker features thoughtful introductions and clear worksheets. Participants will not only gain new insights about their organization's potential, but also forge strategies for implementation and future success.

Multiple Uses for the *Self-Assessment Tool*

- *The leadership team*—the chairman of the board and the chief executive—can lead the organization in conducting a comprehensive self-assessment, refining mission, goals, and results, and developing a working plan of action.

- *Teams throughout the organization* can use the *Tool* to invigorate projects, tailoring the process to focus on specific areas as needed.

- *Governing boards* can use the *Tool* in orientation for new members, as means to deepen thinking during retreats, and to develop clarity on mission and goals.

- *Working groups from collaborating organizations* can use the *Tool* to define common purpose and to develop clear goals, programs, and plans.

Process Guide　　　　　Paperback ISBN 0-7879-4436-X　　$29.95
Participant Workbook　　Paperback ISBN 0-7879-4437-8　　$12.95

1+1 SAT Package = 1 *Process Guide* + 1 *Participant Workbook*
ISBN 0-7879-4730-X　　$34.50 **Save 20%!**

1+10 SAT Package = 1 *Process Guide* + 10 *Participant Workbooks*
ISBN 0-7879-4731-8　　$89.95 **Save 40%!**

FAX
Toll Free
24 hours a day:
800-605-2665

CALL
Toll Free
6am to 5pm
PST:
800-956-7739

MAIL
Jossey-Bass Publishers
350 Sansome St.
San Francisco, CA
94104

WEB
Secure ordering at:
www.josseybass.com

Leading Beyond the Walls

Frances Hesselbein, Marshall Goldsmith,
Iain Somerville, Editors

from the Drucker Foundation's Wisdom to Action Series

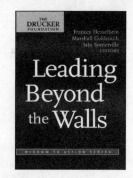

"There is need for acceptance on the part of leaders in every single institution, and in every single sector, that they, as leaders, have two responsibilities. They are responsible and accountable for the performance of their institution, and that has to be concentrated, focused, limited. They are responsible however, also, for the community as a whole. This requires commitment. It requires willingness to accept that other institutions have different values, respect for these values, and willingness to learn what these values are. It requires hard work. But above all, it requires commitment; conviction; dedication to the Common Good. Yes, each institution is autonomous and has to do its own work the way each instrument in an orchestra plays its own part. But there is also the 'score,' the community. And only if the individual instrument contributes to the score is there music. Otherwise there is only noise. This book is about the score."

—Peter F. Drucker

Increasingly, leaders and their organizations work in ways that extend beyond the walls of the enterprise. These partnerships, alliances, and networks allow organizations to achieve new levels of performance. At the same time, they create new challenges. Leaders "beyond the walls" must be adept at building and maintaining relationships, comfortable in working with individuals and organizations they cannot control, and able to move beyond the old preconceptions.

Leading Beyond the Walls presents insights from over twenty-five thought leaders from all three sectors, exploring the challenges and opportunities of partnership as well as the unique practices and perspectives that have helped individuals and organizations become more effective.

Hardcover   ISBN 0-7879-4593-5 $27.00

FAX	CALL	MAIL	WEB
Toll Free	Toll Free	Jossey-Bass Publishers	Secure ordering at:
24 hours a day:	6am to 5pm	350 Sansome St.	www.josseybass.com
800-605-2665	PST:	San Francisco, CA	
	800-956-7739	94104	